Python for Scientists

Third Edition

The third edition of this practical introduction to Python has been thoroughly updated, with all code migrated to Python 3 and made available as Jupyter notebooks. The notebooks are available online with executable versions of all the book's content (and more).

The text starts with a detailed introduction to the basics of the Python language, without assuming any prior knowledge. Building upon each other, the most important Python packages for numerical math (NumPy), symbolic math (SymPy), and plotting (Matplotlib) are introduced, with brand new chapters covering numerical methods (SciPy) and data handling (Pandas). Further new material includes guidelines for writing efficient Python code and publishing code for other users.

Simple and concise code examples, revised for compatibility with Python 3, guide the reader and support the learning process throughout the book. Readers from the quantitative sciences, whatever their background, will be able to quickly acquire the skills needed for using Python effectively.

JOHN M. STEWART was Emeritus Reader in Gravitational Physics at the University of Cambridge, and a Life Fellow at King's College, Cambridge, before his death in 2016. He was the author of *Non-equilibrium Relativistic Kinetic Theory* (Springer, 1971) and *Advanced General Relativity* (Cambridge, 1991), and he translated and edited Hans Stephani's *General Relativity* (Cambridge, 1990).

MICHAEL MOMMERT is Assistant Professor for Computer Vision at the University of St. Gallen, Switzerland, where he combines computer vision and Earth observation to implement efficient learning methods for a wide range of use cases. Before, he was a solar system astronomer and actively wrote scientific open-source code for this community.

Python for Scientists

Third Edition

JOHN M. STEWART

University of Cambridge

MICHAEL MOMMERT

University of St. Gallen, Switzerland

CAMBRIDGE
UNIVERSITY PRESS

CAMBRIDGE
UNIVERSITY PRESS

Shaftesbury Road, Cambridge CB2 8EA, United Kingdom

One Liberty Plaza, 20th Floor, New York, NY 10006, USA

477 Williamstown Road, Port Melbourne, VIC 3207, Australia

314–321, 3rd Floor, Plot 3, Splendor Forum, Jasola District Centre, New Delhi – 110025, India

103 Penang Road, #05–06/07, Visioncrest Commercial, Singapore 238467

Cambridge University Press is part of Cambridge University Press & Assessment,
a department of the University of Cambridge.

We share the University's mission to contribute to society through the pursuit of
education, learning and research at the highest international levels of excellence.

www.cambridge.org
Information on this title: www.cambridge.org/9781009014809
DOI: 10.1017/9781009029728

First and Second editions © John M. Stewart 2014, 2017

Third edition © Cambridge University Press & Assessment 2023

First published 2014
Second edition 2017
Third edition 2023

Printed in the United Kingdom by CPI Group Ltd, Croydon CR0 4YY

A catalogue record for this publication is available from the British Library

A Cataloging-in-Publication data record for this book is available from the Library of Congress

ISBN 978-1-009-01480-9 Paperback

Additional resources for this publication at www.cambridge.org/9781009014809.

Contents

Preface

I bought a copy of *Python for Scientists* at a conference booth in 2016, looking for an affordable and easily readable textbook for a Python course I was teaching at that time. I was intrigued by how straightforwardly even complex things were explained in this book. It was a perfect match for my course and my students, despite my impression that the book was rather heavily focused on mathematical applications.

It has been five years since the second edition of *Python for Scientists* was released. This is a long time in the life cycle of a programming language that is still under active development. It was definitely time for an update.

Unfortunately, John is no longer with us to provide this update himself. Instead, I was honored that this task was offered to me, and I could not decline.

Besides updating the Python code examples shown in the book, I took the opportunity to also update the content of the book with the goal of making it accessible to a broader audience of scientists, especially those with a quantitative focus in their work. This includes a more in-depth discussion of numerical mathematics with NumPy (Chapter 4) and SciPy (Chapter 5), plotting capabilities with Matplotlib (Chapter 6), and, for the first time, data handling with Pandas (Chapter 8), performance computing with Python (Chapter 9), and an outline of software development techniques that are useful to scientists (Chapter 10). However, in order to keep the book reasonably short and affordable, other content, such as the detailed treatment of ordinary and partial differential equations, had to be significantly shortened or removed altogether – Python packages for dealing with such problems exist, but their discussion is beyond the scope of this beginner book.

I sincerely hope the third edition of *Python for Scientists* will be a useful companion on your long journey to becoming a scientific programmer.

Michael Mommert
St. Gallen, November 2022

1 Introduction

1.1 Python for Scientists

The title of this book is *Python for Scientists*, but what does that mean? The dictionary defines "Python" as either (a) a nonvenomous snake from Asia or Saharan Africa or (b) a computer programming language, and it is the second option that is intended here. By "scientist," we mean anyone who uses quantitative models either to obtain conclusions by processing precollected experimental data or to model potentially observable results from a more abstract theory, and who asks "what if?" What if I analyze the data in a different way? What if I change the model?

Given the steady progress in the development of evermore complex experiments that explore the inner workings of nature and generate vast amounts of data, as well as the necessity to describe these observations with complex (nonlinear) theoretical models, the use of computers to answer these questions is mandatory. Luckily, advances in computer hardware and software development mean that immense amounts of data or complex models can be processed at increasingly rapid speeds. It might seem a given that suitable software will also be available so that the "what if" questions can be answered readily. However, this turns out not always to be the case. A quick pragmatic reason is that while there is a huge market for hardware improvements, scientists form a very small fraction of it and so there is little financial incentive to improve scientific software. But for scientists, specialized, yet versatile, software tools are key to unraveling complex problems.

1.2 Scientific Software

Before we discuss what types of scientific software are available, it is important to note that all computer software comes in one of two types: proprietary or open-source. **Proprietary software** is supplied by a commercial firm. Such organizations have both to pay wages and taxes and to provide a return for their shareholders. Therefore, they have to charge real money for their products, and, in order to protect their assets from their competitors, they do not tell the customer how their software works. Thus the end users have little chance of being able to adapt or optimize the product for their own use.

Since wages and taxes are recurrent expenditures, the company needs to issue frequent charged-for updates and improvements (the *Danegeld effect*).

Open-source software, on the other hand, is available for free. It is usually developed by computer-literate individuals, often working for universities or similar organizations, who provide the service for their colleagues. It is distributed subject to anti-copyright licenses, which give nobody the right to copyright it or to use it for commercial gain. Conventional economics might suggest that the gamut of open-source software should be inferior to its proprietary counterpart, or else the commercial organizations would lose their market. As we shall see, this is not necessarily the case.

Next we need to differentiate between two different types of scientific software. The easiest approach to extracting insight from data or modeling observations utilizes prebuilt software tools, which we refer to as "**scientific software tools**." Proprietary examples include software tools and packages like Matlab, Mathematica, IDL, Tableau, or even Excel and open-source equivalents like R, Octave, SciLab, and LibreOffice. Some of these tools provide graphical user interfaces (GUIs) enabling the user to interact with the software in an efficient and intuitive way. Typically, such tools work well for standard tasks, but they do offer only a limited degree of flexibility, making it hard if not impossible to adapt these packages to solve some task they were not designed for. Other software tools provide more flexibility through their own idiosyncratic programming language in which problems are entered into a user interface. After a coherent group of statements, often just an individual statement, has been typed, the software writes equivalent core language code and compiles it on the fly. Thus errors and/or results can be reported back to the user immediately. Such tools are called "interpreters" as they interpret code on the fly, thus offering a higher degree of flexibility compared to software tools with shiny GUIs.

On a more basic level, the aforementioned software tools are implemented in a **programming language**, which is a somewhat limited subset of human language in which sequences of instructions are written, usually by humans, to be read and understood by computers. The most common languages are capable of expressing very sophisticated mathematical concepts, albeit often with a steep learning curve. Although a myriad of programming languages exist, only a handful have been widely accepted and adopted for scientific applications. Historically, this includes C and Fortran, as well as their descendants. In the case of these so-called **compiled languages**, compilers translate code written by humans into machine code that can be optimized for speed and then processed. As such, they are rather like Formula 1 racing cars. The best of them are capable of breathtakingly fast performance, but driving them is not intuitive and requires a great deal of training and experience. This experience is additionally complicated by the fact that compilers for the same language are not necessarily compatible and need to be supplemented by large libraries to provide functionality for seemingly basic functionality.

Since all scientific software tools are built upon compiled programming languages, why not simply write your own tools? Well, a racing car is not usually the best choice for a trip to the supermarket, where speed is not of paramount importance. Similarly, compiled languages are not always ideal for quickly trying out new ideas or writing short scripts to support you in your daily work. Thus, for the intended readers of this book, the direct use of compilers is likely to be unattractive, unless their use is mandatory. We therefore look at the other type of programming language, the so-called **interpreted languages**, which include the previously mentioned scientific tools based on interpreters. Interpreted languages lack the speed of compiled languages, but they typically are much more intuitive and easier to learn.

Let us summarize our position. There are prebuilt software tools, some of which are proprietary and some of which are open-source software, that provide various degrees of flexibility (interpreters typically offer more flexibility than tools that feature GUIs) and usually focus on specific tasks. On a more basic level, there are traditional compiled languages for numerics that are very general, very fast, rather difficult to learn, and do not interact readily with graphical or algebraic processes. Finally, there are interpreted languages that are typically much easier to learn than compiled languages and offer a large degree of flexibility but are less performant.

So, what properties should an ideal scientific software have? A short list might contain:

☐ a mature programming language that is both easy to understand and has extensive expressive ability,

☐ integration of algebraic, numerical, and graphical functions, and the option to import functionality from an almost endless list of supplemental libraries,

☐ the ability to generate numerical algorithms running with speeds within an order of magnitude of the fastest of those generated by compiled languages,

☐ a user interface with adequate on-line help and decent documentation,

☐ an extensive range of textbooks from which the curious reader can develop greater understanding of the concepts,

☐ open-source software, freely available,

☐ implementation on all standard platforms, e.g., Linux/Unix, Mac OS, Windows.

☐ a concise package, and thus implementable on even modest hardware.

You might have guessed it: we are talking about Python here.

In 1991, Guido van Rossum created Python as an open-source, platform-independent, general purpose programming language. It is basically a very simple language surrounded by an enormous library of add-on packages for almost any use case imaginable. Python is extremely versatile: it can be used to build complex software tools or as a scripting language to quickly get some task done. This versatility has both ensured its adoption by power users and led to the assembly of a large community of developers. These properties make Python a very powerful tool for scientists in their daily work and we hope that this book will help you master this tool.

1.3   About This Book

The purpose of this intentionally short book is to introduce the Python programming language and to provide an overview of scientifically relevant packages and how they can be utilized. This book is written for first-semester students and faculty members, graduate students and emeriti, high-school students and post-docs – or simply for everyone who is interested in using Python for scientific analysis.

However, this book by no means claims to be a complete introduction to Python. We leave the comprehensive treatment of Python and all its details to others who have done this with great success (see, e.g., Lutz, 2013). We have quite deliberately preferred brevity and simplicity over encyclopedic coverage in order to get the inquisitive reader up and running as soon as possible.

Furthermore, this book will not serve as the "Numerical Recipes for Python," meaning that we will not explain methods and algorithms in detail: we will simply showcase how they can be used and applied to scientific problems. For an in-depth discussion of these algorithms, we refer to the real *Numerical Recipes* – Press et al. (2007) and all following releases that were adapted to different programming languages – as well as other works.

Given the dynamic environment of software development, details on specific packages are best retrieved from online documentation and reference websites. We will provide references, links, and pointers in order to guide interested readers to the appropriate places. In order to enable an easy entry into the world of Python, we provide all code snippets presented in this book in the form of Jupyter Notebooks on the CoCalc cloud computing platform. These Notebooks can be accessed, run, and modified online for a more interactive learning experience.

We aim to leave the reader with a well-founded framework to handle many basic, and not so basic, tasks, as well as the skill set to find their own way in the world of scientific programming and Python.

1.4   References

Print Resources

Lutz, Mark. *Learning Python: Powerful Object-Oriented Programming*. O'Reilly Media, 2013.

Press, William H, et al. *Numerical Recipes: The Art of Scientific Computing*. 3rd ed., Cambridge University Press, 2007.

2 About Python

Python is currently the most popular programming language among scientists and other programmers. There are a number of reasons leading to its popularity and fame, especially among younger researchers. This chapter introduces the Python programming language and provides an overview on how to install and use the language most efficiently.

2.1   What Is Python?

Python is a general-purpose programming language that is extremely versatile and relatively easy to learn. It is considered a high-level programming language, meaning that the user typically will not have to deal with some typical housekeeping tasks when designing code. This is different from other (especially compiled) languages that heavily rely on the user to do these tasks properly. Python is designed in such a way as to help the user to write easily readable code by following simple guidelines. But Python also implements powerful programming paradigms: it can be used as an object-oriented, procedural, and functional programming language, depending on your needs and use case. Thus Python combines the simplicity of a scripting language with advanced concepts that are typically characteristic for compiled languages. Some of these features – which we will introduce in detail in Chapter 3 – include dynamic typing, built-in object types and other tools, automatic memory management and garbage collection, as well as the availability of a plethora of add-on and third-party packages for a wide range of use cases. Despite its apparent simplicity, these features make Python a very competitive, powerful, and flexible programming language.

Most importantly, Python is open-source and as such freely available to everyone. We detail in Section 2.2 how to obtain and install Python on your computer.

Based on various recent reports and statistics, Python is currently the most popular programming language among researchers and professional software developers for a wide range of applications and problems. This popularity largely stems from the ease of learning Python, as well as the availability of a large number of add-on packages that supplement basic Python and provide easy access to tasks that would otherwise be cumbersome to implement.

But there is also a downside: Python is an interpreted language, which makes it slower than compiled languages. However, Python provides some remedies for this issue as we will see in Chapter 9.

For researchers, Python offers a large range of well-maintained open-source packages, many of which are related to or at least based on the SciPy ecosystem. SciPy contains packages for scientific computing, mathematics, and engineering applications. Despite being the backbone of many Python applications, SciPy is completely open-source and funded in some part through NumFocus, a nonprofit organization supporting the development of scientific Python packages. We will get to know some of the packages that are part of the SciPy universe in Chapters 4, 5, and 8.

2.1.1   A Brief History of Python

The Python programming language was conceived by Guido van Rossum, a Dutch computer scientist, in the 1980s. He started the implementation in 1989 as a hobby project over the Christmas holidays. The first release became available in 1991 and Python 1.0 was released in 1994; Python 2.0 became available in 2000. With a growing user base, the development team also started to grow and gradually all the features that we appreciate about this language were implemented. Python 3.0 was released in 2008, which broke the backwards compatibility with Python 2.x due to some design decisions. The existence of two versions of Python that were incompatible with each other generated some confusion, especially with inexperienced users. However, support for Python 2.x ended in 2020, leaving Python 3.x as the only supported version of Python. The example code shown in this book and the accompanying Jupyter Notebooks (see Section 2.4.2) are based on Python version 3.9.12, but this should not matter as future versions should be compatible with that one.

Van Rossum is considered the principal author of Python and has played a central role in its development until 2018. Since 2001, the Python Software Foundation, a nonprofit organization focusing on the development of the core Python distribution, managing intellectual rights, and organizing developer conferences, has played an increasingly important role in the project. Major design decisions within the project are made by a five-person steering council and documented in Python Enhancement Protocols (PEPs). PEPs mainly discuss technical proposals and decisions, but we will briefly look at two PEPs that directly affect users: the Zen of Python (PEP 20, Section 2.1.2) and the Python Style Guide (PEP 8, Section 3.13).

We would also like to note that in 2012, NumFOCUS was founded as a nonprofit organization that supports the development of a wide range of scientific Python packages including, but not limited to, NumPy (see Chapter 4), SciPy (see Chapter 5), Matplotlib (see Chapter 6), SymPy (see Chapter 7), Pandas (see Chapter 8), Project Jupyter, and IPython. The support through NumFOCUS for these projects includes funding that is based on donations to NumFOCUS; for most of these open-source projects, donations are their only source of funding.

One detail we have skipped so far is why Van Rossum named his new programming language after a snake. Well, he did not. Python is actually named after the BBC comedy TV show *Monty Python's Flying Circus*, of which Van Rossum is a huge fan. In case you were wondering, this is also the reason why the words "spam" and "eggs" are oftentimes used as metasyntactic variables in Python example code in a reference to their famous "Spam" sketch from 1970.

2.1.2 The Zen of Python

The Zen of Python is an attempt to summarize Van Rossum's guiding principles for the design of Python into 20 aphorisms, only 19 of which have been written down. These guiding principles are very concise and distill many features of Python into a few words. The Zen of Python is so important that it is actually published (PEP 20) and its content is literally built into the Python language and can be accessed as follows:

```
import this
```

```
Beautiful is better than ugly.
Explicit is better than implicit.
Simple is better than complex.
Complex is better than complicated.
Flat is better than nested.
Sparse is better than dense.
Readability counts.
Special cases aren't special enough to break the rules.
Although practicality beats purity.
Errors should never pass silently.
Unless explicitly silenced.
In the face of ambiguity, refuse the temptation to guess.
There should be one — and preferably only one — obvious way to
    do it.
Although that way may not be obvious at first unless you're Dutch.
Now is better than never.
Although never is often better than *right* now.
If the implementation is hard to explain, it's a bad idea.
If the implementation is easy to explain, it may be a good idea.
Namespaces are one honking great idea — let's do more of those!
```

Please note that these guidelines focus on the design of the Python programming language, not necessarily the design of code written in Python. Nevertheless, you are free to follow these guidelines when writing your own code to create truly *pythonic* code. The term *pythonic* is often used within the Python community to refer to code that follows the guiding principles mentioned here.

These guiding principles are numerous and some of them might not be immediately clear to the reader, especially if you are new to Python programming. We would summarize the most important Python concepts as follows.

Simplicity Simple code is easier to write and read; it improves readability, shareability, and maintainability, and therefore helps you and others in the short term and long term.

Readability It is nice to write code as compact as possible, but if writing compact code requires some tricks that are hard to understand, you might prefer a more extensive implementation that provides better readability. Why? Imagine that your future self tries to modify some code that you wrote years ago. If your code is well-readable, you will probably have fewer problems understanding what the individual lines of code do.

Explicitness We will explain this idea with an example. Consider you are writing code that is able to read data from different file formats. A decision you have to make is the following: will you create a single function that is able to read all the different file formats, or do you create a number of individual functions, each of which is able to read only a single file format? The *pythonic* way would be the latter: each function that you create will explicitly be able to deal with only a single file format in contrast to a single function that implicitly deals with all file formats. Why is this solution favored? Generally, explicit code is easier to understand and less prone to confusion.

Naturally, these concepts are entangled and closely related to each other. However, there is no need to memorize these concepts. You will internalize those concepts that are relevant to you by writing code and reading code written by others. And, of course, nobody can force you to follow these principles in your own coding; but we hope that this section provides you a better understanding of the Python programming language and its design.

2.2   Installing Python

Depending on the operating system you are using, there are several ways to install Python on your computer, some of which are simpler than others. The easiest and at the same time safest way to install Python is to use the Anaconda environment as detailed below.

Alternatively, you can also install Python from scratch on your computer – unless it is already installed. In the latter case, you should be careful not to interfere with the native Python already installed as it might be required by your operating system. This process might be a bit more complicated, but there are detailed installation guides for all operating systems available online. To be on the safe side, we recommend the installation of Anaconda, which comes with Conda, a tool to set up and utilize virtual environments, in order to prevent interference with other versions of Python that might be installed on your computer. Once Python is installed, additional packages can also be installed using Conda and the *Package installer for Python*, pip.

2.2.1 Anaconda and Conda

Anaconda is a Python distribution package for data science and machine learning applications. Despite this specialization, the Anaconda Individual Edition (also known as the "Anaconda Distribution") constitutes a solid basis for any scientific Python installation.

The Anaconda Distribution is provided and maintained by Anaconda Inc. (previously known as Continuum Analytics). Despite being a for-profit company, Anaconda Inc. distributes the Anaconda Individual Edition for free.

Installing Anaconda

Installing Anaconda is simple and straightforward. All that is required is to download the respective Anaconda Individual Edition installer (see Section 2.6) for your operating system and run it. The installer will walk you through the installation process. Note that you will need to agree to the Anaconda license agreement. At the end of the installation routine, you will be asked whether to make Anaconda Python your default Python version, which is a good idea in most cases. If you now start the Python interpreter (see Section 2.4.1), you will be greeted by Anaconda Python. Congratulations, you have successfully installed Anaconda Python on your computer.

Conda

One advantage of using Anaconda is the availability of Conda, an open-source package and environment manager that was originally developed by Anaconda Inc., but has subsequently been released separately under an open-source license. Although, for a beginner, the simple installation process for Anaconda Python is most likely its most important feature, Conda also solves two problems in the background. As a package manager, it allows you to easily install Python packages with a single command on your command line, e.g.,

```
conda install numpy
```

Almost all major Python packages are available through Conda. Packages are available through Conda-Forge (see Section 2.6), a GitHub (see Section 10.3.1) organization that contains repositories of "Conda recipes" for a wide range of packages. Conda-Forge contains more detailed information on how to install packages through Conda, as well as a list of all packages that are available through Conda.

As an environment manager, Conda allows you to define different environments, each of which can have its own Python installation. Although this is an advanced feature and becomes important when you are dealing with specific versions of your Python packages, there is still some benefit for the Python beginner. Some operating systems use native Python installation to run crucial services; meddling with these Python installations can seriously harm your system. By default, Anaconda creates a *base* environment for the user. Since this environment is independent from your system, there is no danger in meddling with your system Python installation. Thus using Anaconda is safer than using your system Python installation.

It is not complicated to define new Conda environments and to switch between them. However, due to the advanced nature of dealing with different environments, we refer to the Conda documentation to learn more about how to do this.

2.2.2   Pip and PyPI

Pretty much all Python packages are registered with the *Python Package Index*, PyPI, which enables the easy distribution of these packages. Installing packages from PyPI is very easy using the pip package manager, which comes with most Python installations, e.g.,

```
pip install numpy
```

Everybody can publish their code via PyPI; in Section 10.3.2 we will show how this can be achieved. Since PyPI is the official repository of Python packages, pretty much all available packages are installable using pip.

Pip or Conda?

After learning about Conda and pip you might be confused which of these tools you should use to install Python packages. The short answer is, in most cases it does not matter. Especially for beginners, it is perfectly fine and typically also safe to install packages using pip. Pip is typically faster than Conda in installing packages.

This faster installation process comes at a (small) price that won't matter to most users. The price is that Conda is generally safer in installing new packages. Before Conda installs a new package, it will check the version numbers of all packages that are already installed in your current Conda environment and it will check whether these packages in the present versions are compatible with the new package and vice versa. Pip simply checks whether the versions of the installed packages are compatible with the new package – and it will update the already present packages, to make them compatible with the new package. However, pip disregards that there might be requirements by other packages that will break by updating these existing packages. As a result, pip may break packages that were previously installed.

This happens very rarely, since most Python packages are compatible over many different versions. However, in the case of quickly developing projects it is mandatory to use specific versions of packages. In those cases, it is much safer to use Conda to install new packages. For most other users, especially on the beginner level, there should be no major issues.

2.3 How Python Works

In Chapter 1, we already introduced compiled and interpreted programming languages. As a brief reminder, compiled languages take the code written by the user in some high-level programming language and translate it into machine-readable code that is written to an executable file. Interpreted languages, on the other hand, do not require the high-level code provided by the user to be compiled. Instead, the *interpreter* reads the code in chunks and translates them sequentially into some less-basic kind of machine-readable *bytecode* that is directly executed. As you can imagine, compiled languages perform faster than interpreted languages, since the *compiler* already does the hard work to translate user code to efficient machine-readable code, whereas an interpreter has to do this on the fly in a less efficient way.

The following sections will detail how to directly provide code to the interpreter in different ways.

2.4 How to Use Python

There are different ways to use Python, the most important of which we will introduce in the following sections. Which of these options you should use depends on your preferences and the problem you are trying to solve.

In the remainder of this book, we assume that you are using Jupyter Notebooks. This choice is mainly driven by the opportunity to publish all code elements from this book as readily accessible Jupyter Notebooks. You can run these Notebooks (as well as your own Notebooks) online in the cloud, or locally on your computer as detailed below. However, we would like to point out that it is not a requirement for the reader to use these Notebooks in order to follow this book in any way. Feel free to use whichever interface to Python you feel most comfortable with.

2.4.1 The Python Interpreter

The easiest way to use Python is to run its interpreter in interactive mode. On most operating systems, this is done by simply typing `python` into a terminal or powershell window. Once started, you can type Python commands and statements into the interpreter, which are then executed line by line (or block by block if you use indentation).

While this might be useful to quickly try something out, it is not really suited to write long scripts or other more or less complex pieces of code. The interpreter also provides only a bare minimum in terms of support and usability.

The Python interpreter also offers a different way to run Python code that is much better suited for running longer pieces of code. Instead of writing your code line by line into the interpreter, you can simply write your code into an ordinary text file and pass that file to the interpreter in your terminal window or on the command line. You can give your code file any name you want, but by convention, you should use the file ending ".py." You can use the most basic text editor for this purpose: Emacs, Vim, Nano or Gedit on Linux, TextEdit or Sublime on a Mac, or NotePad on Windows. It is important that the resulting Python code file does not contain any fancy formatting, just clean text.

For example, you could create a file named "hello.py" with the following single line of content:

```
print('Hello World!')
```

You can then run this script in a terminal window or powershell by using

```
python hello.py
```

Make sure that Python is properly installed on your system (see Section 2.2) and that you run this command in the same directory where the hello.py file resides. If successful, the output that you receive should look like this:

```
Hello World!
```

And this is your first Python program!

2.4.2   IPython and Jupyter

IPython (Interactive Python) is an architecture for interactive computing with Python: it can be considered as the Python interpreter on steroids. The IPython interpreter has been designed and written by scientists with the aim of offering very fast exploration and construction of code with minimal typing effort, and offering appropriate, even maximal, on-screen help when required. It further supports introspection (the ability to examine the properties of any Python object at runtime), tab completion (autocompletion support during typing when hitting the Tab key), history (IPython stores commands that are entered and their results, both of which can be accessed at runtime), as well as support for parallel computing. Most importantly, IPython includes a browser-based Notebook interface with a visually appealing notebook-like appearance.

The first version of IPython was published in 2001. Project Jupyter evolved from IPython around 2014 as a nonprofit, open-source project to support interactive data science and scientific computing. The Notebook interface was subsequently outsourced from IPython and implemented as part of Jupyter, where it was perfected and extended in different ways. Most notably, Jupyter Notebooks are language agnostic and can be used with different programming languages using so-called kernels. The Python kernel is provided and still maintained by the IPython project.

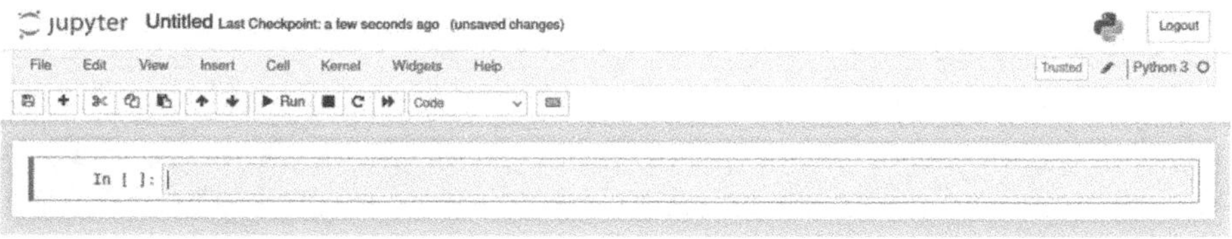

Figure 2.1 A newly created Jupyter Notebook containing a single, empty code cell.

The following sections introduce the most important features of Jupyter.

Jupyter Notebooks

The most relevant feature of Jupyter for you will most likely be the **Jupyter Notebook**, which is an enhanced version of the IPython Notebook. All programming examples are presented in the form of Jupyter Notebooks and imitate their appearance (see Figure 2.1). Furthermore, all code elements shown in this book are available as Jupyter Notebooks online at CoCalc, and also at www.cambridge.org/9781009014809.

Jupyter Notebooks are documents that consist of distinct cells that can contain and run code, formatted text, mathematical equations, and other media. Notebooks are run in your browser through a server that is either hosted locally on your computer or in the cloud (see Section 2.4.4).

To start a Jupyter Notebook server locally, you simply have to run

```
jupyter notebook
```

in a terminal window or powershell. This will run a server in the background that is typically accessible through `http://localhost:8888` (you need to type this into the URL field of your browser to access the Notebook server). You will see a list of files and directories located in the directory you started the server from. From here you can navigate your file system, and open existing Jupyter Notebooks or create new ones. Notebook files use the filename ending `.ipynb`, indicating that they are using the IPython kernel. To open a Notebook, simply click on the file and you will see something that looks like Figure 2.1.

Cloud services hosting Jupyter Notebook servers are a different avenue that allow you to utilize Notebooks without the (minor) hassle of having to install the necessary software on your computer. As a result, Notebooks that run on cloud services (see Section 2.4.4) might look a little bit different to what is shown in Figure 2.1, but rest assured that they can be used in the same way as described in this book.

Notebooks consist of *cells* that are either **code cells** that contain Python code or **markdown cells** that contain text or other media utilizing the markdown language. **Markdown** is a lightweight markup language (pun intended) that enables you to quickly format text and even supports LaTeX inline math. A markdown cheat sheet containing some formatting basics is provided in Table 2.1 for your convenience; for more

Table 2.1 Jupyter Notebook markdown cheat sheet

Markdown	Appearance
# Large Headline ### Medium Headline ##### Small Headline	# Large Headline ## Medium Headline **Small Headline**
normal text *emphasized/italics* text **bold** text `simple one-line code sample`	normal text *emphasized/italics* text **bold** text `simple one-line code sample`

``python
print('multi-line syntax')
print('highlighting', '!')
``
	print('multi-line syntax')
	print('highlighting', '!')

* unordered list item 1 * unordered list item 2 1. ordered list item 1 2. ordered list item 2	• unordered list item 1 • unordered list item 2 1. ordered list item 1 2. ordered list item 2
[https://www.python.org](link)	link
![alt text][https://...image.jpg] ![alt text][/path/to/image.jpg]	insert image from url insert image from file
$\frac{1}{2} x^2 = \int x\, dx$	$\frac{1}{2}x^2 = \int x\, dx$

information on how to use the markdown language, please consult your favorite internet search engine.

To run any cell, i.e., to run the code in a code cell or to render the text in a markdown cell, you can click the corresponding "run" button or simply use the keyboard shortcut shift + enter. If your code cell generates output, this output will be displayed underneath the code cell. Note that each executed code cell will be numbered (e.g., [1] for the code cell that was executed first) at the beginning of that cell and that the corresponding output will carry the same number. This number is stored in the history of the Notebook and can be utilized and indexed during runtime. Note that in the case of markdown cells, the raw input that you provided is simply replaced by the rendered text upon execution.

For as long as a Notebook is open and running, the memory is shared between all cells. That means that if you define an object in one cell and execute that cell, you can access that object from any other cell. This also means that if you change the object in one cell, its state changes in all other cells, too. Thus the order in which cells are executed might be important.

There is no rule for how many lines of code should go into a single code cell. When testing code or performing explorative data analysis, you might end up with a number of single-line code cells. If you develop large-scale numerical models, you might end up with cells containing hundreds of lines of code. The same applies to the number of cells in a Notebook.

We encourage the reader to take full advantage of the features of a Notebook: combine code cells and markdown cells in such a way as to treat the Notebook as a self-explanatory document that contains runnable Python code.

While code cells generally expect to receive valid Python commands, they can also execute commands on the underlying operating system's terminal or command line environment. **Magic commands** provide the user with a way to interact with the operating system and file system from within a Jupyter Notebook. A very long, very detailed description of magic commands can be found by typing %magic, and a compact list of available commands is given by typing %lsmagic. Note that there are two types of magic: **line magic** and **cell magic**. Line magic commands are prefixed by % and operate only on a single line of a cell. Cell magic, on the other hand, is prefixed by %% and operates on the entire cell; cell magic should always appear at the beginning of a cell.

A harmless line magic example is pwd, which comes from the Unix operating system and prints the name of the current directory (**p**resent **w**orking **d**irectory). With magic, pwd can be called by invoking

```
%pwd
```

An example for a cell magic command is %%timeit, which we introduce in Section 9.1.1 to accurately measure the time it takes to run a specific cell.

Magic commands provide a useful set of commands, but this set is limited. There is also the possibility to execute commands directly on the operating system level without having to leave a running Notebook environment. This can be achieved in code cells by prepending an exclamation mark (!). For instance, you can use this mechanism to install missing Python packages from within a Notebook:

```
!pip install <package name>
```

(see Section 2.2.2 for an introduction on pip).

Within this book, we display Notebook code cells as follows:

```
This is a code cell.
```

The output of a cell is displayed differently:

```
This is the code cell's output.
```

Please be aware that the output that you might receive on your computer may differ from the output provided in this book. This is especially true for code elements that rely on random numbers, but also other examples. Finally, please be aware that we had to edit the output provided by Python manually in a few cases to have it displayed properly in this book.

JupyterLab

JupyterLab is an advanced version of the Jupyter Notebook. It provides you with an interface to arrange multiple files – e.g., documents, Jupyter Notebooks, text editors, consoles – on a single screen. The idea behind the JupyterLab environment is to support data analysis by combining different tools into a single environment. To start a JupyterLab server locally, all you need to do is to run

```
jupyter lab
```

in your Linux or Mac terminal or your Windows powershell. The combination of Notebooks and data visualization tools makes JupyterLabs powerful for tasks involving the analysis of data and other tasks. We encourage readers to experiment with this system, but we will not require its use in the following.

JupyterHub

JupyterHub runs a multi-user server for Jupyter Notebooks. This means that multiple users can log into a server to run and share Notebooks. Some research institutes maintain their own JupyterHub to provide their researchers a collaborative work environment. A detailed discussion of JupyterHub is outside the scope of this book, but we would like the reader to be aware of its existence.

2.4.3   Integrated Development Environments

If you prefer a more sophisticated environment for coding, you should have a look at integrated development environments (IDEs), which support you in your software development endeavors by providing online help, checking your syntax on the fly, highlighting relevant code elements, integrating with and supporting version control software, providing professional debugging tools, and many other things.

A wide range of IDEs for Python is available. Here we briefly introduce a small number of freely available open-source IDEs that run on all major operating systems (Linux, Mac OS, and Windows).

A very simple IDE for beginners is **Thonny**. One feature of Thonny that might appeal to beginners is that it comes with an option to install its own Python interpreter; the user will not have to install Python themselves (although this is of course still possible). Furthermore, Thonny provides features that will help you code in Python, better understand your code, and find mistakes in your code during typing.

Spyder is a much more advanced IDE that is tailored to scientific applications with a focus on data science. Spyder is written in Python and for Python. It comes with many features of professional IDEs, like a debugger, and it allows you to work with Jupyter Notebooks.

PyCharm and **VSCode** (Visual Studio Code) are two rather professional IDEs providing all of the aforementioned features plus a wide range of plugins for a variety of use cases. While VSCode, although provided by Microsoft, is completely free of charge, PyCharm has two different versions: a free-to-use Community Edition that comes with all the bells and whistles for Python programming, and a Professional Version that is not free, but comes with additional support for the development of scientific software and web applications.

Finding the right IDE that fits your needs is mostly a matter of taste, habit, and expectations. Feel free to try all of these IDEs and pick the one that suits your needs. Be aware that especially the more professional environments will typically feel less comfortable in the beginning and that it takes some time to get used to setting them up and working with them. However, at some point, you will get used to them and enjoy some of their more advanced features.

However, always keep in mind that there is no requirement to use an IDE to become a good programmer. There are plenty of people out there that write excellent and extremely complex code, using simple text editors like Vim or Emacs (even those can be customized into very efficient programming tools by installing a few extensions) or Jupyter Notebooks. Our bottom line is this: feel free to use whatever tool you feel most comfortable with!

2.4.4   Cloud Environments

Finally, we would like to point out that it is possible to run Jupyter Notebooks in cloud environments. For instance, all Notebooks utilized in this book are available online and can be run on different cloud services. Free computing is available through a number of providers; we would like to point out three examples: Binder, CoCalc, and Google Colab. **Binder** enables you to run Notebooks hosted in Github repositories (see Section 10.3.1) and does, as of writing this, not require any form of registration or user authentication. **CoCalc** provides similar functionality; all Jupyter Notebooks related to this book are hosted at CoCalc. **Google Colab** requires registration with Google services; usage is free to some reasonable extent. The advantage of Colab is its integration in the Google services environment (e.g., it is possible to connect to Google Drive for storing Notebooks and data files) and the option to ask for additional computational resources like GPU support at no charge (as of this writing).

2.5   Where to Find Help?

Before we get started on actual programming with Python, we would like to share a few words on how to get help when you are stuck with an issue. First of all, do not panic: there are many ways for you to get help, depending on your situation.

In case you are unsure about how to use a function or method, or you are trying to find the right function or method for your purpose, you can consult the corresponding **Reference**, which describes its syntax and semantics in detail. The Python Language Reference describes the syntax and core semantics of the language. On the other hand, the Python Standard Library contains details on the workings of the built-in functionality of Python. Both references are important and you might want to browse them to get an idea of their content and utility. In addition to these resources, each major Python package has its own reference document. As a practical example, let us consider the math package reference that is part of the Python Standard Library. For each function in the math module, the reference provides a detailed *docstring* (see Section 3.1) that describes the function's general functionality as well as its arguments. For instance, the *docstring* of math.perm() looks like this:

```
math.perm(n, k=None)

Return the number of ways to choose k items from n items without
    repetition and with order.

Evaluates to n! / (n - k)! when k <= n and evaluates to zero when k >
    n.

If k is not specified or is None, then k defaults to n and the
    function returns n!.

Raises TypeError if either of the arguments are not integers. Raises
    ValueError if either of the arguments are negative.

New in version 3.8.
```

math.perm takes two arguments: a (required) positional argument (see Section 3.8.2), n, and an (optional) keyword argument (see Section 3.8.3), k. The *docstring* defines the functionality of the function and what it returns. Furthermore, it contains information on the exceptions (see Section 3.10.2) that it may raise and a note about when it was implemented into the math module. Based on this information – and after reading the next chapter of this book – it should be straightforward to utilize this function. References can be accessed online by utilizing your favorite search engine, by using the help() function in your Python interpreter, or through your favorite IDE.

If you prefer looking things up in printed books instead of browsing the Internet, you may, of course, also refer to literature (see, e.g., Section 3.14). The advantage here is that function descriptions might be less technical and easier to understand – but on the downside, these descriptions might be incomplete. Nevertheless, literature is definitely a good resource if you are looking for help.

Even if you are perfectly sure about how to use a function, errors may occur. When an error occurs during runtime, Python will tell you about it. It will not only tell you on which line of code what type of error occurred, but also how the program reached that point in your code (this is called the *traceback*; see Section 3.10.1 for more details on this). The latter might sound trivial, but it is actually very useful when dealing with highly modular programs that consist of hundreds or thousands of lines of code.

Every once in a while, every programmer will encounter a problem that they cannot solve without help from others. A perfectly legitimate approach to solving this problem would be to search for a solution on the Internet. An excellent resource, and likely the most common website to pop up as a result of search engine queries, is *StackOverflow*, which is used by beginners and professional programmers alike. You can ask questions on *StackOverflow*, but it is more than likely that the specific problem that you encountered has already been addressed and answered by the community and can therefore be found with most internet search engines. For instance, the last line of your *traceback* (the actual error message; see Section 3.10.1) would be a good candidate to enter into a search engine, potentially leading to a number of cases in which other coders experienced similar issues and presumably were able to solve them. While this sounds trivial, this process of finding the solution to a problem online should be in no way stigmatized. On the contrary, we encourage users in this process, since the potential to learn from others cannot be underestimated.

2.6   References

Online resources

□ Python project resources

Python project homepage
https://python.org

Python Developer's Guide
https://python.org/dev/

Python PEP Index
https://python.org/dev/peps

NumFOCUS project homepage
https://numfocus.org

NumPy project homepage
https://numpy.org

SciPy project homepage
https://scipy.org

Matplotlib project homepage
https://matplotlib.org

SymPy project homepage
`https://sympy.org`

Pandas project homepage
`https://pandas.pydata.org`

Jupyter project homepage
`https://jupyter.org`

IPython project homepage
`https://ipython.org`

□ Installation resources

Anaconda homepage
`https://anaconda.com/`

Anaconda Individual Edition download homepage
`https://anaconda.com/products/individual`

Conda project homepage
`https://conda.io`

Conda-Forge project homepage
`https://conda-forge.org/`

Conda documentation
`https://docs.conda.io/`

Python Package Index (PyPI) homepage
`https://pypi.org/`

□ Integrated development environments

Thonny
`https://thonny.org/`

Spyder
`https://spyder-ide.org/`

PyCharm
`https://jetbrains.com/pycharm/`

Visual Studio Code
`https://spyder-ide.org/`

□ Cloud environments

Binder
`https://mybinder.org/`

CoCalc
`https://cocalc.com/`

       Google Colab

         `https://colab.research.google.com/`

☐ Finding help

       Python Standard Library

         `https://docs.python.org/3/library/`

       Python Language Reference

         `https://docs.python.org/3/reference/`

       StackOverflow

         `https://stackoverflow.com/`

3 Basic Python

Very few people would learn a foreign language by first mastering a grammar textbook and then memorizing a dictionary. Most start with a few rudiments of grammar and a tiny vocabulary. Then, by practice, they gradually extend their range of constructs and working vocabulary. This allows them to comprehend and speak the language very quickly, and it is the approach to learning Python that is being adopted here. The disadvantage is that the grammar and vocabulary are diffused throughout the learning process, but this is ameliorated by the existence of language references, such as those cited in Sections 2.6 and 3.14, to which the reader can refer for further reading. For now, we will start with the very basics of Python and gradually make our way toward the more complex aspects. As a reminder: all code elements from this chapter are available in a Jupyter Notebook (cambridge.org/9781009029728/ch3).

Most of the functions introduced in this chapter are *built-in functions*, meaning that they are available in every Python installation and do not require importing external packages (see Section 3.3). This is in contrast to other functionality requiring explicit importing of external modules and packages as presented in the subsequent chapters.

3.1 Typing Python

Every programming language includes **blocks** of code, which consist of one or more lines of code forming a syntactic unit. Python uses fewer parentheses "()" and braces "{}" than other languages, and instead uses **indentation** as a tool for formatting blocks. After any line ending in a colon (":") an indented block is required. Although the amount of indentation is not specified, the unofficial standard is four spaces. Jupyter Notebooks, IDEs, and any Python-aware text editor will help you to provide proper indentation where required. This very specific meaning of indentation often causes headaches in new Python users who have previously used other programming languages, but you will quickly grow used to this concept.

Python allows two forms of **comments**. A pound or hash symbol "#" indicates that the rest of the current line is a comment and will be ignored by the interpreter:

```
# this is a line comment
```

A different form of comment is provided in the form of the "documentation string" or ***docstring*** that can run over many lines and include any printable character. It is delimited by a pair of triple quotes ("""), e.g.,

```
"""This is a long docstring
that continues
across multiple lines."""
```

Technically, *docstrings* define multiline *strings* (see Section 3.5.7), but since defining objects without assigning them to *identifiers* (see Section 3.2) does no harm, they may be used for multiline comments, too. *Docstrings* are typically used to provide brief documentation on a function or class that you wrote (see Sections 2.5, 3.8, and 3.11).

For completeness, we note that it is possible to place several Python statements on the same line provided we separate them with semicolons:

```
a = 4; b = 5.5; c = 1.5+2j; d = 'a'
```

While this is legitimate Python code, it is rather unusual to put multiple statements on the same line as it severely affects the readability of the code (see Sections 3.13 and 2.1.2 for some motivation on this). Instead, every statement should appear on a new line.

To prevent overlong lines (fewer than 80 characters are preferred according to PEP8; see Section 3.13), long statements can and should be broken up. This can be achieved with the **line continuation symbol** \:

```
a = 1 + 2 + 3 + 4 + 5 + \
    6 + 7 + 8 + 9 + 10
```

or, if a statement is bracketed by parentheses "()", we can split the line at any point between them without the need for the continuation symbol:

```
a = (1 + 2 + 3 + 4 + 5 +
     6 + 7 + 8 + 9 + 10)
```

The latter is typically considered more *pythonic* and should be the preferred way to break up long lines.

3.2 Objects and Identifiers

Python deals exclusively with objects and *identifiers*. An **object** may be thought of as a region of computer memory containing both some data and information associated with that data. Pretty much everything in Python is actually an object. For a simple object, this information consists of its **type**, and its ***identity***[1] (i.e., the location in memory, which is of course machine-dependent). The *identity* is therefore of no interest to most users. They need a machine-independent method for accessing objects. This is provided by an ***identifier***, a label that can be attached to objects. You can think of the *identifier* as the name of a variable, and it is made up of one or more characters. The first must be a letter, or underscore, and any subsequent characters must be digits, letters, or underscores. *Identifiers* are case-sensitive: x and X are different *identifiers*. *Identifiers* that have leading and/or trailing underscores have specialized uses, and should be avoided by the beginner. We must also avoid using predefined words that are already used within Python as *function names* (such as print(), range, or open) or have other meanings (e.g., list, int, or True), since choosing such an *identifier* would disconnect it from its original use case and preclude its future use. However, the choice between, say, xnew, x_new, and xNew is a matter of taste.

The following example explains the details:

```
p = 3.14
p
```

```
3.14
```

We create an object by simply assigning a value (3.14) to the *identifier* p using the assignment operator (=; see below). Note that we never declared the type of the object p, which we would have had to declare in C or other compiled languages. This is no accident or oversight. A fundamental feature of Python is that the type belongs to the object, not to the *identifier*.[2] This means that the object's type only becomes relevant – and is defined – at runtime. This feature is referred to as ***dynamic typing*** and is characteristic of Python. If ambiguous, Python will choose the data type able to represent the full complexity of the value as efficiently as possible. When evaluating an object, as is done in the second line in the code cell above (p), the *identifier* is simply replaced with the object (3.14 in this case). Now we set q = p:

```
q = p
```

The right-hand side is replaced by whatever object p pointed to, and q is a new *identifier* that points to this object, see Figure 3.1). No equality of *identifiers* q and p is implied here! Next, we reassign the *identifier* p to a *string* object (see Section 3.5.7 for details on *strings*):

```
p = 'pi'
```

---

[1] An unfortunate choice of name, not to be confused with the about-to-be-defined *identifiers*.
[2] The curious can find the type of an object with *identifier* p with the command type(p) and its *identity* with id(p).

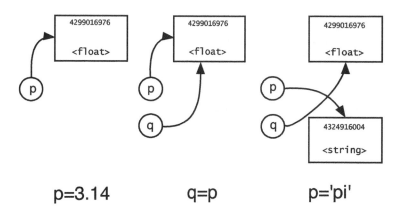

$$p=3.14 \qquad q=p \qquad p=\text{'pi'}$$

Figure 3.1 A schematic representation of assignments in Python. After the first command p=3.14, the *float* object 3.14 is created and *identifier* p is assigned to it. Here the object is depicted by its *identity*, a large number, its address in the memory (highly machine-dependent) where the data are stored, and the type. The second command q=p assigns *identifier* q to the same object. The third command p='pi' assigns p to a new *string* object, leaving q pointing to the original *float* object.

What are the values of p and q now?

```
p
```

```
'pi'
```

p, which used to be a *float* (see Section 3.4.2), is now a *string*. But what about q?

```
q
```

```
3.14
```

The original *float* object is still pointed to by the *identifier* q (see Figure 3.1), and this is confirmed here. Suppose we were to reassign the *identifier* q. Then, unless in the interim another *identifier* had been assigned to q, the original *float* object would have no *identifier* assigned to it and so becomes inaccessible to the programmer. Python will detect this automatically and silently free up computer memory, a process known as **garbage collection**.

Because of its importance in what follows, we emphasize the point that the basic building block in Python is the ***assignment operation***, which, despite appearances, has nothing to do with equality. In pseudocode,

```
<identifier> = <object>
```

which will appear over and over again. As we have already stated, the type of an object "belongs" to the object and not to any *identifier* assigned to it. Henceforth we shall try to be less pedantic!

3.3   Namespaces and Modules

While Python is running, it needs to keep a list of those *identifiers* that have been assigned to objects. This list is called a *namespace*, and, as a Python object, it too has an *identifier*. For example, while working in a Notebook or the interpreter, the *namespace*, __name__, has the unmemorable name __main__.

One of the strengths of Python is its ability to include objects, functions, classes, etc., written either by you or someone else. To enable this inclusion, suppose you have created a file containing objects, e.g., obj1, obj2 that you want to reuse. Common examples for such objects are functions or classes, but they could also contain data. The file should be saved as, e.g., foo.py, where the .py ending is mandatory. (Note that with most text editors you need this ending for the editor to realize that it contains Python code.) This file is then called a **module**. The module's *identifier* is foo, i.e., the filename minus the ending.

This module can be imported into subsequent sessions via

```
import foo
```

(When the module is first imported, it is compiled into *bytecode* and written to a directory named __pycache__/ in a file named after the module and ending in .pyc. On subsequent imports, the interpreter loads this precompiled *bytecode* unless the modification date of foo.py is more recent, in which case a new version of the file foo.pyc is generated automatically.) One effect of this import is to make the *namespace* of the module available as foo. Then the objects from foo are available with, e.g., *identifiers* foo.obj1 and foo.obj2. Note that it is necessary to specify that obj1 and obj2 are defined in the foo *namespace* by explicitly prepending foo. to these *identifiers*. If you are absolutely sure that obj1 and obj2 will not clash with *identifiers* in the current *namespace*, you can import them directly via

```
from foo import obj1, obj2
```

and then refer to them as obj1 and obj2.

It is possible to import all objects from module foo into the current *namespace* using

```
from foo import *
```

but this **should be avoided** for the following reason: if an *identifier* obj1 already existed in the current namespace, this *identifier* will be overwritten by this import process, which usually means that the original object becomes inaccessible. For example, suppose we had an *identifier* gamma referring to a *float*. Then

```
from math import *
```

overwrites this and gamma now refers to the gamma-function. A subsequent

```
from cmath import *
```

overwrites gamma with the complex gamma-function! Note, too, that import statements can appear anywhere in Python code, and so chaos is lurking if we use this option.

Especially for **packages**, which provide common *namespaces* for collections of modules, it makes sense to import only those objects that you really need. In case there are a number of objects that you need, you can also import the module and rename its *namespace*. Common names for packages that we will use extensively later in this book include

```
import numpy as np
```

for the NumPy package (see Chapter 4),

```
import matplotlib.pyplot as plt
```

for the Matplotlib package (see Chapter 6), and

```
import pandas as pd
```

for the Pandas package (see Chapter 8).

We finish our discussion of *namespaces* and modules with a related note. When you write Python code into .py files, it is good practice to wrap relevant code into functions (Section 3.8) and classes (Section 3.11) and to call and utilize those from within a code block that follows an if statement (see Section 3.6) that looks as follows:

```
if __name__ == "__main__":
    <code block>
```

If the .py file is executed from the terminal or command line, the *namespace* is named __main__ and therefore, the code block is executed. However, if the .py file is imported as a module, its *namespace* is not __main__, but the name of the module. Therefore, the code block is not executed, but all the functions and classes within the module are available to the user. In practice, this is incredibly convenient. While developing a suite of objects, e.g., functions, we can keep the ancillary test functions nearby. In production mode via import, these ancillary functions are effectively "commented out."

3.4   Numbers

Python contains three simple types of number objects, and we introduce a fourth, not-so-simple, one.

3.4.1   Integers

Python refers to whole numbers as *integers* (`int`). While earlier versions of Python only supported limited ranges for the values of *integers*, in current versions (Python 3 and later) *integers* are unbounded, meaning that there is no limit on their value. Creating an *int* object is done simply by assigning a whole number to an *identifier*:

```
p = 2
type(p)
```

```
int
```

As we see, p is indeed of type *integer*.

The usual **mathematical operations** of addition (+), subtraction (-), multiplication (*) and division (/) are, of course, implemented and available in basic Python. Naturally, these operators are not only implemented for *integers*, but also for all other applicable data types. In the case of division, even if both p and q are *integers*, the result of the division p/q will be represented by a *float* (a real-number data type, see Section 3.4.2). Furthermore, *integer* division is defined in Python by p//q. The *remainder* of this type of division is available through the modulo operation, p%q. Exponentiation p^q is also available as p**q, and can produce a real number if $q < 0$. Finally, there is one more useful feature that Python inherited from its C roots. Suppose we wish to increment *integer* p by two. Instead of

```
p = p + 2
```

one can also type

```
p += 2
```

The same formalism applies to a number of mathematical operators. Needless to say, the usual mathematical rules apply with respect to the use of brackets. Finally, we would like to point out that additional mathematical functions are available through external packages; good starting points here are the `math` module dealing with real numbers, `cmath` for complex numbers, and the NumPy and SciPy packages (see Chapters 4 and 5, respectively).

3.4.2   Real numbers

Floating-point numbers are readily available as *floats* (`float`). In most installations, the default will be approximately 16 digits of precision for *floats* in the range $(10^{-308}, 10^{308})$. The notation for *float* constants is standard, e.g.,

```
-3.14,  -314e-2, -314.0e-2, -0.00314E3
```

```
(-3.14, -3.14, -3.14, -3.14)
```

all represent the same *float*.

The usual arithmetic rules for addition, subtraction, multiplication, division, and exponentiation are available for *floats* (see Section 3.4.1). For the first three, mixed mode operations are implemented seamlessly, e.g., if addition of an *integer* and a *float* is requested, then the *integer* is automatically converted into a *float* before the operation is applied, a process that is referred to as widening. **Widening** of an *integer* to a *float* is available explicitly, e.g., **float**(4) will return 4.0. **Narrowing** of a *float* to an *integer* is defined by the following algorithm. If x is real and positive, then there exist an *integer* m and a *float* y such that

$$x = m + y \quad \text{where} \quad 0 \leqslant y < 1.0.$$

In Python, this narrowing is implemented via int(x), which returns m. If x is negative, then int(x)=-int(-x), succinctly described as "truncation towards zero," e.g., int(1.4)=1 and int(-1.4)=-1. The use of int() and float() (and similar functions) is also referred to as ***explicit type conversion***.

3.4.3   Booleans

Booleans (bool) are utilized to express the outcome of conditional statements and are widely utilized in the context of controlling the flow of your program (e.g., using if statements; see Section 3.6). A *Boolean* can have either the value **True** or **False** and can be instantiated with a given value:

```
a = True
b = False
a, b
```

```
(True, False)
```

or by evaluating a condition, for instance involving the *less than* comparison operator (<):

```
12 < 10
```

```
False
```

Other **comparison** (or **relational**) **operators** include > (greater than), >= (greater than or equal to), <= (less than or equal to), == (equal to) and != (not equal to). It is possible to combine a number of comparisons, or *Booleans* in general, in simple logical expressions utilizing **and, or**, and **not**. The following code cells show a few examples:

```
10 < 12 and 1 < 2
```

```
True
```

The combined expression is True since both "10 < 12" and "1 < 2" are True.

```
not 10 < 12 or 1 > 2
```

```
False
```

This expression is False since both "not 10 < 12" and "1 > 2" are False. Please note that the not keyword, which simply negates an expression, in this situation only applies to the subsequent expression. The use of parentheses provides a better control over the combination of multiple expressions; compare the following two examples:

```
not (10 < 12 or 1 > 2)
```

```
False
```

In this case, not is applied to the combined expression "10 < 12 or 1 > 2", which is, of course, True.

```
1 < 2 and (not 3 < 2 or 1 == 0)
```

```
True
```

Here, both "1 < 2" and "not 3 < 2 or 1 == 0" are True, since "not 3 < 2" is True.

3.4.4   Complex Numbers

We have introduced three classes of numbers that form the simplest types of Python objects. These are the basis for classes of numbers that are more complicated. For example, *rational* numbers can be implemented in terms of pairs of *integers* (see Section 3.11 for an example implementation of a class dealing with fractions). For our purposes, a probably more useful class is that of complex numbers, implemented in terms of a pair of real numbers. Whereas mathematicians usually denote the **imaginary unit** $\sqrt{-1}$ by i, many engineers prefer j, and Python has adopted the latter approach. Thus a Python *complex* number can be defined explicitly as, e.g.,

```
c = 1.5-0.4j
c
```

```
(1.5-0.4j)
```

Note carefully the syntax: the j (or equivalently J) follows the *float* with no intervening "*." Alternatively, a pair of *floats* a and b can be widened to a complex number via c = complex(a,b). We can narrow a *complex*; e.g., with c, as in the last sentence, c.real returns a and c.imag returns b:

```
c.real, c.imag
```

```
(1.5, -0.4)
```

Both real and imag are attributes of the complex class (see Section 3.11 to learn what attributes are). Another useful object is the conjugate() method, which returns the complex conjugate of c:

```
c.conjugate()
```

```
(1.5+0.4j)
```

conjugate() is a method of the complex class. Methods are class-specific functions and therefore require a pair of parentheses (see Section 3.11 for details), which may be used to pass arguments to the method.

The five basic arithmetic operations work for Python complex numbers and in mixed mode widening are done automatically. The library of mathematical functions for complex arguments is cmath instead of math. However, for obvious reasons, the comparison operations described in Section 3.4.3 are not defined for complex numbers, although the equality and inequality operators are available.

You have now seen enough of Python to use it as a sophisticated five-function calculator, and you are urged to try out a few examples of your own.

3.5   Container Objects

The usefulness of computers is based in large part on their ability to carry out repetitive tasks very quickly. Most programming languages therefore provide *container* objects, often called "arrays," which can store large numbers of objects of the same type and retrieve them via an indexing mechanism. Mathematical vectors would correspond to one-dimensional arrays, matrices to two-dimensional arrays, etc. It may come as a surprise to find that the Python core language has no array concept. Instead, it has *container* objects that are much more general: *lists*, *tuples*, *strings*, and *dictionaries*. It will soon become clear that we can simulate an array object via a *list*, and this is how numerical work in Python used to be done. Because of the generality of *lists*, such simulations took a great deal longer than equivalent constructions in Fortran or C, and this gave Python a deservedly poor reputation for its slowness in numerical work. Developers produced various schemes to alleviate this by implementing the NumPy package for numerical math, which we will introduce in Chapter 4. Arrays in NumPy have much of the versatility of Python *lists*, but are implemented behind the scenes as arrays in C, significantly reducing, but not quite eliminating, the speed penalty. In this section, we describe the core *container* objects in sufficient detail for much scientific work. They excel in the "administrative, bookkeeping chores" where Fortran and C are at their weakest. Number-crunching numerical arrays are deferred to Chapter 4, but the reader particularly interested in numerics will need to understand the content of this section, because the ideas developed here carry forward into that chapter.

3.5.1   Lists

Let's have a look at how *lists* can be used.

```
[1, 4.0, 'a']
```

```
[1, 4.0, 'a']
```

This is our first instance of a Python *list*, an ordered sequence of Python objects that are not necessarily of the same type separated by commas and surrounded by square brackets []. [3] *Lists* themselves are Python objects, and can be assigned a Python *identifier*:

```
u = [1, 4.0, 'a']
v = [3.14, 2.78, u, 42]
len(v)
```

```
4
```

We see that in creating the *list*, an *identifier* is replaced by the object it refers to, e.g., one *list* can be an element in another. This construct of having a *list* as an element in another *list* is called a **nested list**. The beginner should consult Figure 3.1 again. It is the object, not the *identifier*, that matters. In the last line of the code cell, we invoke an extremely useful Python function, **len()**, which returns the length of a sequence (Python functions will be discussed in detail in Section 3.8). The length of *list* v is 4, since *list* u only counts as a single element.

We can replicate *lists* with the multiplication operation, *:

```
v*2
```

```
[3.14, 2.78, [1, 4.0, 'a'], 42, 3.14, 2.78, [1, 4.0, 'a'], 42]
```

---

[3] We define a sequence as a series or succession of items or elements in the most general sense and will use this term synonymously with *lists*, *tuples* (see Section 3.5.6), and later *arrays* (see Section 4.1), as those data types are often interchangeable.

We can concatenate *lists* with the addition operation (*list* **concatenation**), +:

```
v+u
```

```
[3.14, 2.78, [1, 4.0, 'a'], 42, 1, 4.0, 'a']
```

and we can append items to the end of a *list* using the **append()** function, which is only available for *lists*:

```
v.append('foo')
v
```

```
[3.14, 2.78, [1, 4.0, 'a'], 42, 'foo']
```

Note that append() directly modifies the underlying *list*.

3.5.2 List Indexing

We can access elements of u by indexing, u[i] where $i \in [0, len(u))$ is an *integer*. Note that indexing starts with index 0 (u[0]) and ends with index len(u)-1 (u[len(u)-1]):

```
v[0]
```

```
3.14
```

Index 0 refers to the first element of *list* v; index 1 thus points to the second elements, and so on. So far, this is very similar to what is available for arrays in, e.g., C or Fortran. However, a Python *list* such as u "knows" its length, and so we could also index the elements in reverse order, by invoking u[len(u)-k] where $k \in (0, len(u)]$, which Python abbreviates to u[-k]. This turns out to be very convenient. For example, not only is the first element of any *list* w referred to by w[0], but the last element is w[-1]:

```
v[-1]
```

```
'foo'
```

The middle line of Figure 3.2 shows both sets of indices for a *list* of length 8. Using the code snippet above, you might like to guess the objects corresponding to v[1] and v[-3], and perhaps use the Notebook to check your answers.

At first sight, this may appear to be a trivial enhancement, but it becomes very powerful when coupled to the concepts of slicing and mutability, which we address next. Therefore, it is important to make sure you understand clearly what negative indices represent.

3.5.3   List Slicing

Given a *list* u, we can form more *lists* by the operation of slicing. The simplest form of a slice is u[start:end], which is a *list* of length end-start, as shown in Figure 3.2. If the slice occurs on the right-hand side of an assignment, then a **new** *list* is created. For example,

```
nv = v[1:4]
nv
```

```
[2.78, [1, 4.0, 'a'], 42]
```

generates a new *list* with three elements, where nv[0] is initialized with v[1]. Please note that the end point of the slice (index 4) is exclusive and will not be included in the newly generated *list*.

If the slice occurs on the left, no new *list* is generated. Instead, it allows us to change a block of values in an existing *list*:

```
nv[1:] = [1, 2]
nv
```

```
[2.78, 1, 2]
```

Note the notation here: we omit the end index, meaning all the way to the end of the *list*. In the same way, omitting the start index means all items starting from the first e.g., v[:-1] is a copy of v with the last element omitted. Consequently, omitting both indices (v[:]) means the entire *list* with one caveat: since slicing generates a new *list*, v[:] contains the same items as v, but it is a different object (a copy of the original *list*); this is an efficient way to duplicate *lists*.

The more general form of slicing is su = u[start:end:step]. Then su contains the elements u[start], u[start+step], u[start+2*step], ..., as long as the index is less than start+end. Consider the following example:

```
u = [0, 1, 2, 3, 4, 5, 6, 7, 8]
u[2:-1:2]
```

```
[2, 4, 6]
```

A particularly useful choice is step=-1, which allows traversal of the *list* in the reverse direction:

```
u[::-1]
```

```
[8, 7, 6, 5, 4, 3, 2, 1, 0]
```

See Figure 3.2 for an example.

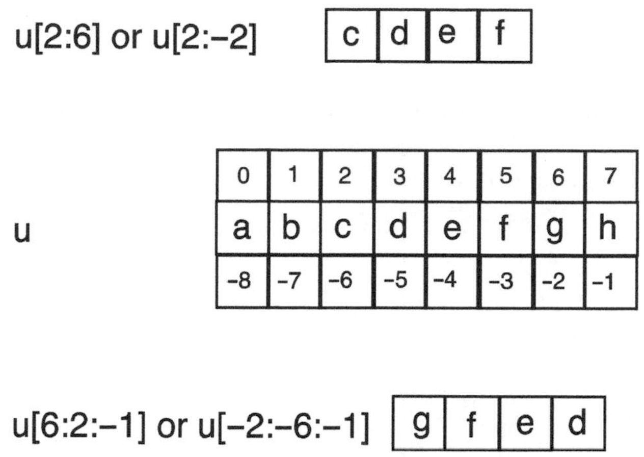

u[2:6] or u[2:−2]

c	d	e	f

u

0	1	2	3	4	5	6	7
a	b	c	d	e	f	g	h
−8	−7	−6	−5	−4	−3	−2	−1

u[6:2:−1] or u[−2:−6:−1]

g	f	e	d

Figure 3.2 Indices and slicing for a *list* u of length 8. The middle line shows the contents of u and the two sets of indices by which the elements can be addressed. The top line shows the contents of a slice of length 4 with conventional ordering. The bottom line shows another slice with reversed ordering.

These are important new constructs that may well be unfamiliar to programmers used to C, Fortran, or other languages. It is worth spending some time to really understand the underlying principles of slicing, as it is also applicable to other sequences such as NumPy arrays (see Section 4.1), which makes it extremely powerful. Play with the examples shown here and carry out further experiments of your own.

3.5.4 List Mutability

For any *container* object u, it may be possible to modify an element or a slice, without any apparent change having been applied to the object's *identifier*. Such objects are said to be *mutable*. As an example, consider a politician's promises. In particular, *lists* are *mutable*. There is a trap here for the unwary. Consider the code:

```
u = [0,1,4,9,16]
v = u
v[2] = 'foo'
v
```

```
[0, 1, 'foo', 9, 16]
```

This code cell should be comprehensible: u is assigned to a *list* object and so is v. Because *lists* are mutable, we may change the second element of the *list* object v. But u is pointing to the same object (see Figure 3.1) and it too shows this change:

```
u
```

```
[0, 1, 'foo', 9, 16]
```

While the logic is clear, this may not be what was intended, for u was never changed explicitly.

It is important to remember the assertion made above: a slice of a *list* is always a **new** object, even if the dimensions of the slice and the original *list* agree. Therefore, compare the previous code cell with the following one:

```
u = [0,1,4,9,16]
v = u[:]
v[2] = 'foo'
u
```

```
[0, 1, 4, 9, 16]
```

Now we generate a new slice object, which is a ***shallow copy***. If u contains an element that is mutable, e.g., another *list* w, the corresponding element of v still accesses the original w. To guard against this, we need a ***deep copy*** to obtain a distinct but exact copy of both u and its current contents. Changes to v do not alter the u-*list* and vice versa.

3.5.5   List Functions

Lists are very versatile objects, and there exist many Python functions that utilize them to perform different tasks. For instance, we already learned about the len() function to derive the length of a *list*. In the following, we will introduce some other useful functions performing on *lists*.

The **sum()** function computes the sum of all elements of a *list*:

```
u = [1, 2, 3, 4, 5]
sum(u)
```

```
15
```

Keep in mind that sum() is not very smart: of course, all the elements of the *list* must be numerical, otherwise the function will result in an error:

```
u = [1, 2, 'foo', 4, 5]
sum(u)
```

```
TypeError                        Traceback (most recent call last)
<ipython-input-35-3323b4f6e688> in <module>
      1 u = [1, 2, 'foo', 4, 5]
----> 2 sum(u)

TypeError: unsupported operand type(s) for +: 'int' and 'str'
```

This also precludes the application of this function on *nested lists*:

```
u = [1, 2, [1, 1], 4, 5]
sum(u)
```

```
TypeError                          Traceback (most recent call last)
<ipython-input-36-1b88faa89e6c> in <module>
      1 u = [1, 2, [1, 1], 4, 5]
----> 2 sum(u)

TypeError: unsupported operand type(s) for +: 'int' and 'list'
```

(See Section 3.10.1 to learn how to interpret these error messages.)

Another useful *list* function is **zip()**, which allows you to combine the elements of two *lists* of equal length in pairs (similar to the way a zipper works):

```
u = [0, 1, 2, 3]
v = ['a', 'b', 'c', 'd']
list(zip(u, v))
```

```
[(0, 'a'), (1, 'b'), (2, 'c'), (3, 'd')]
```

Here we create two *lists* of equal length and zip them together. The result is a *list* of *tuples* (see Section 3.5.6), each of which contains two elements: the first element is from *list* u and the second element is from *list* v. The order of elements from the two *lists* is naturally conserved. Note a little detail here: in order to receive a human readable output from zip() you must apply the list() function to turn its elements into a *list*.

The **filter()** function allows you to filter elements from a *list* that meet a specific condition. This condition can be expressed by a Python function (see Section 3.8). For now consider the following example of a function (less_than_5()) that returns the value True if the value provided to the function is less than 5, or False otherwise. The filter() function can now be utilized to extract exactly those elements from a *list* that are less than 5:

```
u = [1, 0, 3, 5, 6, 9]

def less_than_5(x):
    """a function that returns True if x<5"""
    return x < 5

list(filter(less_than_5, u))
```

```
[1, 0, 3]
```

In a similar way, the map() function allows one to apply a function to every single element of a *list*. In the following example, we apply a function that squares the value of its argument:

```python
def square(x):
    """a function that returns the square value"""
    return x**2

list(map(square, u))
```

```
[1, 0, 9, 25, 36, 81]
```

As a result, we obtain a new *list* containing the squares of the elements of the original *list* in the corresponding order. The map() function can, of course, also be used to perform element-wise comparisons:

```python
list(map(less_than_5, u))
```

```
[True, True, True, False, False, False]
```

Now how can we use map() to check whether all elements of a *list* (not just individual ones) have values less than 5? Here we need the **all()** function, which takes in a *list* of *Booleans* and returns True only if all of them are True:

```python
all(list(map(less_than_5, u)))
```

```
False
```

Similarly, we can check whether any of the *list* elements are True utilizing the **any()** function:

```python
any(list(map(less_than_5, u)))
```

```
True
```

Finally, we note that all of the functions that we introduced here for *lists* work exactly the same way on *tuples* (see Section 3.5.6). For NumPy arrays (see Section 4.1) similar functions are available from the NumPy package.

3.5.6   Tuples

The next *container* to be discussed is the *tuple*. Syntactically, it differs from a *list* only by using "()" instead of "[]" as delimiters. Indexing and slicing work as for *lists* as do the functions introduced for *lists* in Section 3.5.5. However, there is a fundamental difference. We cannot change the values of its elements; a *tuple* is **immutable**. At first sight, the *tuple* would appear to be entirely redundant. Why not use a *list* instead? The rigidity of a *tuple*, however, has an advantage. We can use a *tuple* where a scalar quantity is expected, and in many cases we can drop the brackets () when there is no ambiguity, and indeed this is the most common way of utilizing *tuples*. Consider the following code cell, where we have written two examples for *tuple* assignment that lead to the same result:

```
(a, b, c, d) = (4, 5.0, 1.5+2j, 'a')
a, b, c, d = 4, 5.0, 1.5+2j, 'a'
```

In both lines we make multiple scalar assignments with a single assignment operator. This becomes extremely useful in the common case where we need to swap two objects, or equivalently two *identifiers*, say a and b. The conventional way to do this is:

```
temp = a
a = b
b = temp
```

This would work in any language, assuming `temp`, a, and b all refer to the same type. However,

```
a, b = b, a
```

does the same job in Python, is clearer, more concise, and works for arbitrary types.

Another common use for *tuples* is the ability to pass a variable number of arguments to a function, as discussed in Section 3.8. We also would like to point out that *tuples* are more memory efficient, but we defer this discussion to Section 9.1.3.

Finally, we note a feature of the notation that often confuses the beginner. We sometimes need a *tuple* with only one element, say foo. The construction (foo) strips the parentheses and leaves just the element. The correct *tuple* construction is (foo,).

3.5.7 Strings

Although we have already seen *strings* in passing, we note that Python regards them as *immutable container* objects for alphanumeric characters. There is no comma separator between items. The delimiters can be either single quotes or double quotes, but not a mixture. The advantage is that the unused delimiter can occur within the *string*; e.g.,

```
s1 = "It's time to go"
s2 = ' "Bravo!" he shouted.'
```

Indexing and slicing work in the same way as for *lists*.

There are two very useful conversion functions that can be associated with *strings*. The function **str()** when applied to a Python object will produce a string representation of that object. The function **eval()** acts as the inverse of `str()`. Consider the following code cell:

```
L = [1, 2, 3, 5, 8, 13]
ls = str(L)
ls
```

```
'[1, 2, 3, 5, 8, 13]'
```

This creates the *string* representation of a *list*; we can now use `eval()` to create a new *list* from this representation and compare it to the original *list*:

```
eval(ls) == L
```

```
True
```

*String*s will turn out to be very useful for the input of data, and, most importantly, producing formatted output from the `print()` function (see Section 3.9.2). The *string* class contains a wide range of useful methods for dealing with sequential and unstructured data. We introduce only a few examples here.

Consider the case that you have some tabular data stored in such a way that each row is a string (we look at a single row called `row` in this example) that contains the different fields separated by commas. In order to separate the fields, you can use the **split()** method:

```
row = "1,45,23.2,   London   ,2.45,#FF0000,16.3453"
l = row.split(',')
l
```

```
['1', '45', '23.2', '   London   ', '2.45', '#FF0000', '16.3453']
```

In this case, since the fields are separated by commas, we must specify the delimiter symbol when calling the method by invoking `split(',')`. The data contains *integers*, *floats*, and *strings*. The fourth field (index 3) of l contains a *string* with some leading and trailing whitespaces; those can be easily removed with the **strip()** method:

```
l[3].strip()
```

```
'London'
```

By default, `strip()` will remove leading and trailing whitespaces, but it is also possible to remove other characters like underscores by invoking `row.strip('_')`. Let's assume that you would like to replace the *string* '#FF0000' with something more meaningful like `'red'`; the **replace()** method will replace each occurrence of the former with the latter throughout the *string*:

```
row.replace('#FF0000', 'red')
```

```
'1,45,23.2,  London  ,2.45,red,16.3453'
```

These are probably the most common and useful *string* modification methods; we refer to the *string* class reference that is part of the Python built-in reference (see Section 3.14) for an extensive list. We close the discussion of *strings* with a note that *strings* containing only numeric characters can be easily converted to numerical data types with explicit type conversion (see Section 3.4.2), e.g., using `int(l[0])` or `float(l[2])`.

3.5.8   Dictionaries

As we have seen, a *list* object is an ordered collection of objects, A *dictionary* object is an unordered collection. Instead of accessing the elements by virtue of their position, we must assign a *key*, an *immutable* object, for instance a *string*, which identifies the element. Thus a *dictionary* is a collection of pairs of objects, where the first element in the pair is a unique **key** and the second is referred to as the corresponding **value**. A *key–value* pair is referred to as an **item** written as "`key: value`". The *dictionary* delimiters are the braces { }. Here is a simple example that illustrates two different ways to define the same *dictionary*:

```
params = {'alpha': 1.3, 'beta': 2.74}
params = dict(alpha=1.3, beta=2.74)
params
```

```
{'alpha': 1.3, 'beta': 2.74}
```

We fetch *items* via *keys* rather than position, e.g., `params['alpha']` will return `1.3`. Dictionaries are mutable, so we can add new *items* and modify existing *items*:

```
params['alpha'] = 2.6
params['gamma'] = 0.999
params
```

```
{'alpha': 2.6, 'beta': 2.74, 'gamma': 0.999}
```

This illustrates the main numerical use of *dictionaries*, to pass around an unknown and possibly variable number of parameters. Another important use will be keyword arguments in functions (see Section 3.8). Dictionaries are extremely versatile and commonly utilized in many Python programs and scripts.

3.5.9   Sets

Sets can be thought of as dictionaries that only contain *keys* but no *values*. As such, they are unordered collections of unique *keys* just like sets in the mathematical sense:

```
a = {1, 2, 3, 4, 4, 5}
a
```

```
{1, 2, 3, 4, 5}
```

Note how the *key* 4 appears twice in the definition of the *set*, but is present only once in the resulting *set*. Python *sets* provide functionality based on their mathematical equivalent. Given a second *set*, we can derive the **union()** of the two *sets*:

```
b = {4, 5, 5, 6, 7, 8, 'apple'}
a.union(b)
```

```
{1, 2, 3, 4, 5, 6, 7, 8, 'apple'}
```

and their **intersection()**:

```
a.intersection(b)
```

```
{4, 5}
```

3.6   Python `if` Statements

Normally, Python executes statements in the order that they are written. The `if` statement is the simplest way to modify this behavior, and exists in every programming language. In its simplest form, the pseudo-Python syntax is

```
if <Boolean expression>:
    <block 1>
<block 2>
```

Here, the expression must produce a `True` or `False` result. If `True`, then `block 1` is executed, followed by `block 2`, the rest of the program; if the expression is `False`, then only `block 2` is executed. Note that the `if` statement ends with a colon (:) indicating that an indented block must follow. The absence of delimiters such as braces makes it much easier to follow the logic, but the price required is careful attention to the indentation. Any Python-aware editor should take care of this automatically.

A generalization of the `if` statement is

```
if <Boolean expression 1>:
    <block 1>
```

```
elif <Boolean expression 2>:
    <block 2>
else:
    <block 3>
<block 4>
```

which executes either block 1, block 2, or block 3, followed by block 4. Let's look at this code cell in detail. If the first expression is True, block 1 is executed and then block 4. The second expression is not executed, nor is the else block (block 3) touched on. However, if the first expression is False, then the **elif** (short for else-if) expression is tested; if True, then block 2 is executed and then block 4. Finally, if both expressions are False, then the **else** block, block 3, is executed followed by block 4. It is important to note that only one of the "branches" of the if statement is executed. Furthermore, the number of elif branches is not limited, but there must be only one (or none at all) else branch.

Here is a real-world example involving a complete if statement:

```
a = 5

if a > 5:
    print("a is greater than 5")
elif a < 5:
    print("a is less than 5")
else:
    print("a is equal to 5")

print("now we know the result and move on...")
```

```
a is equal to 5
now we know the result and move on...
```

(We will introduce the print() function in Section 3.9.2.)

A situation that arises quite often is a construction with terse expressions, e.g.,

```
if a >= 0:
    y = 1
else:
    y = 2
```

As in the C-family of languages, there is an abbreviated form. The snippet above can be shortened in Python to

```
y=1 if a>=0 else 2
```

Please keep in mind our Zen of Python (see Section 2.1.2), especially the two points *Simple is better than complex* and *Readability counts*. This example is simple, but shortening if statements in real-life code can quickly become ugly and hard to decipher. Use it wisely!

3.7   Loop Constructs

Computers are capable of repeating sequences of actions with great speed, and Python has two loop constructs, for and while loops.

3.7.1   The for Loop

For loops are the simplest loop constructs and therefore exist in all programming languages: as for loops in the C-family and as do loops in Fortran. The Python for loop construct is a generalized, sophisticated evolution of these. Its simplest form is

```
for <iterator> in <iterable>:
    <block>
```

Here, the *iterable* is any *container* object. The *iterator* is any quantity that can be used to access, term by term, the elements of the *container* object. For instance, if the *iterable* is an ordered *container*, like a *list* (e.g., l=[1,2,3]) then the *iterator* would be assigned the elements of l sequentially in each iteration. The changing value of the *iterator*, cycling through the *iterable* can then be utilized in the loop's block.

This sounds very abstract and needs to be elucidated. We start with a simple, but unconventional example:

```
x = 4

for x in "abc":
    print(x)

print(x)
```

```
a
b
c
c
```

Keep in mind that before we start the for loop, we assign an *integer* value to x. In each iteration of the loop, x (the *iterator*) will retrieve one element from the *iterable*, which in this case is a *string* (remember that *strings* work similarly to *lists*; see Section 3.5.1), and execute the block, which consists here only of a print() function that displays x. After finishing the loop, we print x again and find that it still has the same value as in the final iteration; the *integer* value that we assigned before the loop has been overwritten.

At first sight it looks as though the *iterator* and *iterable* must be single objects, but we can circumvent this requirement by using *tuples*. For example, suppose Z is a *list* of *tuples* each of length 2. Then a loop with two *iterators* can be constructed via the following:

```
Z = [('a', 1), ('b', 2), ('c', 3)]

for (x, y) in Z:
    print(x, y)
```

```
a 1
b 2
c 3
```

and be perfectly permissible. For another generalization, consider the zip() function introduced in Section 3.5.5.

Before we can exhibit usage that is more traditional, we need to introduce the built-in Python **range()** function. range is an *iterable* that generates *items*, in this case *integers*, on demand. Its general form is range(start, end, step) that generates *integers* [start, start+step, start+2*step, ...] one at a time as long as each *integer* is less than end. In order to retrieve a full *list* of all *integers*, you can wrap range() in a list() call. Here, step is an optional argument, which defaults to one, and start is optional, defaulting to zero. Thus list(range(4)) yields [0, 1, 2, 3]. range() is very powerful in combination with for loops as it allows to easily iterate over indices, e.g., of a *list*:

```
l = [0, 1, 2, 3, 4]

for i in range(len(l)):
    l[i] += 1

l
```

```
[1, 2, 3, 4, 5]
```

A word of caution: The block can change the *iterator* and, in theory, also the *iterable* that is iterated over. Consider this simple example:

```
l = [0, 1, 2, 3, 4]

for i in range(len(l)):
    if i+1 < len(l):
        l[i+1] *= 2
    print(l[i])
```

```
0
2
4
6
8
```

While it seems tempting to utilize this fact, it should be avoided at all cost as it may lead to erratic and unexpected behavior, the debugging of which will be a nightmare.

3.7.2   The `while` Loop

The other extremely useful loop construct supported by Python is the `while` loop. While the `for` loop iterates over a *container* object, the `while` loop repeats a code block until a condition is met:

```python
i = 0

while i < 5:
    print(i)
    i += 1

print('done!')
```

```
0
1
2
3
4
done!
```

The condition $i < 5$ is tested after each iteration. Note that once the *integer* i reaches the value of five, the code block is not evaluated and skipped. A common but dangerous use case for `while` uses no condition at all: `while True` will loop eternally if not stopped by a `break` statement (see Section 3.7.4).

3.7.3   The `continue` Statement

The loop structures that we saw so far have a fixed control flow and are not very flexible. The `continue` statement allows for skipping remainders of a code block once invoked. Consider the following example of a loop through a range of *integers*:

```python
for i in range(10):
    if i > 5:
        continue
```

```
    print(i)

print('done!')
```

```
0
1
2
3
4
5
done!
```

For each value of i, as the program cycles through *integer* values ranging from zero to nine, it is checked whether i > 5 in the if-clause. If this condition is met, the continue statement is called; if not, the remainder of the for-block is executed, consisting of a print() call, printing the value of i. Once the loop has finished, the word 'done!' is printed. The output of this code cell shows how continue works: if continue is called, the remainder of the for-block is ignored and Python immediately resumes with the next iteration. As a result, only *integers* i less than 6 are printed as those do not meet the condition i > 5.

3.7.4   The break Statement

The break statement allows for premature ending of the loop. The basic syntax is shown using a different implementation of the previous example (see Section 3.7.3):

```
for i in range(10):
    if i > 5:
        break
    print(i)

print('done!')
```

```
0
1
2
3
4
5
done!
```

Here, break immediately stops the entire for loop and does not resume with the next iteration. Both continue and break provide powerful means to manipulate the control flow in loop structures. Of course, both statements can be used together in the same loop to provide the user with a high degree of flexibility.

3.7.5   List Comprehensions

A task that arises surprisingly often is the following. We have a *list* l1, and need to construct a second *list* l2 whose elements are a fixed function of the corresponding elements of the first. The conventional way to do this (without the use of the map() function introduced in Section 3.5.5) is via a for loop. For example, let us produce an item-wise squared *list*:

```
l1 = [2, 3, 5, 7, 11, 14]
l2 = []

for i in range(len(l1)):
    l2.append(l1[i]**2)


l2
```

```
[4, 9, 25, 49, 121, 196]
```

However, Python can execute the same loop in a single line via a *list comprehension*:

```
l2 = [x**2 for x in l1]
```

Not only is this shorter, it is faster, as we will detail in Section 9.1.3.

List comprehensions are considerably more versatile than this. Suppose we want to build l2, but only for the odd numbers in l1:

```
[x**2 for x in l1 if x%2]
```

```
[9, 25, 49, 121]
```

As you can see, we can combine *list comprehensions* with an inline if statement.

Suppose we have a *list* of points in the plane, where the coordinates of the points are stored in *tuples*, and we need to form a *list* of their Euclidean distances from the origin:

```
import math

lpoints = [(1, 0), (1, 1), (4, 3), (5, 12)]
[math.sqrt(x**2 + y**2) for (x, y) in lpoints]
```

```
[1.0, 1.4142135623730951, 5.0, 13.0]
```

Next, suppose that we have a rectangular grid of points with the *x*-coordinates in one *list* and the *y*-coordinates in the other. We can build the distance *list* as follows:

```
l_x = [0, 2, 3, 4]
l_y = [1, 2]
[math.sqrt(x**2 + y**2) for x in l_x for y in l_y]
```

```
[1.0, 2.0, 2.23606797749979, 2.8284271247461903,
 3.1622776601683795, 3.605551275463989,
 4.123105625617661, 4.47213595499958]
```

List comprehension is a Python feature that, despite its initial unfamiliarity, is well worth mastering. However, as we will see in Section 9.1.4, for some of the use cases that we presented here, it is strongly recommended to use NumPy functionality as it is much faster and easier to read.

Also, another reminder on the Zen of Python (see Section 2.1.2), especially the points *Simple is better than complex* and *Readability counts*. *List comprehensions* can quickly become hard to understand. Do not use them for overly complex tasks.

3.8   Functions

A function is a device that groups together a sequence of statements that can be executed an arbitrary number of times within a program. To increase generality, we may supply input arguments that can change between invocations. A function may, or may not, return data.

In Python, a function is, like everything else, an object. We will explore first the basic syntax and the concept of *scope* and only finally, in Sections 3.8.2 to 3.8.5, the nature of input arguments. (This may seem an illogical order, but the variety of input arguments is extremely rich.)

3.8.1   Syntax and Scope

A Python function may be defined *anywhere* in a program before it is actually used; there is no need to define it at the beginning of a code file. The basic syntax is outlined in the following piece of pseudocode:

```
def <name>(<arglist>):
    """docstring"""
    <body>
```

The `def` denotes the start of a function definition; <name> assigns an *identifier* or name to address the object. The usual rules on *identifier* names apply, and of course the *identifier* can be changed later. The brackets "()" are mandatory. Between them, we may insert zero, one or more object identifiers, separated by commas, which are called arguments (see below). The final colon is mandatory.

Next follows the *docstring*, which describes what the function does in a concise way, and finally the *body* of the function, the statements to be executed. As we have seen already, such blocks of code have to be indented. The conclusion of the function body is indicated by a return to the same level of indentation as was used for the `def` statement. In rare circumstances, we may need to define a function, while postponing the filling-out of its body. In this preliminary phase, the body should consist of the single statement `pass`. It is not mandatory, but conventional and highly recommended, to include a *docstring* (see Section 3.13).

The body of the function definition introduces a new private *namespace* that is destroyed when the execution of the body code terminates (see Section 3.3 for an introduction to *namespaces*). When the function is invoked, this *namespace* is populated by the *identifiers* introduced as arguments in the `def` statement, and will point to whatever the arguments pointed at when the function was invoked. The *namespace* of the function is within the **scope** of each of these *identifiers*. A *scope* consists of the places (or *namespaces*) in which identifiers are looked up. New *identifiers* introduced in the body also belong in the function's *namespace*; they can only be invoked from within the function. Of course, the function is defined within a *namespace* (outside the function) that contains other external *identifiers*. These external *identifiers* are also within the *scope* of the function. This means that if you use an *identifier* that is not defined within the function's *namespace*, Python will search for this *identifier* outside the function. Those *identifiers* from outside the function that have the same names as the function arguments or *identifiers* already defined in the body do not exist in the private *namespace*, because they have been replaced by those private identifiers. The others are visible in the private *namespace*, but it is strongly recommended not to use them unless the user is absolutely sure that they will point to the same object on every invocation of the function. Summarized, this means that within a function, Python can see both *identifiers* that are defined within the same function and outside. However, *identifiers* within a function cannot be seen from the outside. For a detailed discussion of the concept of *scopes*, please refer to Lutz (2013). In order to ensure portability when defining functions, try to use only the *identifiers* contained in the argument *list* and those that you have defined within, and that are intrinsic to, the private *namespace*.

Usually we require the function to produce some object or associated *identifier*, say y, and this is done with a line `return y`. The function is exited after such a statement and so the **return** statement will be the last executed, and is hence usually the last statement in the function body. In principle, y should be scalar, but this is easily circumvented by using a *tuple*. For example, to return three quantities, say u, v, and w one should use a *tuple*, e.g., `return (u, v, w)` or even `return u, v, w`. If, however, there is no return statement, Python inserts an invisible **return None** statement. Here None is a special Python *identifier* that refers to an empty or void object, and is the "value" returned by the function.

Here are some simple toy examples to illustrate these features:

```python
x = 23

def add_one(x):
    """ Takes x and returns x + 1. """
    x += 1
    return x

add_one(0.456)
```

```
1.456
```

Ignoring the first line of this code cell for now, the following happens. We define the function add_one(x) with one positional argument (x, more on positional arguments in a bit). The function body contains a brief *docstring*, adds one to x and then returns the result. So far, the function has only been defined, but not executed. That happens in the final line of the code cell. Called with the *float* value 0.456, the result is 1.456.

Let's get back to the first line of the code cell. It defines an *identifier* x with value 23. What will be the value of x after we defined and executed a function that also contains an *identifier* x?

```python
x
```

```
23
```

Here x remains unchanged at 23. The fact that function add_one() also contains an *identifier* named x does not concern the *identifier* x that was defined outside the function: anything that happens to x inside the function is limited to the function's *namespace* and will not affect *identifiers* on the outside.

Next consider a faulty example:

```python
def add_z(x):
    """ Adds z to x and returns x+z. """
    return x+z

add_z(0.456)
```

```
NameError                          Traceback (most recent call last)
<ipython-input-54-df0717a7367f> in <module>
      2     """ Adds z to x and returns x+z. """
      3     return x+z
----> 4 add_z(0.456)
```

```
<ipython-input-54-df0717a7367f> in add_z(x)
      1 def add_z(x):
      2     """ Adds z to x and returns x+z. """
----> 3     return x+z
      4 add_z(0.456)

NameError: name 'z' is not defined
```

Here, we define a function that adds to its positional argument x an *identifier* z that is not defined within its *namespace* (please see Section 3.10 for a discussion of Python errors). The function looks for an *identifier* z in the enclosing *namespace*. None can be found and so Python stops with an error. If, however, we introduce an instance of z before calling the function:

```
z = 1
add_z(0.456)
```

```
1.456
```

then the function works as expected. However, this is nonportable behavior. We can only use the function inside *namespaces* where an instance of z has already been defined. There are a few cases where this condition will be satisfied, but in general this type of function should be avoided as it might lead to unexpected behavior.

Better coding is shown in the following example, which also shows how to return multiple values via a *tuple*, and also that functions are objects:

```
def add_x_and_y(x, y):
    """ Add x and y and return them and their sum. """
    z = x + y
    return x, y, z

a, b, c = add_x_and_y(1, 0.456)
a, b, c
```

```
(1, 0.456, 1.456)
```

The *identifier* z is private to the function, and is lost after the function has been left. Because we assigned c to the object pointed to by z, the object itself is not lost when the *identifier* z disappears. The next code cell demonstrates that functions are objects, and we can assign new *identifiers* to them (it may be helpful to look again at Figure 3.1 at this point):

```
f = add_x_and_y
f(0.456, 1)
```

```
(0.456, 1, 1.456)
```

So far, the objects used as arguments have been *immutable*, and so have not been changed by the function's invocation. This is not quite true if the argument is a mutable *container*, as is shown in the following example:

```
l = [0, 1, 2]

def add_with_side_effects(m):
    """ Increment first element of list. """
    m[0] += 1

add_with_side_effects(l)
l
```

```
[1, 1, 2]
```

The content of *list* l has been changed, with no assignment operator outside the function body and no return statement. This is a *side effect* that is harmless in this context, but can lead to subtle hard-to-identify errors in real-life code. The cure is to make a private copy within the function's body:

```
l = [0, 1, 2]

def add_without_side_effects(m):
    """ Increment first element of list. """
    mc = m[:]
    mc[0] += 1
    return mc

print(add_without_side_effects(l))
print(l)
```

```
[1, 1, 2]
[0, 1, 2]
```

In some situations, there will be an overhead in copying a long *list*, which may detract from the speed of the code, and so there is a temptation to avoid such copying. However, before using functions with side effects, remember the adage "premature optimization is the root of all evil," and use them with care.

We will now investigate the different types of arguments that are available for Python functions.

3.8.2   Positional Arguments

This is the conventional case, common to all programming languages. As an example, consider

```
def spam(a,b,c):
    <body>
```

Every time `spam` is called, precisely three arguments must be supplied. An example might be `spam(3, 2, 1)`, and the obvious substitution by order takes place. Another way of calling the function might be `spam(c=1,a=3,b=2)`, which allows a relaxation of the ordering. It causes an error to supply any other number of arguments.

3.8.3   Keyword Arguments

Another form of function definition specifies keyword arguments, e.g.,

```
def eggs(d=21.2, e=4, f='a'):
    <block>
```

In calling such a function, we can give all arguments, or omit some, in which case the default value will be taken from the `def` statement. For example, invoking `eggs(f='b')` will use the default values d=21.2 and e=4 so as to make up the required three arguments. Since these are keyword arguments, the order does not matter.

It is possible to combine both of these forms of arguments in the same function, provided all of the positional arguments come before the keyword ones. For example:

```
def spam_and_eggs(a, b, c, d=21.2, e=4, f='a')
    <block>
```

Now, in calling this function, we must give between three and six arguments, and the first three refer to the positional arguments.

3.8.4   Arbitrary Number of Positional Arguments

It frequently happens that we do not know in advance how many arguments will be needed. For example, imagine designing a `print()` function (see Section 3.9.2), where you cannot specify in advance how many items are to be printed. Python uses *tuples* to resolve this issue. Here is a much simpler example to illustrate syntax, method, and usage. We are given an arbitrary collection of numbers, for which we want to compute the arithmetic mean:

```
def average(*args):
    """ Return mean of a non-empty tuple of numbers. """
    s = sum(args)
    return s/len(args)

print(average(1, 2, 3, 4))
print(average(1, 2, 3, 4, 5))
```

```
2.5
3.0
```

As *args is simply a *tuple*, we can use the sum() function to sum up its elements and then simply divide by the number of elements to derive the mean. It is customary, but not obligatory, to call the *tuple* args in the definition. The asterisk * is, however, mandatory; the notation specifies that the function takes any number of positional arguments.

3.8.5 Arbitrary Number of Keyword Arguments

Python has no problem coping with a function that takes a fixed number of expected positional arguments, followed by an arbitrary number of positional arguments, followed by an arbitrary number of keyword arguments. The key here is the convention of "positional before keyword," meaning that positional arguments are always listed before keyword arguments and that *args always follows after expected positional arguments. As the previous section showed, the additional positional arguments are packed into a *tuple* (identified by an asterisk). The additional keyword arguments are wrapped into a *dictionary* that is typically indicated by **kwargs (note the extra asterisk). The following example exemplifies the process:

```
def show(a, b, *args, **kwargs):
    print(a, b, args, kwargs)

show(1.3, 2.7, 3, 'a', 4.2, alpha=0.99, gamma=5.67)
```

```
1.3 2.7 (3, 'a', 4.2) {'alpha': 0.99, 'gamma': 5.67}
```

Beginners are not likely to want to use all of these types of arguments proactively. However, they will see them occasionally in the *docstrings* of library functions, and so it is useful to know what they are.

3.8.6 Anonymous Functions

It should be obvious that the choice of a name for a function's arguments is arbitrary, $f(x)$ and $f(y)$ refer to the same function. On the other hand, we saw in the code snippet for the function add_x_and_y() in Section 3.8.1 that we could change the name to f() with impunity. This is a fundamental tenet of mathematical logic, usually described in the formalism of the *lambda-calculus* or *λ-calculus*. There will occur situations in Python coding where the name of the function is totally irrelevant, and Python can mimic the lambda calculus. Using a *lambda function*, we could have coded the function add_x_and_y() from Section 3.8.1 as follows:

```
f = lambda x, y: (x, y, x+y)
f(1, 2)
```

```
(1, 2, 3)
```

Lambda functions are expressions that consist of a single expression, unlike functions that contain blocks of statements. They consist of the keyword lambda, one or more arguments, a colon (:), and the expression involving the arguments. *Lambda functions* are typically used as inline function definitions containing rather simple functionality. Their use is convenient, but in most cases, an explicit function definition is the more *pythonic* way.

3.9   Python Input/Output

Every programming language needs to have functions that either accept input data or output other data, and Python is no exception. Input data usually comes from either the keyboard or a file, while output data is usually "printed" either to the screen or written to a file. File input/output, typically abbreviated as I/O, can be either in human-readable form or binary data. In the following, we introduce methods for input/output operations.

3.9.1   Keyboard Input

Here we look at a small amount of data, input from the keyboard. There are several ways to do this, and so we have chosen the simplest solutions. Let us start with a snippet for children:

```
name = input("What is your name? ")
print("Your name is " + name)
```

On execution, the first line containing **input()** issues the prompt question, and the keyboard input is encapsulated as a *string*. Thus the second line makes sense – we are printing the concatenation of two *strings*.

3.9.2   The print() Function

We have utilized the print() function already in different code snippets leading up to this point, so let us introduce it properly. The print() function displays sequences of characters on the screen to present the information contained in objects to the human user. The function expects a variable number of arguments, implicitly a *tuple*. Consider the following example:

```
it = 12
y = 3.412
print("After iteration", it, "the solution was", y)
```

```
After iteration 12 the solution was 3.412
```

We provide a *tuple* containing *strings*, an *integer*, and a *float* to the print() function in the form of a *tuple*. Here we have no control over the formatting of the two numbers, and this is a potential source of problems, e.g., when producing a table, where uniformity is highly desirable. The preferred way to customize the output of the print() function is to provide it with a single argument in the form of a formatted *string*. Python offers two ways for formatting *strings*: *string* formatting expressions and *string* formatting method calls. In this book, we will utilize the latter, which should be the preferred way for formatting *strings* nowadays. The former approach, which is based on the C printf model, is nevertheless still valid and widely used: we will briefly outline this approach at the end of this section.

Formatted strings utilize the format method of the *String* class from which *strings* are instantiated. The simplest way to adopt the previous example would look as follows:

```
print("After iteration {} the solution was {}".format(it, y))
```

```
After iteration 12 the solution was 3.412
```

We apply the format method to a *string* in which braces "{}" serve as placeholders for the arguments provided to the format method in the order in which they appear. Arguments can also be references by index:

```
print("After iteration {0} the solution was {1}".format(it, y))
```

or by keyword:

```
print("After iteration {iteration} the solution was {value}".format(
    iteration=it, value=y))
```

While the results of all these examples are identical to the unformatted print() call, the power of format lies in its flexibility. For each argument data type, a wide range of customization options are available by modifying the corresponding placeholder. In the following, we will briefly present the most common formatting options and point to the formatter options of the *string* class for an in-depth discussion.

In general, *string* formatter placeholders have the following structure:

```
{<identifier><:formatspec>}
```

where `identifier` can be omitted if there is one placeholder for each argument provided to the `format` method. If not omitted, `identifier` stands for the index of an argument or a *key* contained in a *dictionary* provided as the argument to the `format` method. `identifier` may contain brackets [] to reference elements of a *list* (e.g., "{0[0]} < {0[1]}".format([1, 3])) or attribute calls (e.g., for an object `coo` with attributes x and y: "{0.x} and {0.y}".format(coo)). The optional `:formatspec` part defines the exact formatting rules for each placeholder, following this general structure:

```
:<fill><align><sign><width><,><.precision><typecode>
```

All of these components are optional and their availability depends on the `typecode` (see below). `width` defines the length in characters that is occupied by this placeholder; `align` may be [<, >, ^] for [left aligned, right aligned, centered] output; `fill` defines a character that is used to fill the unused space (blanks are used by default). For numerical arguments, `sign` can be used to display signs: + will force to always display a sign, – will only display negative signs, and a blank will display a blank in case of positive numbers and minus sign in case of negative numbers; "," will enable the use of thousands separators. In the case of *floats*, `.precision` defines the number of digits after the decimal point to be displayed. Finally, `typecode` defines the type of the argument to be displayed; the most common choices are s for *strings*, d for *integers*, f for *floats* in floating-point decimal representation and e (and E) for *floats* in floating-point exponential representation. The following code cell and corresponding output (shown here side by side) showcases examples for different formatting options; note that we also show different `identifier` options that do not affect the formatting of the string:

```
# strings
print('ab{:5s}ef'.format('cd'))                    abcd   ef
print('ab{0:*^5s}ef'.format('cd'))                 ab*cd**ef
print('ab{[a]:_>5s}ef'.format({'a': 'cd'}))        ab___cdef
# integers
print('{:8d}'.format(362500))                         362500
print('{:>8,d}'.format(362500))                      362,500
print('{0:>05d}'.format(13))                       00013
print('{0:>+5d}'.format(-13))                        -13
print('{0:>+5d}'.format(13))                         +13
print('{0:> 5d}'.format(13))                          13
# floats
print('{:^10.3f}'.format(3.14159))                   3.142
print('{0:8,.3f}'.format(1234.56789))              1,234.568
print('{0:8,.3e}'.format(1234.56789))              1.235e+03
```

Finally, we also briefly introduce *string* formatting expressions, which are still widely used. Using this approach, our simple example from the beginning looks like this:

```
print("After iteration %d the solution was %f" % (it, y))
```

```
After iteration 12 the solution was 3.412000
```

First of all, note the different syntax: instead of calling a *string* method (.format()), formatting expressions utilize the % operator to define a convenient way for multiple *string* substitutions in a single call. Similarly to the formatting method approach, placeholders are defined in the target string, which are then substituted with *identifiers* provided by the % operator. Note that each placeholder here must carry a typecode. The definition of typecodes and other formatting options is almost identical to those above and almost as flexible:

```
print("After iteration %03d the solution was %.2f" % (it, y))
```

```
After iteration 012 the solution was 3.41
```

So why prefer the formatting method over formatting expressions? We have to admit that the advantages of the formatting method are small (in terms of flexibility in formatting and providing values for the placeholders), but it is generally more *pythonic* and as such should be given preference.

3.9.3 File Input/Output

In the context of scientific programming, it is probably more important to be able to read data to and from files than to ask a human during runtime for manual data input.

File input/output operations in Python utilize file objects that must be opened to operate on them. The following code cell creates a simple ASCII file named `test.txt` in the current working directory and writes some text into the file:

```
f = open('test.txt', 'w')
f.write('this is a test\n')
f.close()
```

In a very similar way, we can read data from the same file and print its content to the screen:

```
f = open('test.txt', 'r')
print(f.read())
f.close()
```

```
this is a test
```

The first line of both code cells uses the **open()** function to open a file object for file test.txt in different **processing modes**; the processing mode to write to a file is 'w', whereas the processing mode to read a file is 'r'. One more important processing mode for ASCII files is 'a' for appending to an existing file. While both 'a' and 'w' will create files if they do not yet exist, only 'a' will append to a file that already exists, whereas 'w' will simply overwrite already existing files. The same processing modes are also available for binary files, using the processing mode labels 'wb', 'ab', and 'rb'.

File objects provide a range of methods to manipulate files. **write()** will append a *string* to the file object; note that in contrast to the print() function, the write() method will not automatically close with a linebreak, so those must be appended manually at the end of each line as '\n'. If you have a *list* of *strings*, the **writelines()** method will help you to write all of them in a single method call. Similarly, the read() method will read the entire file content into a single *string*, while the **readlines()** method reads each line of the file into a separate *string* that is part of a *list*. Finally, the **close()** method will close the file object; note that calling close() explicitly is good practice, but in case you forget to close the file, this will be done automatically by Python once your code finishes running. Another elegant way to handle file objects is utilizing *context managers*:

```python
with open('test', 'a') as f:
    f.write('more test\n')
```

The **with** statement identifies the **context manager**. File object f is only available within the context manager code block and will be automatically closed upon leaving the code block. Context managers are the preferred way to deal with file objects as they improve the readability and coherence of your code.

3.10   Error Handling

In case you already played with some of the Python code examples provided thus far, you probably have come across some error messages. In this section, we will learn how to read error messages and how to deal with errors in your code.

3.10.1   Traceback

Python tries its best to help you identify code passages that cause errors by providing a *traceback*, which can be thought of as an elaborate error message. When you see a *traceback* for the first time it can be quite overwhelming, so let's have a look at a simple example in which we call an *identifier* that has not yet been defined:

```python
print(xyz)
```

```
NameError                          Traceback (most recent call last)
<ipython-input-1-b6499aa2e891> in <module>
----> 1 print(xyz)
NameError: name 'xyz' is not defined
```

In this trivial case, the *traceback* consists of four lines: the first line names the actual error type (see Section 3.10.2) and identifies the output as a *traceback*, the second line indicates the module in which the error occurred, the third line indicates the line of the error (the first line of the previous code cell), and the fourth line indicates the actual error and provides some more details.

A key feature of the *traceback* is that it *traces back* the error through your code, allowing you to understand what led your code to crash. To showcase the idea behind this, consider the following example in which we call a function that tries to perform a division by zero:

```
def invert(x):
    return 1/x

invert(0)
```

```
ZeroDivisionError                  Traceback (most recent call last)
<ipython-input-97-f981e239492b> in <module>
      1 def invert(x):
      2     return 1/x
----> 3 invert(0)

<ipython-input-97-f981e239492b> in invert(x)
      1 def invert(x):
----> 2     return 1/x
      3 invert(0)

ZeroDivisionError: division by zero
```

This *traceback* is longer than the previous example: the first line now contains a different error type and the following lines indicate the order of calls leading up to the error. The bottom line of the code cell, which is the first line to be executed after reading the function, calls `invert`, on the second line of which the `ZeroDivisionError` happens. While this example is brief, *traceback* can be easily several tens of lines long. The actual error that is reported, happens always on the last code line reported, guiding you to the faulty part of your code. The actual appearance of the *traceback* may vary with the version of Python you are using.

3.10.2   Errors, Exceptions, and Warnings

Whenever Python encounters an error, it triggers an *exception*, which can be dealt with in different ways. In the case of the *tracebacks* shown in Section 3.10.1, these *exceptions* are handled by the default *exception* handler of Python, which prints the error message including the *traceback* and immediately terminates the execution of the code. The most common *exceptions* are as follows:

IndentationError a line of code uses an unexpected level of indentation;

IndexError an index is out range for the given sequence, e.g., `list(range(5))[6]`;

KeyError a *key* (e.g., of a *dict*) is not available, e.g., `{0:'a', 1:'b'}[2]`;

NameError an *identifier* of this name is not available;

SyntaxError unintelligible syntax, e.g., `print(('test);`

TypeError an operation is applied to an object of the wrong type, e.g., `range('a');`

ValueError an operation is applied to an object with the wrong *value*, e.g., `int('a')`.

However, *exceptions* can also be intercepted during runtime as part of your code, allowing Python to deal with (not fully) unexpected situations. Consider the previous example of the `invert` function: it is possible that this function is called with zero as its argument, causing the termination of the code execution. Since this scenario cannot be ruled out, Python provides a means to handle this case with a `try-except` block:

```python
def invert_safe(x):
    try:
        return 1/x
    except ZeroDivisionError:
        return None

print(invert_safe(0))
print(invert_safe(2))
```

```
None
0.5
```

In this updated version, function `invert_safe` contains a `try-except` block, which is started by a **try** statement and ends with an **except** clause. The idea is that Python will try to execute the code in the `try` block; if no error occurs in this block, the `except` clause is simply ignored. However, if it encounters an error that is listed after the `except` clause (multiple comma-separated errors are possible), the corresponding code block is executed (in this case, `None` is returned). Error handling with `try-except` blocks enables the programmer to handle common errors and prevent their code from crashing if expected issues occur.

Exceptions can also be raised by programmers to indicate that something unexpected is happening. For instance, let's consider the case that the value of x must be less than 5; the following lines will raise a `ValueError` together with a meaningful error message:

```
x = 6

if x >= 5:
    raise ValueError('x must be less than 5 ({} provided)'.format(x))
```

```
ValueError                         Traceback (most recent call last)
<ipython-input-100-14d7daf3900b> in <module>
      1 x = 6
      2 if x >= 5:
----> 3     raise ValueError('x must be less than 5 ({} provided)'.
      format(x))

ValueError: x must be less than 5 (6 provided)
```

Finally, for the sake of completeness, we will also mention *warnings*, which inform the user of some unexpected behavior, but will not affect the execution of code. A common example for *warnings* are `DeprecationWarnings` that are typically raised from within modules that are about to change in future releases. As with the check engine light in your car, the most common interaction with *warnings* is to simply ignore them. All *warning* messages can be suppressed with help from the `warnings` module:

```
import warnings
warnings.filterwarnings("ignore")
```

While useful at times, please be warned that by suppressing all incoming *warnings*, some important issues might go undetected; *warnings* are typically there for a reason.

3.11   Introduction to Python Classes

Classes are extremely versatile structures in Python. The basic idea behind them is that you may have a fixed data structure or object that occurs frequently, together with operations directly associated with it. The Python class encapsulates both the object and its operations. Our introductory presentation by way of a scientific example is concise but contains many of the features most commonly used by scientists. In this pedagogic context, we shall use a class implementing fractions. We have in mind to implement a Frac as a pair of *integers* num and den, where the latter is nonzero. We have to be careful, however, because 3/7 and 24/56 are usually regarded as the same number, meaning that the class requires a method for reducing the fraction. We also require methods for simple arithmetic operations, addition and multiplication, as well as methods for generating a human-readable representation of a fraction and converting the fraction to a real number. The following snippet shows a simple `Frac` class implementing this functionality:

```python
class Frac:
    """Fractional class, consisting of a pair of integers."""

    def __init__(self, num, den):
        """Constructor; catch case denominator == 0."""
        self.num = num
        if den == 0:
            raise ValueError("Denominator cannot be zero.")
        self.den = den

    def __repr__(self):
        """Generate a string representation of a Frac. """
        return "{:d}/{:d}".format(self.num, self.den)

    def __mul__(self, another):
        """Multiply two Fracs to produce a Frac. """
        return Frac(self.num*another.num, self.den*another.den)

    def __add__(self, another):
        """Add two Fracs to produce a Frac. """
        return Frac(self.num*another.den+self.den*another.num,
                    self.den*another.den)

    def reduce(self):
        """Reduce numerator and denominator based on the greatest
        common divisor, derived with the Euclidean algorithm."""
        a, b = self.num, self.den
        while b != 0:
            (a, b) = (b, a%b)
        self.num = int(self.num/a)
        self.den = int(self.den/a)
        return self

    def to_real(self):
        """ Return floating point value of Frac. """
        return float(self.num)/float(self.den)
```

The first novelty here is the `class` statement, which ends with a terminating colon, indicating that the actual class is defined through indentation. As part of the class `Frac`, we define six methods – **methods** are functions (thus the def statements) that belong to a Python class. Each method contains a short *docstring*, providing crucial information, and its code uses additional indentation. The first method, __init__(), would in other languages be called a *"constructor."* The __init__() method is automatically invoked when a new *instance* of the corresponding class is created – in this case, it takes a pair of *integers* and creates a Frac instance. The mandatory name __init__() is strange, but, as we shall see, it is never used outside the class definition. The convention of leading and trailing double-underscores indicates a reserved method that has a special meaning in Python.

The first argument in most class methods is usually called self, and it too never appears outside the class definition. **self** is a reference to the current class instance, once an instance has been created. This all looks very unfamiliar, so let's see how we can instantiate a Frac instance:

```
a = Frac(3,7)
```

This is asking for a Frac object for the *integer* pair 3 and 7 to be referenced by the *identifier* a. Implicitly, this line invokes the __init__() method with self replaced by a, and num and den replaced by 3 and 7. It then assigns num to a.num (since self references to the instance, which is a) and den to a.den, but only if den!=0; otherwise, a ValueError with a meaningful error message is raised (see Section 3.10.2). a.den and a.nom are class **attributes**, which are class-specific variables that can be accessed in this way outside the class definition:

```
a.den
```

```
7
```

The purpose of the method __repr__ is to output a meaningful *string* representation of any Frac *instance*. This can be invoked by simply stating the *identifier* (a) in a Notebook, or utilizing the print() function. In that case, the self statement in the method code is replaced by a:

```
a
```

```
3/7
```

While these first two methods are more or less essential, we may define methods to carry out class operations. Here, we implement multiplication and addition, which appear as class methods __mul__() and __add__(), respectively. Again, we find this peculiar naming convention. Why not just call them mul and add? These particular naming conventions have special meanings; in the case of __mul__(), we do not necessarily need to call a.__mul__(b), but we can use the actual arithmetic operator for this method call, a*b. Multiplication of two Frac objects requires the definition of the class method __mul__(). When we invoke a*b where b is a different *instance* of class Frac, this function is invoked with self replaced by the left operand, here a, and another replaced by the right operand, here b. Note how the numerator and denominator of the product are computed, and then __init__() is called with the result to create a new Frac object, so that c = a*b would create a new Frac with *identifier* c. As the code snippet shows, addition is handled in exactly the same way:

```
b = Frac(1, 2)
c = a*b
d = a+b
print(a, b, c, d)
```

```
3/7 1/2 3/14 13/14
```

We also defined a reduce() method that utilizes the Euclidean algorithm to find the greatest common divisor to reduce the fraction:

```
e = Frac(3, 27)
e.reduce()
```

```
1/9
```

Finally, we defined a method to_real() that converts a fraction to a real number:

```
print(b.to_real())
print(type(b.to_real()))
```

```
0.5
float
```

Note how the return value of the to_real() method indeed returns a *float* value.

Classes are extremely versatile and useful as they enable Python to be used in an *object-oriented* way (see the following section for details on this).

3.12   The Structure of Python

Near the end of Section 3.2, we pointed out the relationship between *identifiers* and objects, and we now return to this topic. In our pedagogic example of a Python class Frac in Section 3.11, we noted that an *instance* of a Frac, e.g., a=Frac(3,7), produces an *identifier* a referring to an object of class Frac. Now a Frac object contains data, here a pair of *integers*, together with a set of methods to operate on them. We access the data relevant to the *instance* via the "***dot mechanism***," e.g., a.num. Similarly, we access the associated methods via, e.g., a.to_real().

So far, this is merely gathering previously stated facts. However, Python is packed with objects, some very complicated, and this *dot mechanism* is used universally to access the objects' components. We have already seen enough of Python to point out some examples.

Our first example is that of complex numbers described in Section 3.4.4. Suppose we have set c = `1.5-0.4j` or equivalently c = `complex(1.5,-0.4)`. We should regard complex numbers as being supplied by class `Complex`, although to guarantee speed they are hard-coded into the system. Now just as with the `Frac` class, we access the data via `c.real` and `c.imag`, while `c.conjugate()` produces the complex conjugate number `1.5+0.4j`. These are further examples of *instances* and attributes. Python is *object oriented*.

Our next example refers to modules described in Section 3.3. Like most other features in Python, a module is an object. Thus `import math as m` includes the `math` module and gives it the *identifier* m. We can access data as, e.g., `m.pi`, and functions by, e.g., `m.gamma(2)`.

Once you master the concept of the dot mechanism, understanding Python should become a lot clearer. See, e.g., the discussion of *container* objects in Section 3.5. All of the more sophisticated packages, e.g., *NumPy*, *Matplotlib*, *SymPy*, and *Pandas*, rely on it.

3.13 A Python Style Guide

In the previous sections, we learned the basics of the Python programming language. In theory, this is sufficient to write your own code for scientific applications. However, especially to researchers, the motto *sharing is caring* applies: code is often exchanged with other researchers, modified and extended to other use cases. As motivated by the *Zen of Python* (see Section 2.1.2), well-written and well-documented code is more easily used by others (and by your future self). For this reason, every Python programmer should strive to follow some simple guidelines to make their code easy to read and understand. An extensive guide for how to write good Python code is provided as part of PEP8 (see Section 3.14). Here, we summarize only a few important guidelines that should be easy to follow:

- ☐ Keep your code tidy and well-readable. This ensures that others will be able to make sense of your intentions and your code. It further simplifies debugging and makes your life easier.

- ☐ Provide comments in your code. Do not comment every line. Instead, provide short descriptions for blocks of code. For complicated lines of code, consider providing a short motivation for why you use this specific approach. Use *docstrings* in your function definitions.

☐ Be consistent. Python provides you with a great deal of freedom for your programming style. For instance, consider a simple sum: you can type it as "x+y" or as "x + y". Both versions are perfectly valid. The former has the advantage of requiring less space and is the preferred way as per PEP8. But in the end, it is up to you to decide which version you prefer. However, you should not mix both versions as it complicates reading your code.

☐ Group your code into blocks, separated by blank lines. Code blocks are natural units as they can be used to fulfill a given purpose or solve a specific problem. Add a comment to the top of each block (see above) and end it with a blank line. This significantly improves readability of your code and makes it easier to orient yourself in large programs.

☐ Use indentation wisely. It is widely customary to use four whitespaces of indentation. Never use tabs.[4] If you are breaking a line of code within a pair of brackets, start the new line at the column that follows the opening brackets (see Section 3.1 for an example).

☐ Wrap overlong lines. PEP8 recommends a maximum line length of 79 characters. This limit is (at least in part) due to historical reasons. For your personal programming, you do not have to follow this guideline, but we recommend using some consistent line length limit. The problem with overlong lines is that IDEs and text editors will eventually wrap them automatically, which may lead to complications in reading them.

☐ Pick meaningful names for your *identifiers*. The times of Fortran, where all *identifiers* should be as short as possible, are over. Use names that allow you to remember what the purpose of the object or function is, without making them too long!

This list could be continued eternally. However, we think it would be better for you to define the details of your programming style yourself.

3.14   References

Online resources

☐ General Python Resources

Python Project Website
`https://www.python.org`

Python Documentation Overview
`https://docs.python.org/3/`

Python Tutorial
`https://docs.python.org/3/tutorial/index.html`

---

[4] Most editors and IDEs will convert tabs into whitespaces, which is, of course, perfectly legitimate.

Python Library Reference
`https://docs.python.org/3/library/index.html`

Python Language Reference
`https://docs.python.org/3/reference/index.html`

Python Glossary
`https://docs.python.org/3/glossary.html`

☐ Typing Python

Lexical Analysis
`https://docs.python.org/3/reference/lexical_analysis.html`

☐ Objects and Identifiers

Data Model
`https://docs.python.org/3/reference/datamodel.html`

☐ Namespaces and Modules

Execution Model
`https://docs.python.org/3/reference/executionmodel.html`

The Import System
`https://docs.python.org/3/reference/import.html`

Modules
`https://docs.python.org/3/tutorial/modules.html`

☐ Numbers

Numbers
`https://docs.python.org/3/tutorial/introduction.html#numbers`

Floating Point Arithmetic
`https://docs.python.org/3/tutorial/floatingpoint.html`

Built-in Types
`https://docs.python.org/3/library/stdtypes.html`

☐ Container Objects

Sequence Types
`https://docs.python.org/3/library/stdtypes.html#sequence-types-list-tuple-range`

Lists
`https://docs.python.org/3/tutorial/introduction.html#lists`

Data Structures
`https://docs.python.org/3/tutorial/datastructures.html`

☐ Python `if` Statements

Loop Constructs

Looping Techniques
https://docs.python.org/3/tutorial/datastructures.html#looping-techniq
ues

More Control Flow Tools
https://docs.python.org/3/tutorial/controlflow.html

List Comprehension
https://docs.python.org/3/tutorial/datastructures.html#list-comprehens
ions

☐ Functions

Defining Functions
https://docs.python.org/3/tutorial/controlflow.html#defining-functions

More on Defining Functions
https://docs.python.org/3/tutorial/controlflow.html#more-on-defining-fu
nctions

☐ Python I/O

Input and Output
https://docs.python.org/3/tutorial/inputoutput.html

☐ Errors, Exceptions, and Warnings

Errors and Exceptions
https://docs.python.org/3/tutorial/errors.html

☐ Introduction to Python Classes/The Structure of Python

Classes
https://docs.python.org/3/tutorial/classes.html

☐ A Python Style Guide

PEP 8 – Style Guide for Python Code
https://peps.python.org/pep-0008/

Coding Style

https://docs.python.org/3/tutorial/controlflow.html#intermezzo-coding-
style

☐ Further Useful Resources

Brief Tour of the Standard Library
https://docs.python.org/3/tutorial/stdlib.html

Brief Tour of the Standard Library – Part II
`https://docs.python.org/3/tutorial/stdlib2.html`

Python HOWTOs
`https://docs.python.org/3/howto/index.html`

Print Resources

Lutz, Mark. *Learning Python: Powerful Object-Oriented Programming*. O'Reilly Media, 2013.

4 NumPy: Numerical Math

NumPy (Harris et al., 2020) is an add-on package that forms the core of the NumPy/ SciPy ecosystem and is supported by the *NumFocus* organization (see Section 2.1.1). It brings enhancements that allow Python to be used constructively for scientific computing, by offering a performance close to that of compiled languages but with the ease of the Python language. NumPy implements the fundamental infrastructure for a number of other scientific packages, the *array* object, and some useful basic functionality for the processing and analysis for large amounts of data. This chapter is merely an introduction to NumPy; for a complete guide, please refer to Oliphant (2015).

Before we start, we must import the NumPy package. The preferred approach is to preface the code with

```
import numpy as np
```

Then a NumPy function `func` needs to be written as **np.<func>**. Of course, the user is free to rename the package *namespace*, but the use of `np` can be considered traditional in the community and we will follow this tradition throughout this book and the accompanying Notebook (cambridge.org/9781009029728/ch4).

4.1   Arrays

The basic object in NumPy is the **np.ndarray** class, or simply the *array* (*ndarray* stands for *n*-dimensional *array*). For the remainder of this book we will define *arrays* to refer to instances of the `ndarray` class. *Arrays* are (possibly multidimensional) sequences of objects, all of which share the same data type, that have a size that is fixed upon creation. (Note that Python *lists* do not impose homogeneity on their items, and that a *list* object can enlarge dynamically via the intrinsic `append()` function; see Section 3.5.1.) The homogeneity requirement ensures that each item occupies the same amount of memory. This enables the NumPy designers to implement many operations involving *array*s as precompiled C code. Because of this, operations on *array*s can be executed much more efficiently and with much less support code than that required for Python *lists*. Let us illustrate this point with an often-quoted simple example. Suppose that a is a large Python *list* and we want to increment each element of the *list* by one. Using the *pythonic approach* of Chapter 3, we might use a simple `for`-loop that iterates over a and increments each element individually. We measure the time it takes to finish this operation with the `time` module (we will introduce a more elegant way to measure runtimes in Section 9.1.1):

```
import time
a = list(range(10000000))
b = []
starttime = time.time()

for i in range(len(a)):
    b.append(a[i]+1)

print(time.time()-starttime, 'seconds')
```

```
3.5564627647399902 seconds
```

While this runtime may not sound like a lot (and may actually be shorter on your computer), the following implementation using NumPy *arrays* will already show you why NumPy is so powerful:

```
a = np.array(a)
starttime = time.time()
b = a + 1
print(time.time()-starttime, 'seconds')
```

```
0.680443286895752 seconds
```

The use of a NumPy *array* reduces the runtime significantly and instead of having to deal with a loop, the syntax is short and easy to understand.

4.1.1   One-Dimensional Arrays

Vectors are simply one-dimensional *arrays* that form the basic building blocks for numerical computation. We look first at how to construct them, what their properties are and then at how to use them. It makes sense here to distinguish three types of constructors: to build a vector from another *container* object, from scratch, or to "look like" another object.

Arrays are easily **created from other container objects**, e.g., *lists*, *tuples*, or other *arrays*, using the function **np.array()**. Consider the following example in which we create an *array* x from a *list* l:

```
l = [1, 2, 3.0]
x = np.array(l)
x
```

```
array([1., 2., 3.])
```

First of all, Python indicates that this object is of type *array* to prevent confusion with *lists* and other *container* objects. Also, note how in the resulting *array* all elements of the *list*, which contains both *floats* and *integers*, are converted to *floats* (note the decimal points); this is done since all elements of an *array* must have the same data type – in fact, the *array* itself has a data type. np.array() will try to guess an appropriate type. In this case, *float* was chosen as it is the least complex data type to accommodate both *floats* and *integers*. This automatic choice can be overridden by specifying the **dtype** parameter upon creation of the *array*. Possible choices include bool, int, float, complex, and even user-defined types. In this following example, we create an *array* of complex numbers from 1:

```
np.array(1, dtype=complex)
```

```
array([1.+0.j, 2.+0.j, 3.+0.j])
```

The data type of an *array*, as well as many other useful properties, is accessible through **attributes**. For instance, the data type is accessible through the dtype attribute:

```
x.dtype
```

```
dtype('float64')
```

Note that the data type is not simply *float* but *float64*, which is a NumPy data type indicating a *float* with 64-bit precision (see the NumPy resources in the References for an overview of available types). Other useful attributes include the number of dimensions (**ndim**, trivial in the case of vectors), the number of elements (**size**), and the shape (**shape**) of the *array*:

```
print(x.ndim)
print(x.size)
print(x.shape)
```

```
1
3
(3,)
```

For a full list of attributes, please refer to the ndarray reference.

Ndarray also provides a range of **methods**. For instance, an existing *array* can be recast with a different data type using the **astype()** method:

```
x.astype(int)
```

```
array([1, 2, 3])
```

Many other methods are also available as package-level functions in NumPy. Therefore, we simply list some common methods and refer to the discussion of the corresponding functions in the following sections: for *array* shape manipulations, np.reshape(), np.transpose(), np.flatten(), and np.squeeze() are available (Section 4.1.5), while common mathematical functions include np.mean(), np.std(), np.max(), np.argmin(), np.argsort(), np.sum(), and np.clip (see Section 4.5). We show just a few examples here to provide the user with an idea of their use as methods (np.linspace() will be introduced below):

```python
x = np.linspace(0, 10, 11)
print(x.mean())      # mean of array
print(x.max())       # max of array
print(x.argmax())    # index of max element
print(x.clip(2, 6))  # clip array values to range [2,6]
```

```
5.0
10.0
10
[2. 2. 2. 3. 4. 5. 6. 6. 6. 6. 6.]
```

Also, note that most *built-in functions* that work on sequence *containers* like *lists* and *tuples* also work on *arrays* (see Sections 3.5.1 and 3.5.5):

```python
print(len(x))
print(sum(x))
print(max(x))
```

```
11
55.0
10.0
```

In the same way, important concepts like slicing (Section 3.5.3) and indexing (Section 3.5.2) work for *arrays* in the same way as for other *container* objects:

```python
x[2:5], x[0]
```

```
(array([2., 3., 4.]), 0.0)
```

NumPy provides a number of functions that **create *arrays* from scratch**. Perhaps the most useful constructor is **np.linspace()**, which builds an equally spaced *array* of *floats*. In its simplest use case, the function takes a start value, a stop value, and the number of steps as arguments:

```python
np.linspace(0, 1, 10)
```

```
array([0.        , 0.11111111, 0.22222222, 0.33333333, 0.44444444,
       0.55555556, 0.66666667, 0.77777778, 0.88888889, 1.        ])
```

Note that the final element of the resulting *array* has the same value as the assigned stop value. This is the case since the keyword argument endpoint defaults to True, meaning that the final element has the same value as the stop value. However, if endpoint=False, the stop value is exclusive:

```
np.linspace(0, 1, 10, endpoint=False)
```

```
array([0. , 0.1, 0.2, 0.3, 0.4, 0.5, 0.6, 0.7, 0.8, 0.9])
```

With the retstep keyword argument, we can obtain a *tuple* containing the generated *array* and the step size taken:

```
np.linspace(0, 1, 10, endpoint=False, retstep=True)
```

```
(array([0. , 0.1, 0.2, 0.3, 0.4, 0.5, 0.6, 0.7, 0.8, 0.9]), 0.1)
```

The function **np.logspace()** is similar, but the numbers are equally spaced on a logarithmic scale (note that the start and stop values must be provided in units of $\log_{10}$):

```
np.logspace(0, 3, 10)
```

```
array([   1.        ,    2.15443469,    4.64158883,   10.          ,
         21.5443469 ,   46.41588834,  100.          ,  215.443469  ,
        464.15888336, 1000.        ])
```

Somewhat closer to the range() function of Python is the function **np.arange()**, which returns an *array* rather than a *list*. In contrast to np.linspace(), np.arange() takes a step size instead of the number of steps as an argument:

```
np.arange(1, 10, 1)
```

```
array([1, 2, 3, 4, 5, 6, 7, 8, 9])
```

Note that the stop value is by default excluded by this function; unlike np.linspace(), there is no explicit way to include the stop value in the *array*. Python will try to deduce the type of the *array*, e.g., int, float, or complex, from the input arguments, but this choice can be overridden by specifying the dtype argument:

```
np.arange(1, 10, 1, dtype=complex)
```

```
array([1.+0.j, 2.+0.j, 3.+0.j, 4.+0.j, 5.+0.j, 6.+0.j, 7.+0.j,
       8.+0.j, 9.+0.j])
```

Also, we would like to point out that the step size defaults to unity if only two positional arguments are provided:

```
np.arange(1, 10)
```

```
array([1, 2, 3, 4, 5, 6, 7, 8, 9])
```

Three further vector constructors turn out to be surprisingly useful. For instance, **np.zeros()**:

```
np.zeros(5, dtype=float)
```

```
array([0., 0., 0., 0., 0.])
```

constructs an *array* of *floats*, filled with zeros. The function **np.ones()** does the same but packs the *array* with ones, and **np.empty()** constructs an *array* of the same length but leaves the values of the contents unspecified. In addition to these three functions, there also exist **look alike-constructors** that create the corresponding *arrays* shaped after an *array* that is provided to them. For instance, both lines in this example result in *arrays* of the same shape as x, but filled with zeros:

```
np.zeros(x.shape)
np.zeros_like(x)
```

```
array([0., 0., 0., 0., 0., 0., 0., 0., 0., 0.])
```

4.1.2   Basic Array Arithmetic

Arithmetical operations between *arrays of the same size* can be performed as follows:

```
a = np.linspace(0, 1, 5)
c = np.linspace(1, 3, 5)
print(a+c)
print(a*c)
print(a/c)
```

```
[1.   1.75 2.5  3.25 4.  ]
[0.   0.375 1.   1.875 3.  ]
[0.          0.16666667 0.25      0.3         0.33333333]
```

Let us look in detail at the result of the summation operation. The sum is an *array* of the same size as its operands. The ith component is the sum of the i-components of a and c. In this sense, the + operator is said to act ***component-wise***. All of the arithmetical operations in this code snippet are acting component-wise, as do other operators like ****** (exponentiation) and **%** (modulo).

Incidentally, there is an efficiency issue, relevant for large *arrays*, which should, perhaps, be highlighted here. Suppose that instead of a+c we had set a = a+c. Python would have created a temporary *array* to hold the sum required on the right-hand side, filled it, then attached the *identifier* a to it, and finally deleted the original a-*array*. It is faster to use a += c, which avoids the creation of a temporary *array*. Similar constructions are available for the other arithmetic operators acting on vectors. There is, however, a pitfall for the unwary. In Python, if a scalar a has type int and a second scalar b has type float, then the operation a += b widens the type of a to float. In fact, this is not the case for NumPy *arrays*, if the += operator is used! The reader is encouraged to try

```
a = np.ones(4, dtype=int)
b = np.linspace(0, 1, 4)
a += b
```

```
UFuncTypeError                    Traceback (most recent call last)
<ipython-input-30-319837fad535> in <module>
      1 a = np.ones(4, dtype=int)
      2 b = np.linspace(0, 1, 4)
----> 3 a += b
UFuncTypeError: Cannot cast ufunc 'add' output from
dtype('float64') to dtype('int64') with casting rule 'same_kind'
```

to see that the type of a is unchanged. However, the result will not be narrowed back to int by truncation towards zero. Instead, an *exception* will be raised, warning about this issue. Finally, be aware that the operation a + b (which creates a new *array*) does not suffer from this issue, since the new *array* is simply widened.

In general, arithmetical operations between vectors of different sizes that produce another vector cannot be defined unambiguously, and so cause an error. However, such operations between an *array* and a scalar can be given an unambiguous meaning:

```
a = np.linspace(0, 1, 5)
print(a*2)
print(a**2)
print(a/2)
```

```
[0.  0.5 1.  1.5 2. ]
[0.     0.0625 0.25   0.5625 1.    ]
[0.    0.125 0.25 0.375 0.5  ]
```

For someone unaware of the workings of NumPy, the results should be surprising since operations between an *array*, here a, and a scalar, here 2, are not defined. However, NumPy is able to handle this situation efficiently and performs the operation component-wise.

We now have enough information to consider a simple but nontrivial example, the smoothing of data by three-point averaging. Suppose f refers to a Python vector of data. We might smooth the data at interior points as follows:

```
f = np.sin(np.linspace(0, 2*np.pi, 100))
f_av = f.copy()    # make a copy, just as for lists
for i in range(1, len(f)-1): # loop over interior points
    f_av[i] = (f[i-1] + f[i] + f[i+1])/3
```

(We will learn about np.pi in Section 4.3 and np.sin() in Section 4.2.1.) This works well for small *arrays* but becomes very slow for larger vectors. Consider instead:

```
f_avnp = f.copy()    # as above
f_avnp[1:-1] = (f[:-2] + f[1:-1] + f[2:])/3
```

This ***vectorized code*** will execute much faster for large *arrays* since the implied loop will be executed using precompiled C code. One way to get the slicings correct is to note that in each slice [a:b], the difference a-b is the same, i.e., 2.

Finally, we need to point out to beginners that there is an ***extremely important difference*** between *arrays* and *lists*. If l is a Python *list*, then l[:] is ***always*** a (shallow) copy, but for NumPy *arrays*, slicings ***always*** reference the original *array*. That is why we had to enforce an explicit (deep) copy in the code snippets above.

4.1.3 Two (and More)-Dimensional Arrays

We turn next to *arrays* with two and more dimensions. Fortunately, having mastered the basic definitions, it is easy to see that the definitions are consistent with those for vectors, and that much of what we have already learned about one-dimensional *arrays* or vectors carries through. As we already saw in the discussion of one-dimensional *arrays* (see Section 4.1.1), a general NumPy *array* carries three important attributes: ndim, the number of dimensions or ***axes***; shape, a *tuple* of dimension ndim that gives the extent or length along each axis; and dtype, which gives the type of each element. Let us see them in a familiar context:

```
v = np.linspace(0, 1.0, 11)
v.ndim, v.shape, v.dtype
```

```
(1, (11,), dtype('float64'))
```

Here, the *array* has a shape of (11,) (a *tuple* with one element is almost, but not quite, synonymous with the number 11), meaning a vector of length 11. To get a better understanding of shapes, we now consider a two-dimensional *array*. A conceptually simple method of **generating two-dimensional arrays** explicitly is from a *list* of *lists*, e.g.,

```
x = np.array([[0, 1, 2, 3], [4, 5, 6, 7], [8, 9, 10, 11]])
x
```

```
array([[ 0,  1,  2,  3],
       [ 4,  5,  6,  7],
       [ 8,  9, 10, 11]])
```

The displayed representation of the *array* clarifies how the initializing *list* has to be structured: the outer *list*'s elements form the rows of a two-dimensional matrix, whereas the inner *list*'s elements contain the different elements of each row. If we interpret this object as a matrix, it has three rows and four columns. We can compare this interpretation with the object's *shape*:

```
x.shape
```

```
(3, 4)
```

In the two-dimensional case, the *shape* of an *array* agrees with the matrix notation of (*number of rows*, *number of columns*). Generally, we refer to the rightmost axis of an *array* (the one containing four elements in this case) as the *trailing axis*; this will be important when we introduce broadcasting (see Section 4.1.4). Higher dimensional *arrays* can be built following the same logic:

```
im = np.array([[[1, 0, 0], [1, 1, 0]],
               [[1, 0, 1], [0, 0, 1]]])
im.shape
```

```
(2, 2, 3)
```

Three-dimensional *arrays* such as this one are typical for representing images. You can consider this as a two-dimensional *array*, representing the image plane, each element of which is a vector containing RGB (red-green-blue) values for each pixel. We will discuss this representation some more in Section 6.6.

For any dimensionality, the shape of an *array* should be regular; irregular or "**ragged**" shapes are not permitted. For instance, an *array* cannot be generated from irregularly shaped nested *lists*:

```
np.array([[1, 2, 3], [4, 5], [6, 7, 8]])
```

(For the sake of completeness: it is actually possible to generate an *array* from such a *list* by using **dtype=object**, but the result would be an *array* of *lists* that would not follow the typical *array* behavior in all cases.)

The next snippet shows how we can access individual rows and columns:

```
print(x[2])       # 3rd row
print(x[:,1])     # 2nd column
print(x[2][1])    # specific element
print(x[2,1])     # specific element
```

```
[ 8   9 10 11]
[1 5 9]
9
9
```

The good news is that the Python indexing (Section 3.5.2) and slicing (Section 3.5.3) conventions still apply. The first item extracts the third row (index 2) and the second item extracts the second column (index 1) from x. The last two items show ways to access an individual element of x. In the first, we create an intermediate temporary vector from the last row, and then access an element of that vector. It is, however, more efficient, especially for large *arrays*, to access the required element directly, as in the last entry.

In general, the same constructors that we introduced for vectors (see Section 4.1.1) are able to generate multi-dimensional *arrays*. For instance, we can generate a (3×3×3) *array* only containing zeros using:

```
np.zeros((3, 3, 3))
```

Note how the shape of the *array* is passed to the function as a *tuple*. In the same way, np.ones(), np.empty(), and, of course, the corresponding look-alike functions can be utilized. Nevertheless, be aware that np.linspace(), np.logspace(), and np.arange() can only generate vectors – however, those can be reshaped into multi-dimensional *arrays* utilizing np.reshape() and other shape-changing methods (see Section 4.1.5).

NumPy also provides functionality to **create matrices from coordinate vectors**. Suppose we are given vectors of x-values x_i, where $0 \leqslant i < m$, and y-values y_k, where $0 \leqslant k < n$, and we want to represent a function $u(x, y)$ by grid values $u_{ik} = u(x_i, y_k)$. Mathematically, we might use a $m \times n$ *array* ordered in *matrix form*, e.g., for $m = 3$ and $n = 4$:

$$
\begin{array}{cccc}
u_{00} & u_{01} & u_{02} & u_{03} \\
u_{10} & u_{11} & u_{12} & u_{13} \\
u_{20} & u_{21} & u_{22} & u_{23}
\end{array}
$$

We are thinking of x increasing downwards and y increasing rightwards. However, in the image-processing world, many prefer to require x to increase rightwards and y to increase upwards, leading to *image form*

$$
\begin{array}{ccc}
u_{03} & u_{13} & u_{23} \\
u_{02} & u_{12} & u_{22} \\
u_{01} & u_{11} & u_{21} \\
u_{00} & u_{10} & u_{20}
\end{array}
$$

Clearly, the two *arrays* are linear transformations of each other. Because examples in the literature often use *arrays* corresponding to symmetric matrices, the differences are rarely spelled out explicitly. We therefore need to exhibit care.

Since assembling **grid values** u_{ik} from vectors x and y can be rather complex, NumPy provides tools for this purpose. For vectors, we learned about the NumPy functions `np.linspace()` and `np.arange()`. For two-dimensional *arrays*, there are four possible intervals. As a concrete example, we try to explicitly construct a grid with $-1 \leqslant x \leqslant 1$ and $0 \leqslant y \leqslant 1$ and a spacing of 0.25 in both directions, and perform a simple arithmetical operation on it.

Perhaps the easiest to understand is the **np.meshgrid()** constructor. We first construct vectors `xv` and `yv`, which define the two coordinate axes for the intervals, then two *arrays* `xa` and `ya` on which y and x respectively are held constant. Finally, we compute their product:

```
xv = np.linspace(-1, 1, 5)
yv = np.linspace(0, 1, 3)
xa, ya = np.meshgrid(xv, yv)
print("xa = \n", xa)
print("ya = \n", ya)
print("xa*ya = \n", xa*ya)
```

```
xa =
 [[-1.  -0.5  0.   0.5  1. ]
  [-1.  -0.5  0.   0.5  1. ]
  [-1.  -0.5  0.   0.5  1. ]]
ya =
 [[0.  0.  0.  0.  0. ]
  [0.5 0.5 0.5 0.5 0.5]
  [1.  1.  1.  1.  1. ]]
xa*ya =
 [[-0.  -0.   0.   0.   0. ]
  [-0.5 -0.25 0.   0.25 0.5 ]
  [-1.  -0.5  0.   0.5  1. ]]
```

Notice from the shape of `xa` or `ya` that `np.meshgrid()` uses *image form*.

The **np.mgrid** and `np.ogrid` operators use rather different syntax, cobbled together from slicing notation, and the representation of complex numbers. We illustrate this first in one dimension:

```
np.mgrid[-1:1:9j]
```

```
array([-1.  , -0.75, -0.5 , -0.25,  0.  ,  0.25,  0.5 ,  0.75,  1.  ])
```

```
np.mgrid[-1:1:0.25]
```

```
array([-1.  , -0.75, -0.5 , -0.25,  0.  ,  0.25,  0.5 ,  0.75])
```

Note that the first code cell, with pure imaginary spacing, mimics the effect of the one-dimensional `np.linspace()`, while the second emulates `np.arange()`. Although unfamiliar, this notation is succinct and generalizes to two or more dimensions, where it uses *matrix form*:

```
xm, ym = np.mgrid[-1:1:5j, 0:1:3j]
print("xm = \n", xm)
print("ym = \n", ym)
print("xm*ym = \n", xm*ym)
```

```
xm =
 [[-1.  -1.  -1. ]
 [-0.5 -0.5 -0.5]
 [ 0.   0.   0. ]
 [ 0.5  0.5  0.5]
 [ 1.   1.   1. ]]
ym =
 [[0.  0.5 1. ]
 [0.  0.5 1. ]
 [0.  0.5 1. ]
 [0.  0.5 1. ]
 [0.  0.5 1. ]]
xm*ym =
 [[-0.  -0.5 -1. ]
 [-0.  -0.25 -0.5 ]
 [ 0.   0.   0. ]
 [ 0.   0.25  0.5 ]
 [ 0.   0.5   1. ]]
```

This is shorter than the first code snippet of this section, but achieves the same result up to a linear transformation.

For large *arrays*, especially with more dimensions, much of the data in `xm` and `ym` may be redundant. This deficiency is addressed by the **np.ogrid** variant, which also uses *matrix form*:

```
xo, yo = np.ogrid[-1:1:5j, 0:1:3j]
print("xo = \n", xo)
print("yo = \n", yo)
print("xo.shape = ", xo.shape, " yo.shape = ", yo.shape)
print("xo*yo = \n", xo*yo)
```

```
xo =
 [[-1. ]
  [-0.5]
  [ 0. ]
  [ 0.5]
  [ 1. ]]
yo =
 [[0.  0.5 1. ]]
xo.shape =  (5, 1)  yo.shape =  (1, 3)
xo*yo =
 [[-0.   -0.5  -1.  ]
  [-0.   -0.25 -0.5 ]
  [ 0.    0.    0.  ]
  [ 0.    0.25  0.5 ]
  [ 0.    0.5   1.  ]]
```

You should verify that xo and yo have shapes chosen so that the broadcasting rules apply, and that xm*ym (from the last snippet) and xo*yo are identical.

4.1.4   Broadcasting

Suppose that y is an *array* with precisely the same shape as x. Then x+y, x-y, x*y and x/y are *arrays* of the same shape, where the operations are carried out component-wise, i.e., component by component. In certain circumstances, these operations are well-defined even when the shapes of x and y differ, and this is called *broadcasting*. We generalize to a situation where we have a number of *arrays*, not necessarily of the same shape, to which we are applying arithmetical operations. At first sight, broadcasting seems somewhat strange, but it is easier to grasp if we remember two rules:

☐ The *first rule of broadcasting* is that if the *arrays* do not have the same number of dimensions, then a "1" will be repeatedly prepended to the shapes of the smaller *arrays* until all the *arrays* have the same number of axes.

☐ The *second rule of broadcasting* ensures that *arrays* with a size of 1 along a particular dimension or axis act as if they had the size of the *array* with the largest size along that dimension. The value of the *array* element is assumed to be the same along that dimension for the "broadcasted" *array*.

As a simple example, consider the *array* v = np.linspace(0, 10, 11) with shape (11,). What does 2*v mean? Well, 2 has shape (0,) and so by the first rule we augment the shape of "2" to (1,). Next, we use the second rule to increase the shape of "2" to (11,), with identical components. Finally, we perform component-wise multiplication to double each element of v:

```
v = np.linspace(0, 10, 11)
2*v
```

```
array([ 0.,   2.,   4.,   6.,   8., 10., 12., 14., 16., 18., 20.])
```

The same holds for other arithmetic operations. However, if w is a vector with shape (5,), the broadcasting rules do not allow for the construction of v*w:

```
w = np.arange(5)
v*w
```

```
ValueError                       Traceback (most recent call last)
<ipython-input-40-429aa0d280e3> in <module>
      1 w = np.arange(5)
----> 2 v*w
ValueError: operands could not be broadcast together with
shapes (11,) (5,)
```

Since the shape of w violates the broadcasting rules, v*w results in a `ValueError`.

To see *array* arithmetic with broadcasting in action, consider the following examples:

```
x = np.array([[0, 1, 2], [3, 4, 5], [6, 7, 8]])
r = np.array([0, 1, 2])
c = np.array([[0], [1], [2]])
r*x
```

```
array([[ 0,   1,   4],
       [ 0,   4, 10],
       [ 0,   7, 16]])
```

Here, r is reshaped (since it has the lower dimensionality) from shape (3,) to (1, 3) before the multiplication so that the sequence [0, 1, 2] is multiplied to each "row" of x. A different example:

```
x*c
```

```
array([[ 0,   0,   0],
       [ 3,   4,   5],
       [12, 14, 16]])
```

In this example, c already has the same number of dimensions as x so only the second rule of broadcasting applies here so that the "column vector" [0, 1, 2] is multiplied to each "column" of x.

```
r*c
```

```
array([[0, 0, 0],
       [0, 1, 2],
```

```
     [0, 2, 4]])
```

In this final example, r is reshaped from shape (3,) to (1, 3) and now has the same dimensionality as c, which is of shape (3, 1). The multiplication of both now leads to an *array* of shape (3, 3).

There is one more thing to point out based on the following result:

```
x*r
```

```
array([[ 0,  1,  4],
       [ 0,  4, 10],
       [ 0,  7, 16]])
```

Note that since x*r equals r*x, x*r is **not** the same as matrix multiplication, nor is x*x a matrix multiplication. For these, try **np.dot(x,r)** or dot(x,x). A brief introduction to matrix arithmetic will be given in Section 4.7.

4.1.5   Array Manipulations

NumPy provides a number of tools to **change the shape** of *arrays*. One of these tools is **np.reshape()**, which takes an existing *array* (or even a *list*) and a *tuple*, and, if possible, recasts the *array* into another, the shape of which is determined by the *tuple*. A common example is:

```
np.reshape(range(6), (2,3))
```

```
array([[0, 1, 2],
       [3, 4, 5]])
```

but a potentially more useful idea is

```
np.reshape(np.linspace(0, 1.0, 9), (3, 3))
```

```
array([[0.   , 0.125, 0.25 ],
       [0.375, 0.5  , 0.625],
       [0.75 , 0.875, 1.   ]])
```

Naturally, the number of elements of the new shape, as described through the *tuple*, must exactly match the number of elements of the original *array*. For instance, the following attempt to create a 3×3 matrix out of an *array* with 10 elements will fail and result in a *ValueError*:

```
np.reshape(np.arange(10), (3,3))
```

```
ValueError                         Traceback (most recent call last)
<ipython-input-47-76bc63b294f5> in <module>
```

```
----> 1 np.reshape(np.arange(10), (3,3))

<__array_function__ internals> in reshape(*args, **kwargs)

.../numpy/core/fromnumeric.py in reshape(a, newshape, order)
    297            [5, 6]])
    298    """
--> 299    return _wrapfunc(a, 'reshape', newshape, order=order)
    300
    301
.../core/fromnumeric.py in _wrapfunc(obj, method, *args, **kwds)
     56
     57    try:
--> 58        return bound(*args, **kwds)
     59    except TypeError:
     60        # A TypeError occurs if the object does have ...
ValueError: cannot reshape array of size 10 into shape (3,3)
```

For the user's convenience, the function can automatically derive the length of a single axis if the **wildcard value −1** is provided. The following code cell will generate a 4×3 *array* since the size of the trailing axis (number of columns) is fixed to 3 and the original *array* has a size of 12:

```
np.reshape(np.arange(12), (−1, 3))
```

```
array([[ 0,  1,  2],
       [ 3,  4,  5],
       [ 6,  7,  8],
       [ 9, 10, 11]])
```

Finally, we would like to point out that np.reshape(), just like all of the following functions introduced in this section, is also implemented as a method of the *array* class, enabling the following use:

```
x = np.arange(12).reshape(3, 4)
x
```

```
array([[ 0,  1,  2,  3],
       [ 4,  5,  6,  7],
       [ 8,  9, 10, 11]])
```

It is important to note here that the reshape() method, other than the np.reshape() function, does not require a *tuple* as argument; instead, the length of each axis can be passed as an individual *integer*.

One important aspect of reshaping *arrays* is the ***index order*** in which the reshaping is done. By default, all NumPy reshaping functions and methods assume a C-like index order in which the last axis index changes fastest while the first axis index changes slowest. The opposite is also possible, where the first index changes fastest and the last index changes slowest; this is referred to as the Fortran-like index order. When reshaping, the index order can be set with the order argument: 'C' for the C-like order (which is also the default order) and 'F' for the Fortran-like order. To visualize the difference between the two orders, the following code cell performs the same reshaping operation as the previous cell, but using the Fortran-like index order:

```
np.arange(12).reshape((3, 4), order='F')
```

```
array([[ 0,  3,  6,  9],
       [ 1,  4,  7, 10],
       [ 2,  5,  8, 11]])
```

While the shape of the resulting *array* is identical, the order of elements changed. Interpreting the result as a matrix, the Fortran-like index order "fills in column-by-column," whereas the C-like index order "fills in row-by-row." While the different orders might come in handy at some point, we would like to point out that since C-like index ordering is the default in NumPy, one typically will not encounter too many situations in which to think about what ordering scheme to use to retrieve consistent results. In case a different ordering scheme seems to be the right choice, the order argument is supported by most *array* creation and manipulation functions and methods.

Now, let's consider some other shape modification functions. Sometimes it is useful to be able to flatten an *array*, which means to reshape it in vectorial form. This can be easily achieved with the function **np.ravel()**:

```
np.ravel(x)
```

```
array([ 0,  1,  2,  3,  4,  5,  6,  7,  8,  9, 10, 11])
```

Note that the same result can also be achieved with:

```
x.reshape(-1)
```

NumPy provides a function to derive the transpose of an *array*, **np.transpose()**:

```
np.transpose(x)
```

```
array([[ 0,  4,  8],
       [ 1,  5,  9],
       [ 2,  6, 10],
       [ 3,  7, 11]])
```

The transpose is also accessible as a class method (x.transpose()) and even as an attribute of the *array* class, **x.T**.

A number of different *array* **transformations for rearranging elements** are available, which are especially useful for *arrays* that contain image data of the shape $h \times w \times c$, where h and w are the height and width, respectively, of the image in pixel units and c is the number of channel (e.g., three for RGB images). **np.flip()** can be used to flip *arrays* along a specified axis. For *arrays* containing image data, a flip along axis zero means an up-down flip, whereas a flip along axis one means a left-right flip:

```
im = np.arange(4).reshape(2, 2)
print('original:\n', im)
print('flip u-d:\n', np.flip(im, axis=0))
print('flip l-r:\n', np.flip(im, axis=1))
```

```
original:
 [[0 1]
  [2 3]]
flip u-d:
 [[2 3]
  [0 1]]
flip l-r:
 [[1 0]
  [3 2]]
```

This example uses the special case of a single-channel (grayscale) image; for color images, the results follow the same rules (and `axis=2` would simply reverse the order of the color channels). Note that flips in both directions can also be achieved with the convenience functions **np.flipud()** and **np.fliplr()**. Finally, **np.rot90()** performs rotations of integer multiples of 90 degrees. For instance, the following code line will rotate the *array* by 90 degrees (k=1 × 90 degrees):

```
np.rot90(im, k=1, axes=(0, 1))
```

```
array([[1, 3],
       [0, 2]])
```

The argument `axes` here defines the plane in which the rotation is supposed to happen. In this trivial case of a two-dimensional *array*, the choice is simple: `axes=(0, 1)`. In case of an image *array* following the general shape $h \times w \times c$, the same choice for `axes` would indeed rotate the image perpendicular to the image plane and leave the channels untouched. Note that negative values for **k** lead to rotations in the opposite direction and that values for **k** greater than 3 lead to the same results as **k % 4**.

NumPy provides a number of ways to **join** *arrays*. The most basic function for joining *arrays* is **np.concatenate()**. The function takes as positional argument a sequence (i.e., a *list*, *tuple*, or *array*) of sequences, and as keyword argument an axis index (zero by default) referencing the axis along which the input sequences will be joined. The following example shows how to join a *tuple* of *lists* into a vector:

```
np.concatenate(([0, 1, 2], [3, 4], [5, 6, 7, 8], [9]))
```

```
array([0, 1, 2, 3, 4, 5, 6, 7, 8, 9])
```

Note that the individual *lists* are of variable length. Concatenating sequences of variable shape is only possible if their only variable axis is the same axis along which the sequences are joined. For instance, consider the following nested *lists* (of shape 2×2 and 2×3) that we try to concatenate along axis one, i.e., we join them horizontally:

```
np.concatenate(([[1, 2, 3], [6, 7, 8]], [[4, 5], [9, 10]]), axis=1)
```

```
array([[ 1,  2,  5,  6,  7],
       [ 3,  4,  8,  9, 10]])
```

Despite their different shapes, we can join those *lists* – but only along axis one – whereas joining them along axis zero results in a `ValueError`:

```
np.concatenate(([[1, 2, 3], [6, 7, 8]], [[4, 5], [9, 10]]), axis=0)
```

```
ValueError                          Traceback (most recent call last)
<ipython-input-69-0c15b65cb492> in <module>
----> 1 np.concatenate(([[1, 2, 3], [6, 7, 8]],
                         [[4, 5], [9, 10]]), axis=0)
<__array_function__ internals> in concatenate(*args, **kwargs)
ValueError: all the input array dimensions for the concatenation
axis must match exactly, but along dimension 1, the array at
index 0 has size 3 and the array at index 1 has size 2
```

While `np.concatenate()` joins sequences along existing axes, **np.stack()** creates a new axis along which a sequence is stacked:

```
np.stack(([[0, 1], [2, 3]], [[4, 5], [6, 7]], [[8, 9], [10, 11]]),
         axis=0)
```

```
array([[[ 0,  1],
        [ 2,  3]],

       [[ 4,  5],
        [ 6,  7]],

       [[ 8,  9],
        [10, 11]]])
```

```
np.stack([[[0, 1], [2, 3]], [[4, 5], [6, 7]], [[8, 9], [10, 11]]],
         axis=1)
```

```
array([[[ 0,  1],
        [ 4,  5],
        [ 8,  9]],

       [[ 2,  3],
        [ 6,  7],
        [10, 11]]])
```

```
np.stack([[[0, 1], [2, 3]], [[4, 5], [6, 7]], [[8, 9], [10, 11]]],
         axis=2)
```

```
array([[[ 0,  4,  8],
        [ 1,  5,  9]],

       [[ 2,  6, 10],
        [ 3,  7, 11]]])
```

The convenience functions **np.vstack()**, **np.hstack()**, and **np.dstack()** are available for concatenating *arrays* and other sequences of *arrays* along the vertical, horizontal, and depth dimensions, respectively. Note that although their naming might suggest a behavior that is similar to np.stack(), the three functions actually provide the same results as np.concatenate() with axis arguments zero (vertical stacking), one (horizontal), and two (depth).

Finally, NumPy provides functions to deal with empty axes. Sometimes it is necessary to create *arrays* with seemingly weird shapes for specific purposes (e.g., broadcasting). For instance, it might be necessary to create an *array* of the form array([[0], [1], [2], [3], [4]]). There are numerous ways to create this *array*, but one of the more elegant ways involves **np.expand_dims()**. As its name suggests, this function expands the shape of an *array* by adding axes. The desired *array* can be easily generated:

```
np.expand_dims(np.arange(5), axis=1)
```

```
array([[0],
       [1],
       [2],
       [3],
       [4]])
```

Any number of axes can be added by providing a *tuple* of axis indices to the axis keyword argument. The opposite operation – getting rid of seemingly unnecessary axes – is possible with **np.squeeze()**:

```
np.squeeze([[0], [1], [2], [3], [4]], axis=1)
```

```
array([0, 1, 2, 3, 4])
```

Finally, we can **modify individual elements of *arrays***; this is possible despite the fact that *arrays* are immutable since the functions introduced here create modified copies of the original *array*. The examples provided below refer to the two-dimensional case, which is very common; with the explanations provided below it should be trivial to figure out higher-dimensional cases.

np.append() will append values to the end of an *array* on an *axis* of your choice. While this sounds somewhat similar to the append() function that exists for *lists*, there are a few caveats to keep in mind. First of all, since *arrays* must not be ragged, the shape of the sequence (typically an *array* or a *list*) to be appended must fit the shape of the *array* to which it is appended. This requirement excludes the *axis* on which the sequence is to be appended. This sounds rather complicated, so let's consider our example *array* x, which is of shape (3, 4). First, we want to append a new row to x, which means that we want to append to *axis* zero. The sequence we want to add thus has to be of shape (1, 4); the length of the first axis is unity, since this is the *axis* to which we want to append and the length of 4 in the second *axis* is given by the shape of x. Hence, we can perform this operation with:

```
np.append(x, [[10, 20, 30, 40]], axis=0)
```

```
array([[ 0,  1,  2,  3],
       [ 4,  5,  6,  7],
       [ 8,  9, 10, 11],
       [10, 20, 30, 40]])
```

Note that the sequence [[10, 20, 30, 40]] is of the desired shape (1, 4) and x is not changed by the function call, which returns a modified copy of x. Now consider the case that we would like to append a new column (*axis* one). Following the same logic as above, our sequence to be appended must be of shape (3, 1):

```
np.append(x, [[10], [20], [30]], axis=1)
```

```
array([[ 0,  1,  2,  3, 10],
       [ 4,  5,  6,  7, 20],
       [ 8,  9, 10, 11, 30]])
```

Bringing sequences into the right shape can be a hassle, but the **np.reshape()** method can be of great help here; the following code cell will provide the same result as the previous cell:

```
np.append(x, np.array([10, 20, 30]).reshape(3, 1), axis=1)
```

Be aware that the `axis` keyword argument is optional; if omitted, both the *array* and the sequence will be flattened before the append operation:

```
np.append(x, [[10], [20], [30]])
```

```
array([ 0,  1,  2,  3,  4,  5,  6,  7,  8,  9, 10, 11, 10, 20, 30])
```

The function **np.insert()** allows you to insert a sequence at a given index position on a given *axis*. This function is much less strict in its formatting requirements, as the user provides all necessary parameters as arguments: np.insert(<array>, <index position>, <sequence>, <axis>). In order to add a row after the first row of x, we can use the following:

```
np.insert(x, 1, [10, 20, 30, 40], axis=0)
```

```
array([[ 0,  1,  2,  3],
       [10, 20, 30, 40],
       [ 4,  5,  6,  7],
       [ 8,  9, 10, 11]])
```

Note that in contrast to np.append(), we simply provide the new row as a vector *array*. Similarly, we can add a new column after the first column of x:

```
np.insert(x, 1, [10, 20, 30], axis=1)
```

```
array([[ 0, 10,  1,  2,  3],
       [ 4, 20,  5,  6,  7],
       [ 8, 30,  9, 10, 11]])
```

`axis` is again a keyword argument; if omitted, the *array* will be flattened before the sequence is inserted at the position index:

```
np.insert(x, 1, [10, 20, 30])
```

```
array([ 0, 10, 20, 30,  1,  2,  3,  4,  5,  6,  7,  8,  9, 10, 11])
```

We would also like to point out that the position index can be replaced with a *slice* or a sequence of *integers*, referring to a range of positions (see below for a related example).

Finally, **np.delete()** allows you to remove elements (or sub-*arrays*) from an *array* that are identified based on the position index on a given *axis*. For instance, we can delete the center row (index 1) from x:

```
np.delete(x, 1, axis=0)
```

```
array([[ 0,  1,  2,  3],
       [ 8,  9, 10, 11]])
```

Using *slices* instead of a positional index, you can also remove sub-*arrays*:

```
np.delete(x, np.s_[2:], axis=1)
```

```
array([[0, 1],
       [4, 5],
       [8, 9]])
```

Here, **np.s_** is a means to build standalone index *tuples* for *arrays*. Keep in mind that directly indexing those parts of an *array* that you would like to keep might be easier to read and more efficient than np.delete():

```
x[:,:2]
```

```
array([[0, 1],
       [4, 5],
       [8, 9]])
```

4.2   Working with Arrays

4.2.1   Mathematical Functions and Operators

NumPy offers a wide range of functions that operate on *arrays* and in most cases also on *lists* (which are then internally converted to *arrays*) and scalars. A large fraction of these functions fall under the category of *universal functions* or **ufuncs**, which are functions that, when applied to a scalar, generate a scalar, but when applied to an *array* produce an *array* of the same size, by operating component-wise. An overview of different *ufuncs* is shown in Table 4.1.

While many functions are unique, there is a significant overlap with the math module or other basic Python modules. For instance, there is a function math.sqrt() and a function np.sqrt(), both of which compute square roots. The difference between the two functions is that only np.sqrt() can compute component-wise square roots from an *array*, whereas math.sqrt() only works on scalars. Since NumPy functions are also compatible with scalar inputs, we recommend to use the NumPy versions of these functions in all cases.

Using *ufuncs* is simple. They can be easily imported from NumPy and used on scalar objects:

```
np.sqrt(9)
```

```
3.0
```

Table 4.1 A collection of commonly used *ufuncs* that can be applied to scalars and *arrays* of different shapes sorted by different categories. Arguments are provided in parentheses and symbols in square brackets represent alternative ways to call a function if all arguments are NumPy *arrays*. Each function can be called as np.<function name>.

Operators:		
add(x,y) [x+y]	subtract(x,y) [x-y]	multiply(x,y) [x*y]
divide(x,y) [x/y]	power(x,y) [x**y]	remainder(x,y) [x%y]
abs(x)	sign(x)	floor(x)
sqrt(x)	conjugate(x)	gcd(x,y)
exp(x)	log(x)	log10(x)

Trigonometry:		
sin(x)	cos(x)	tan(x)
arcsin(x)	arccos(x)	arctan(x)
sinh(x)	cosh(x)	tanh(x)
arcsinh(x)	arccosh(x)	arctanh(x)
arctan2(x,y)	deg2rad(x)	rad2deg(x)

Comparisons:		
greater(x,y) [x>y]	greater_equal(x,y) [x>=y]	equal(x,y) [x==y]
less(x,y) [x<y]	less_equal(x,y) [x<=y]	not_equal(x,y) [x!=y]
logical_and(x,y) [a&b]	logical_or(x,y) [x|b]	logical_not(x)

and *arrays*:

```
np.sqrt(np.arange(5))
```

```
array([0.        , 1.        , 1.41421356, 1.73205081, 2.        ])
```

Note that *ufuncs* applied to *arrays* perform their operations in an component-wise fash ion and return an *array* of the same shape. If a *ufunc* takes two objects as arguments, those should be of the same shape or must be broadcastable to a common shape.

One important comment on **trigonometric functions**. As in most other programming languages, trigonometric *ufuncs* require arguments in *radians* – not *degrees*. Please keep this in mind when using those to save yourself long hours of debugging code that otherwise works perfectly fine. Take advantage of the np.deg2rad() and np.rad2deg() functions to convert between both definitions.

One point that is not made clear in the documentation of Python functions in general is the domain and range of each of these functions. For example, how does NumPy interpret $\sqrt{-1}$? In basic Python, math.sqrt(-1) will produce an error and the program will stop. However, cmath.sqrt(-1) returns 1j, for the argument is widened to a complex value. *ufuncs* behave differently, and the type of the argument is critical. Note that np.sqrt(-1+0j) takes a complex square root and returns 1j, but np.sqrt(-1) produces a *warning* and returns np.nan.

4.2.2   Sums and Products

We can sum the elements of any *array* x with **np.sum(x)**. If x has more than one dimension (we use two for illustrative purposes), then np.sum(x, axis=0) sums over the individual rows (along the columns), and np.sum(x, axis=1) sums over the columns (along the rows):

```python
a = [[1, 2], [3, 4]]
print('sum over all elements:', np.sum(a))
print('sum over rows:', np.sum(a, axis=0))
print('sum over columns:', np.sum(a, axis=1))
```

```
sum over all elements: 10
sum over rows: [4 6]
sum over columns: [3 7]
```

With the same syntax, the function **np.cumsum(x)** produces an *array* of the same shape as x but with cumulative sums. The functions **np.prod()** and **np.cumprod()** do the same but for products.

4.2.3   Comparing Arrays

In almost every nontrivial program, there will be user-defined functions, and it is highly desirable that, where appropriate, they behave like *ufuncs*, in the sense that when applied to *arrays* of consistent dimensions, they return *arrays* of an appropriate dimension without invoking explicit loops over the components. In many cases, e.g., where only arithmetical operations and *ufuncs* are involved, this will be manifestly true.

However, if comparisons of *arrays* and other logical statements are involved, this may not be the case. Consider, e.g., the "top hat" function:

$$h(x) = \begin{cases} 0 & \text{if } x < 0, \\ 1 & \text{if } 0 \leqslant x \leqslant 1, \\ 0 & \text{if } x > 1. \end{cases}$$

Using the techniques of Chapter 3, we might try to apply this definition via the code

```python
def h(x):
    """Hat function implemented with basic Python."""
    if x < 0.0:
        return 0.0
    elif x <= 1.0:
        return 1.0
    else:
        return 0.0

v = np.linspace(-2, 2, 401)
h(v)
```

```
ValueError                        Traceback (most recent call last)
<ipython-input-87-62eb3b65da55> in <module>
      8
      9 v = np.linspace(-2, 2, 401)
---> 10 h(v)
<ipython-input-87-62eb3b65da55> in h(x)
      1 def h(x):
---> 2     if x < 0.0:
      3         return 0.0
      4     elif x <= 1.0:
      5         return 1.0
ValueError: The truth value of an array with more than one
element is ambiguous. Use a.any() or a.all()
```

However, this fails, and the reason is very simple. If x has more than one element, then x<0.0 is ambiguous. If x is a scalar, then x<0 is unambiguous. It must evaluate to True or False. But what if x is a vector, i.e., a one-dimensional *array*? Clearly, the right-hand side of the inequality is a scalar, and a moment's thought should suggest that the assertion should be interpreted component-wise, so as to produce a vector of outcomes. Let us test this hypothesis:

```
x = np.arange(10)
x < 5
```

```
array([ True,  True,  True,  True,  True, False, False, False,
       False, False])
```

Indeed, the result of x < 5 is a vector of length 10 of type *bool*, a **logical *array***, of which precisely the first five components are True.

The next code snippet demonstrates an extremely useful feature of NumPy:

```
y = x.copy()
y[x < 5] = -y[x < 5]
y
```

```
array([ 0, -1, -2, -3, -4,  5,  6,  7,  8,  9])
```

We may treat logical *arrays* such as x < 5 as slice definitions on one or both sides of an assignment. First we make a copy y of x. The right-hand side of the next line first selects those components of y that are less than 5, i.e., those for which the corresponding component of x < 5 is True, then multiplies them by −1. The assignment then inserts precisely the modified components back into y. Thus we have computed $y = |x|$ using implicit, C-style, loops. The reason for the copy is to leave the original x unchanged.

Acting on scalars, we can combine logical operators, e.g., x>0 and x<1, by chaining them

```
s = 0.1
s>0 and s<1
```

```
True
```

or using

```
0<s<1
```

```
True
```

Acting on *arrays*, we cannot use the keywords and and or to combine logical *array* expressions in the same way. To combine such expressions and evaluate them in an element-wise fashion on *arrays*, we must use the ***bitwise operators***: **&** (and) and **|** (or):

```
(x>1) & (x<7)
```

```
array([False, False,  True,  True,  True,  True,  True, False,
       False, False])
```

Please note that the use of parentheses around the individual comparisons is mandatory in this case. As we expected, the result of this statement is an *array* of *booleans*. This notation, which applies to NumPy *arrays* and other advanced data types like Pandas *DataFrames* and *Series* (see Sections 8.2 and 8.1) but not *lists*, is very powerful, as is shown in the next section.

Instead of comparing *arrays* component-wise, we could ask whether *all* or *any* elements of the *array* meet a certain condition. This can be easily addressed with the functions **np.all()** and **np.any()**:

```
print('any x > 0:', np.any(x > 0))
print('all x > 0:', np.all(x > 0))
```

```
any x > 0: True
all x > 0: False
```

Not all elements in x are greater than zero since one of them equals zero.

4.2.4   Advanced Array Indexing

We saw in Sections 3.5.1 and 4.1 that *lists* and *arrays* support indexing and slicing. To provide even more flexibility, *arrays* also support indexing based on logical *arrays* and *lists* of *booleans* of the same size that can be used to quickly filter data. Based on the code cells presented in the previous section, consider the following example, which will filter values greater than 1 and less than 7:

```
x[(x>1) & (x<7)]
```

```
array([2, 3, 4, 5, 6])
```

This is possible since (x>1) & (x<7) simply generates an *array* of *booleans*, which acts as a mask on the values of x: in the resulting *array* only those values are contained that are True since they match the condition. This type of indexing is extremely versatile, so let's consider some more examples.

It is possible to design your own *list* of *booleans* and use it for indexing:

```
l = [True, True, False, False, True, True, False, False, True, True]
x[l]
```

```
array([0, 1, 4, 5, 8, 9])
```

That means that any process that generates a *list* or *array* can be exploited here[1]:

```
c = [True if i % 2 ==0 else False for i in range(len(x))]
x[c]
```

```
array([0, 2, 4, 6, 8])
```

Finally, any function or method that generates a *boolean* output can be utilized. In the following example, we generate a copy of x and set one of its values to nan (see Section 4.3). With indexing, we extract all values from the new *array* that are not nan:

```
y = x.copy().astype(float)
y[3] = np.nan
print('y:', y)
print('y cleaned:', y[~np.isnan(y)])
```

```
y: [ 0.  1.  2. nan  4.  5.  6.  7.  8.  9.]
y cleaned: [0. 1. 2. 4. 5. 6. 7. 8. 9.]
```

---

[1] Of course, the same result can be achieved much more easily with x[::2], but the idea here is to show that *list comprehensions* (Section 3.7.5) can be utilized, too.

There are two things to note here. First, we need to change the data type of our copy of x to *float* since nan is defined as a *float* and cannot be used in an *array* of data type *integer*. Secondly, we have to explain that the tilde operator (~) in front of the np.isnan() function (see Section 4.3) call negates its results in an element-wise fashion. Thus ~np.isnan(y) creates an *array* of *booleans* that is True for each element of y that is not nan and vice versa, which is then used to mask out values from y that are nan. In one final example, we combine some of the approaches that we saw earlier:

```
y[~np.isnan(y) & (y**2>25)]
```

```
array([6., 7., 8., 9.])
```

Indexing based on *lists* and *arrays* of *booleans* is very common when dealing with large amounts of data and we will encounter it again in Chapter 8, where we discuss the Pandas package. One reason for its importance is that (typically) the notation is easy to read and, more importantly, the indexing process is extremely fast as it heavily relies on NumPy's C backbone.

4.2.5   Sorting and Searching

The ability to sort NumPy *arrays* is always useful. For numerical sorting, the **np.sort()** function can be used:

```
x = np.array([4, 1, 7, 2, 9, 3])
np.sort(x)
```

```
array([1, 2, 3, 4, 7, 9])
```

The function sorts the elements of x in ascending order and returns a sorted copy of this *array*, which means that its content is untouched. Different sorting algorithms can be utilized (*quicksort* is used by default) and in the case of multidimensional *arrays*, those can be sorted along specific axes.

For some applications, you are more interested in how to reorder the index of an *array* so that it is ordered instead of actually obtaining an ordered *array*. The sequence of indices of an *array* to bring it in order can be obtained with **np.argsort()**:

```
z = np.argsort(x)
print('indices:', z)
print('ordered array:', x[z])
```

```
indices: [1 3 5 0 2 4]
ordered array: [1 2 3 4 7 9]
```

In this case, z is an *array* of indices that order x; we can use z to obtain an ordered version of x.

To **search** for elements that meet specific conditions, a selection of functions is offered by NumPy, a small subset of which we introduce here. Trivial functions include **np.argmin()** and **np.argmax()**, which identify the index of the element corresponding to the minimum and maximum value, respectively. More complex queries are possible with the **np.where()** function, which works very similarly to the indexing method introduced in Section 3.5.2, but provides some more flexibility. It is possible to provide two *arrays* to this function and based on some condition, it will choose whether to pick an element from the first or the second *array*. In this example, we pick an element from x if its value is less than 5 or the corresponding value from x*10 otherwise:

```
np.where(x<5, x, x*10)
```

```
array([ 4,  1, 70,  2, 90,  3])
```

Note that the *array* from which the *boolean* sequence is derived can be unrelated to those *arrays* from which values are extracted – they simply must have the same shape[2]:

```
y = np.arange(6)
np.where(x<5, y, y*10)
```

```
array([ 0,  1, 20,  3, 40,  5])
```

4.3   Constants

The NumPy **constant nan**, or *not a number*, refers to a float of indeterminate value. Further arithmetic may be performed on it, but the result will always be np.nan.

In NumPy, direct division by zero 1.0/0.0 produces an ZeroDivisionError and the execution halts. However, if it occurs indirectly, e.g., within a loop, this is not the case. Consider the following example:

```
x = np.linspace(-2, 2, 5)
x, 1.0/x
```

```
RuntimeWarning: divide by zero encountered in true_divide
(array([-2., -1.,  0.,  1.,  2.]), array([-0.5, -1. ,  inf, 1. ,
    0.5]))
```

which produces a *warning* and array([-0.5,-1.,inf,1.,0.5]). Here inf behaves pretty much like infinity in further calculations. It is available as **np.inf**; its negative is given by **np.NINF** (there is an unfortunate asymmetry in notation here). Other important constants are **np.pi** and **np.e**, which can be readily used.

---

[2] This also holds for the indexing method introduced above.

4.4   Random Numbers

Random numbers are necessary for a wide range of applications; for instance, those that describe stochastic processes. NumPy provides different random number generators as part of the **np.random** module.

The default way to generate random numbers involves the instantiation of a random number generator (rng) using **np.random.default_rng()**:

```
from numpy.random import default_rng

rng = default_rng()
rng.random()
```

```
0.1982743
```

The **random()** method generates a random number from the interval $[0, 1)$ of the type *float* based on a uniform distribution. By providing an integer as argument, it generates a one-dimensional *array* of random numbers from this interval:

```
rng.random(3)
```

```
array([0.75351311, 0.53814331, 0.32973172])
```

and by providing a *tuple*, it generates a multi-dimensional *array* of arbitrary shape:

```
rng.random((3, 3))
```

```
array([[0.7884287 , 0.30319483, 0.45349789],
       [0.1340417 , 0.40311299, 0.20345524],
       [0.26231334, 0.75036467, 0.28040876]])
```

Since the resulting random numbers are stored in an *array*, it is easy to scale them onto a different interval; for instance, consider the interval $[5, 20)$:

```
5 + rng.random(3)*15
```

```
array([ 9.15336806,  7.40978013, 19.5488812 ])
```

If the user instead of *floats* prefers *integers*, the `integers()` method can be used, which allows for defining a range of values (keyword argument `low` and `high`) and the size of the output *array*:

```
rng.integers(low=10, high=100, size=(3,3))
```

```
array([[47, 56, 36],
       [20, 48, 66],
       [51, 79, 42]])
```

Of course, the user is not limited to generating uniformly distributed random numbers of different data types. Methods are available to sample from the most common probability distributions. We showcase the use of the Normal distribution and leave it to the reader to explore other distributions. The parameters of the **normal()** method, `loc` and `scale`, refer to the Normal distribution's mean and standard deviation, respectively. An optional `size` keyword argument is also available to generate arbitrarily shaped *arrays* of random numbers. To sample 10 random values from a Normal distribution with mean value 5 and standard deviation 1, this code cell will do the trick:

```
rng.normal(loc=5, scale=1, size=10)
```

```
array([5.66306337, 4.48599363, 3.35192483, 5.16746474,
       5.10901409, 3.77264795, 4.31677334, 4.92795632,
       4.05524838, 4.90173003])
```

Finally, we will introduce the concept of random seeds. Each random generator uses a **seed value** starting from which random numbers are generated. Since the seed values used on different systems might vary, running the same code that utilizes the same random number generator on two different computers might lead to different results. This is somewhat the idea behind random numbers, but it renders the reproducibility of the results of stochastic processes almost impossible. To enable reproducibility, it is possible to manually set a seed value, which means that random numbers are generated always in the same order.[3] It is good practice to fix the seed value at the beginning of your code if it includes stochastic elements. The reproducibility of the results will help you in debugging your code, and others in understanding your code and results.

To set a seed value, you simply need to initialize your random number generator with this value. For instance, if your seed value is 42 (a very common choice that is somehow related to life, the universe, and everything), all you need is:

```
rng_seeded = default_rng(42)
```

If you now generate a set of random numbers, you will receive the following result:

```
rng_seeded.random(3)
```

```
array([0.77395605, 0.43887844, 0.85859792])
```

There seems to be no difference to generating random numbers without a seed value. However, now try the following: reset the seed value and generate three consecutive scalar *floats*.

```
rng_seeded = default_rng(42)

for i in range(3):
    print(rng_seeded.random())
```

---

[3] This may sound diametrically opposed to the concept of random numbers, but be aware that the numbers generated still follow a random pattern, but simply occur in a fixed order.

```
0.7739560485559633
0.4388784397520523
0.8585979199113825
```

Note that these random numbers are identical to the ones generated by the previous code block – but this time they were generated as individual numbers and not in the form of an *array*. Indeed, by (re)setting a seed value, random numbers are generated in a fixed order. If a different seed value is chosen, other random numbers will be generated; be aware that the difference between two seed values has no impact on "how different" two sets of random numbers generated based on them are.

For the sake of completeness, we will also point out NumPy legacy methods for generating random numbers, as they are still being widely used. Common examples include **np.random.rand()** and **np.random.normal()** for generating uniformly distributed random numbers and random numbers following a Normal distribution, respectively. Seed values can be fixed with **np.random.seed()**. The use of these methods is almost identical to those methods introduced above. Although these methods are still being used (including in this book), the reader should consider using the random number generator methods introduced above, as those provide more flexibility.

4.5   Simple Statistics

NumPy provides a wide range of functions related to statistical analysis, of which we can only introduce a subsample. Please be aware that the SciPy package extends the functionality presented here with respect to statistics (see Section 5.7). All functions introduced below can be called as np.<function name> and can be applied to *arrays*, *lists*, and scalar values.

Most functions are extremely straightforward to use and do not require long introductions. For instance, the basic maximum function, **np.max()**:

```
x = np.array([[5,4,1], [7,3,2]])
np.max(x)
```

```
7
```

We already introduced the concept of axis, which allows you to specify an axis along which the maximum is calculated. Consider the following cases:

```
print('axis=0:', np.max(x, axis=0))
print('axis=1:', np.max(x, axis=1))
```

```
axis=0: [7 4 2]
axis=1: [5 7]
```

The same logic applies to functions such as **np.min()**, **np.mean()**, **np.median()**, **np.std()** (standard deviation), and **np.var()** (variance).

The averaging function **np.average()** is slightly different from np.mean() in that it provides an optional weights argument. If provided, it must be an *array* with either the same shape as the input *array* or a shape appropriate to the chosen axis. The result is an appropriately weighted average, as is exemplified in the following code cell, which assumes some measurements x and corresponding uncertainties xerr, the inverse squares of which we use as weights:

```
x = [3.1, 2.7, 2.5, 3.1, 2.9]
xerr = np.array([0.05, 0.15, 0.6, 0.1, 0.05])
print('unweighted:', np.average(x))
print('weighted:', np.average(x, weights=1/xerr**2))
```

```
unweighted: 2.8600000000000003
weighted: 2.995014662756598
```

Of course, if an element of the data provided to one of these functions is nan, the outcome of this function will be nan, too. To deal with this issue, many functions have alternative implementations that ignore values that are nan, including **np.nanmin()**, **np.nanmax()**, **np.nanmean()**, **np.nanmedian()**, **np.nanstd()**, and **np.nanvar()**. In order to identify values that are nan, **np.isnan()** returns an *array* of *booleans* of the same shape as the input *array*, with a True entry for each instance of nan. The function **np.isfinite(x)** does the opposite, returning False for each nan or inf.

One function that proves useful in the exploration of new data is **np.histogram()**, which generates a histogram from a data *array*. The output of this function consists of a *tuple* containing two *arrays*: the frequency distribution across the bins, and the locations of the bin edges (the length of this latter *array* equals the number of bins plus one). The bins keyword argument defines the bins of the histogram; if an integer value is provided to bins, this value is adopted as the number of bins and they are evenly spread from the minimum value to the maximum value:

```
x = np.random.normal(size=100)
hist, bins = np.histogram(x, 10)
print('hist:', hist)
print('bins:', bins)
```

```
hist: [ 3  4  7  9 18 24 11 11  9  4]
bins: [-2.67309102 -2.20990876 -1.74672651 -1.28354426 -0.820362
       -0.35717975  0.1060025   0.56918475  1.03236701  1.49554926
        1.95873151]
```

The first line here generates some random numbers based on a Normal distribution (see Section 4.4). In this case, we generate a histogram with 10 bins (11 edges). If you prefer to define the edges of your bins yourself, you can do so by assigning a *list* to `bins`:

```python
hist, bins = np.histogram(x, [-3, -1, 0, 1, 3])
print('hist:', hist)
print('bins:', bins)
```

```
hist: [15 44 28 13]
bins: [-3 -1  0  1  3]
```

Note that the bins do not necessarily all need to be of the same size. Another useful property of `np.histogram()` is the ability to return a density instead of a frequency across the bins:

```python
hist, bins = np.histogram(x, [-3, -1, 0, 1, 3], density=True)
print('hist:', hist)
print('sum over hist:', np.sum(hist*(bins[1:]-bins[:-1])))
```

```
hist: [0.075 0.44  0.28  0.065]
sum over hist: 1.0
```

Naturally, the sum of the density multiplied with the bin widths amounts to unity.

Finally, NumPy also contains a number of functions for correlating data that we briefly mention here. **np.correlate()** computes the cross-correlation between two one-dimensional *arrays*:

```python
np.correlate([1, 2, 3], [4, 5, 6])
```

```
array([32])
```

The function **np.corrcoef()** computes the Pearson product-moment correlation coefficients between two *arrays*:

```python
np.corrcoef([1, 2, 3], [4, 5, 6])
```

```
array([[1., 1.],
       [1., 1.]])
```

Finally, **np.cov()** computes the covariance matrix between two *arrays*:

```python
np.cov([1, 2, 3], [4, 5, 6])
```

```
array([[1., 1.],
       [1., 1.]])
```

4.6 Polynomials

Polynomials in a single variable occur very frequently in data analysis, and NumPy offers several approaches for manipulating them. A concise way to describe a polynomial is in terms of its coefficients, e.g.,

$$c_0 x^4 + c_1 x^3 + c_2 x^2 + c_3 x + c_4 \leftrightarrow \{c_0, c_1, c_2, c_3, c_4\} \leftrightarrow [c_0, c_1, c_2, c_3, c_4]$$

stored as a Python *list*.

4.6.1 Converting Data to Coefficients

A rather abstract approach to define a polynomial is to specify a *list* of its roots. This defines the coefficient *list* only up to an overall factor, and the function **np.poly()** always chooses c[0]=1, i.e., a *monic* polynomial:

```
roots = [0, 1, 1, 2]
coeffs = np.poly(roots)
coeffs
```

```
array([ 1., -4., 5., -2., 0.])
```

The resulting *array* contains the coefficients of the four order polynomial $f(x) = x^4 - 4x^3 + 5x^2 - 2x$.

More often we have a *list* or *array* x of *x*-values and a second one y of *y*-values and we seek a "best fit" *least squares approximation* by an unknown polynomial of given order n. This is called *polynomial interpolation* and the function **np.polyfit()** does precisely that. For the sake of simplicity, consider the function $f(x) = x^2 + 1$; we provide a small number of values x and corresponding values y from which we derive the polynomial coefficients presuming a third-order polynomial function:

```
x = [0, 2, 3, 5]
y = [1, 5, 10, 26]
np.polyfit(x, y, 3)
```

```
array([-3.45782877e-16,  1.00000000e+00, -7.79648189e-15,
        1.00000000e+00])
```

Rounding of these coefficients leads to the correct function, $f(x) = x^2 + 1$.[4]

4.6.2 Converting Coefficients to Data

If you are given the coefficient *array*, then **np.roots()** delivers the roots:

```
np.roots(coeffs)
```

---

[4] The numerical solution of problems may lead to uneven solutions. Although clearly greater than zero from a mathematical standpoint, values of the order of 10^{-15} are of the same order of magnitude as typical numerical noise and may therefore be assumed zero.

```
array([2.+0.00000000e+00j, 1.+2.83263462e-08j, 1.-2.83263462e-08j,
       0.+0.00000000e+00j])
```

Although the resulting *array* is of a complex nature, the imaginary parts are negligibly small. Considering only the real parts, the resulting roots are identical to those in the *list* from which the coefficients were generated above.

More usefully, given the coefficient *array* and a single *x*-value or an array of *x*-values, **np.polyval()** returns the corresponding *y*-values:

```
np.polyval(coeffs, [0, 1, 2, 3])
```

```
array([ 0., 0., 0., 12.])
```

4.6.3 Manipulating Polynomials in Coefficient Form

The functions **np.polyadd()**, **np.polysub()**, **np.polymult()**, and **np.polydiv()** handle the four basic arithmetic functions. The function **np.polyder()** obtains the *x*-derivative of a given polynomial, while **np.polyint()** performs *x*-integration, where the arbitrary constant is set to zero. We leave the exploration of these functions to the inclined reader and point to the corresponding NumPy reference.

4.7 Linear Algebra

4.7.1 Basic Operations on Matrices

For *arrays* of the same shape, addition and multiplication by a scalar have already been defined and they act component-wise. This is completely consistent with interpreting the mathematicians' concept of a *matrix* as a two-dimensional *array*. There is, however, a problem with multiplication of such *arrays*. The standard NumPy operation acts component-wise, which is very different from the accepted definition of matrix multiplication. Consider the multiplication on the left-hand side of the following equation:

$$\begin{pmatrix} 1 & 2 \\ 3 & 4 \end{pmatrix} \begin{pmatrix} 5 \\ 6 \end{pmatrix} = \begin{pmatrix} 17 \\ 39 \end{pmatrix}.$$

Naively, one could expect to express this multiplication with the following code cell:

```
A = np.array([[1, 2], [3, 4]])
b = np.array([[5], [6]])
A * b
```

```
array([[ 5, 10],
       [18, 24]])
```

Of course, this results in an incorrect solution. The problem is that the multiplication operator (∗) is defined for component-wise multiplication, but not for matrix multiplication. As such, it applies the rules of broadcasting (Section 4.1.4) and results in a two-dimensional *array*.

To apply the matrix multiplication here, one can use the **np.matmul()** function, which can be represented with the **@** operator (A @ b here); the np.dot() function could also be used but is discouraged in this case:

```
A = np.array([[1, 2], [3, 4]])
b = np.array([[5], [6]])
np.matmul(A, b)
```

```
array([[17],
       [39]])
```

This provides the expected result. In the following, we will introduce some more functionality that is related to matrices and linear algebra.

Suppose that A is a NumPy *array* with two dimensions:

```
A
```

```
array([[1, 2],
       [3, 4]])
```

The transpose of A is available as **A.transpose()**, or more succinctly as **A.T** (here we call the transposed *array* as an attribute of instance A):

```
A.T
```

```
array([[1, 3],
       [2, 4]])
```

Note that NumPy does not distinguish between column and row vectors. This means that if u is a one-dimensional *array* or vector, then u.T = u.

We already know how to build zero matrices, e.g., z = np.zeros((4, 4)). The function **np.identity()** creates identity matrices, e.g.

```
np.identity(3)
```

```
array([[1., 0., 0.],
       [0., 1., 0.],
       [0., 0., 1.]])
```

A more general form of this is the **np.eye()** function. np.eye(m,n,k,dtype=float) returns an $m \times n$ matrix, where the kth diagonal consists of ones and the other elements are zero. By adding up eye-type *arrays*, one can build up banded matrices:

```
2*np.eye(3, 4, -1) + 3*np.eye(3, 4, 0) + 4*np.eye(3, 4, 1)
```

```
array([[3., 4., 0., 0.],
       [2., 3., 4., 0.],
       [0., 2., 3., 4.]])
```

Next, consider a different situation where we have a set of m vectors v1, v2, ...,vm all of length n and we want to construct an $m \times n$ matrix with the vectors as rows. This is accomplished easily with the np.vstack() function (see Section 4.1.5):

```
v1 = np.array([1, 2, 3])
v2 = np.array([4, 5, 6])
np.vstack((v1, v2))
```

```
array([[1, 2, 3],
       [4, 5, 6]])
```

Note that because the actual number of arguments for np.vstack() is variable, we must wrap them in a *tuple* first, because np.vstack() takes precisely one argument.

4.7.2   Matrix Arithmetic

NumPy contains a module **np.linalg** that handles operations on matrices that are more specialized. Suppose that A is a square $n \times n$ matrix. The determinant of A is given by **np.linalg.det()**:

```
import numpy.linalg as la
A = np.array([[4, 2, 0], [9, 3, 7], [1, 2, 1]])
la.det(A)
```

```
-48.00000000000003
```

Assuming A is nonsingular, its inverse is obtained with **np.linalg.inv()**:

```
Ainv = la.inv(A)
np.matmul(A, Ainv)
```

```
array([[ 1.00000000e+00,  0.00000000e+00, -2.22044605e-16],
       [ 0.00000000e+00,  1.00000000e+00, -2.77555756e-17],
       [ 0.00000000e+00,  0.00000000e+00,  1.00000000e+00]])
```

Within the numerical noise, this is the identity matrix.

The function **np.linalg.eig()** can be used to numerically compute eigenvalues and eigenvectors. This function delivers the eigenvectors as columns of an n-row matrix. Each column has unit Euclidean length, i.e., the eigenvectors are normalized.

```
A = np.array([[-2, -4, 2], [-2, 1, 2], [4, 2, 5]])
evals, evecs = la.eig(A)
eval1 = evals[0]
evec1 = evecs[:,0]
eval1, evec1
```

```
(-5.000000000000005, array([ 0.81649658,  0.40824829, -0.40824829]))
```

We can check the normalization (we use **np.linalg.norm()** to compute the norm of a vector):

```
la.norm(evec1), np.matmul(evec1, evec1)
```

```
(0.9999999999999999, 0.9999999999999999)
```

and the eigenvalue property:

```
np.matmul(A, evec1) - eval1*evec1
```

```
array([ 4.44089210e-15,  1.77635684e-15, -3.10862447e-15])
```

which is a zero-vector within the numerical noise.

There are many more functions available in the linalg module, which we encourage the reader to explore.

4.7.3 Solving Linear Systems of Equations

A very common problem is the need to obtain a "solution" **x** to a linear system of equations

$$Ax = b, \tag{4.1}$$

where A is a matrix and **x** and **b** are vectors. **np.linalg.solve()** does that for you.

The simplest case is where A is $n \times n$ and is nonsingular, while **x** and **b** are n-vectors. Then the solution vector **x** is well-defined and unique. It is straightforward to obtain a numerical approximation to it, as the next code cell shows. We shall treat two cases simultaneously, with

$$A = \begin{pmatrix} 3 & 2 & 1 \\ 5 & 5 & 5 \\ 1 & 4 & 6 \end{pmatrix}, \quad \mathbf{b} = \begin{pmatrix} 5 \\ 5 \\ -3 \end{pmatrix} \quad \text{and} \quad \mathbf{b} = \begin{pmatrix} 1 \\ 0 \\ -\frac{7}{2} \end{pmatrix}$$

```
A = np.array([[3, 2, 1], [5, 5, 5], [1, 4, 6]])
b = np.array([[5, 1], [5, 0], [-3, -7.0/2]])
la.solve(A, b)
```

```
array([[ 1. ,  1.5],
       [ 2. , -2. ],
       [-2. ,  0.5]])
```

We can check the solutions:

```
np.matmul(A, la.solve(A, b)) - b
```

```
array([[ 0.00000000e+00, -6.66133815e-16],
       [ 0.00000000e+00, -6.66133815e-16],
       [-8.88178420e-16,  4.44089210e-16]])
```

Once more, all elements are zero within the numerical noise.

This is but the briefest introduction to the linear algebra capabilities of NumPy. For more tools, please refer to the references provided and check out the SciPy capabilities related to linear algebra (Section 5.6).

4.8   File Input/Output

In this section, we look at how to communicate with humans or other programs and how to store intermediate results. We can distinguish at least two scenarios and we consider simple examples of input and output processes for them. The first supposes that we are given a text file that contains numbers, and we wish to read those into NumPy *arrays*. Conversely, we might want to output numbers to a text file. The second scenario is similar but for reasons of speed and economy of space, we wish to use binary files that can be processed by another NumPy program, possibly on a different platform.

In the following, we try to convince the reader to take advantage of the file I/O functionality provided by NumPy whenever possible. However, we also would like to point out that even more flexible methods are available as part of the Pandas package (see Section 8.6).

4.8.1   Text File Input/Output

For the sake of brevity, we simply assume that as the result of some kind of analysis, we are reporting three *float* values for each of four time steps. Given NumPy *arrays* containing them (we use random numbers here), we aim to produce a file called data.txt with a comma-separated tabular representation of the data that can be read both by humans and by other programs. We can formulate this task only utilizing core Python functionality (as introduced in Section 3.9.3):

```python
results = np.random.rand(4, 3)

with open('data.txt', 'w') as outfile:
    outfile.write("#i,x,y,z\n")
    for i, row in enumerate(results):
        outstr = '{:d},'.format(i)
        for col in row:
            outstr += '{:.4f},'.format(col)
        outfile.write(outstr[:-1]+'\n')
```

After generating some artificial data in the first line, we open the file `data.txt` in *write* mode using a context manager (Section 3.9.3), and write a meaningful headline; then we loop through the data in both axes, writing them into a *string* for each line; and finally we write those to the file. The resulting file may look like this[5]:

```
#i,x,y,z
0,0.5660,0.7940,0.1326
1,0.1995,0.6625,0.9750
2,0.3359,0.8355,0.8288
3,0.0465,0.6019,0.4465
```

This format might look familiar to those who frequently deal with data files. It is often referred to as a **comma-separated values** or **csv** file, which is typically used as the filename ending to reveal its nature.

To parse the file back into a NumPy *array* using basic Python, a few steps are required. After opening the file, it has to be read line-by-line and the numerical values must be parsed one at a time and then stored in an *array* of the correct shape:

```python
data = np.empty((4,3), dtype=float)

with open('data.txt', 'r') as infile:
    for i, row in enumerate(infile.readlines()):
        if '#' in row: continue  # ignore header line
        for j, val in enumerate(row.split(',')):
            if j > 0:  # ignore index
                data[i-1,j-1] = float(val)

data
```

---

[5] It may look different on your computer since the numbers are generated by a random number generator.

```
array([[0.566 , 0.794 , 0.1326],
       [0.1995, 0.6625, 0.975 ],
       [0.3359, 0.8355, 0.8288],
       [0.0465, 0.6019, 0.4465]])
```

Now let's find out how we can solve the same tasks with the help of NumPy. We start by writing data to a file with the **np.savetxt()** function. In its simplest form, np.savetxt() only requires a file object generated with open() and the *array* to be written to file. In order to recreate the formatting of the file, some optional arguments can be used: header to provide a header line, fmt to set the formatting of the individual values, and delimiter to set the delimiter character:

```
results = np.random.rand(4, 3)
results = np.insert(results, 0, np.arange(4), axis=1)

with open('data2.txt', 'w') as outfile:
    np.savetxt(outfile, results, header='i,x,y,z',
               delimiter=',', fmt='%.4f')
```

The resulting file looks like this (naturally, the random numbers are now different):

```
# i,x,y,z
0.0000,0.0512,0.7331,0.9968
1.0000,0.3581,0.6672,0.4414
2.0000,0.4502,0.2560,0.6469
3.0000,0.5883,0.4981,0.0087
```

which is close enough to the original file. Note that the np.savetxt() function call does all the formatting and file i/o operations instead of requiring two loops as when using only basic Python.

What about reading in this file? We can use the **np.loadtxt()** function here. It takes as *positional argument* the filename and provides a range of optional arguments of which we utilize delimiter to set the delimiter character and usecols to indicate the column indices to be read in:

```
np.loadtxt('data2.txt', delimiter=',', usecols=(1,2,3))
```

```
array([[0.0512, 0.7331, 0.9968],
       [0.3581, 0.6672, 0.4414],
       [0.4502, 0.256 , 0.6469],
       [0.5883, 0.4981, 0.0087]])
```

Note that a single function call to np.loadtxt() is able to load the data into an *array* without requiring any post-processing steps. This example hopefully clarifies why

NumPy I/O should be preferred over basic Python routines whenever possible. No need to say that NumPy I/O is, of course, much faster on large data files than processing those files with basic Python.

4.8.2   Binary File Input/Output

If performance is an issue and human readability of the data file is not required, you should consider writing your data into binary files. Since different platforms encode numbers in different ways, there is a danger that binary files may be highly platform-dependent. NumPy has its own binary format, which should guarantee platform independence. However, these files cannot be read easily by other non-Python programs.

A single vector or *array* is easily written or read. Using the *array* definitions above, we would write the *array* to file with **np.save()**:

```
np.save('array.npy', x)
```

and we could recover the array with **np.load()**:

```
x = np.load('array.npy')
```

File opening and closing is handled silently provided we use the .npy postfix in the file name.

Although not part of the NumPy package, we would like to point out that more complex data *containers* and all kinds of Python objects can be easily "pickled." **Pickles** are serialized Python objects that are stored in binary files. Consider the following example code to write a *dictionary* to a pickle:

```
import pickle

a = {1: 'one', 2: 'two', 3: 'three'}

pickle.dump(a, open('test.pkl', 'wb'))
```

The **pickle.dump()** function will serialize *dictionary* a and write it to a file (test.pkl; note that the file object has to be opened in binary write mode, wb). To un-pickle the data, you can use the **pickle.load()** function in the same way:

```
pickle.load(open('test.pkl', 'rb'))
```

```
{1: 'one', 2: 'two', 3: 'three'}
```

Pickles can contain any Python object, including classes and their instances. Unfortunately, this makes them somewhat unsafe as *pickle* files can be hacked and malicious code can be inserted that runs when un-pickling the file. Therefore, it is considered unsafe to load *pickle* files from untrusted sources.

4.9   Special Array Types

For the sake of completeness, we briefly introduce two more concepts that are available in NumPy but which have lost some of their importance with the emergence of Pandas *DataFrames* and other concepts (Chapter 8): *masked arrays* and *structured arrays*. We briefly outline how these specialized *arrays* work and how they can be used.

4.9.1   Masked Arrays

Masked arrays are exactly what their name suggests. They are *arrays* that come with a *mask* that enables the user to ignore some of their elements. Consider the following example:

```
import numpy.ma as ma

x = ma.masked_array([1, 2, 3, 4, 5],
                    mask=[False, False, False, True, True])
x
```

```
masked_array(data=[1, 2, 3, --, --],
             mask=[False, False, False,  True,  True],
             fill_value=999999)
```

Masked arrays are available from the **np.ma** module. Their creation is very similar to that of regular *arrays*, but they provide the option to provide a binary mask *array* of the same shape; a `True` element refers to one that is masked, while a `False` element is not masked. This is reflected by the *string* representation of the *masked array*. The *fill value* refers to a placeholder value that may replace the masked values. In order to retrieve only the unmasked values of the *array*, the **compressed()** method can be used:

```
x.compressed()
```

```
array([1, 2, 3])
```

If, instead, you prefer that masked values are filled with the *fill value*, you can use the **filled()** method:

```
x.filled()
```

```
array([     1,      2,      3, 999999, 999999])
```

The main advantage of *masked arrays* is that you can use most NumPy functions and they will be able to ignore masked values without any additional effort:

```
np.mean(x)
```

```
2.0
```

The main use cases of *masked arrays* are incomplete or corrupt data sets, problems to which they pose an elegant remedy. A less elegant but still decent way to deal with such data sets can be achieved through careful pre-processing of the data.

4.9.2 Structured Arrays

Structured arrays can be thought of as data tables: they contain rows of data that follow a very strict schema. Each field in this schema has a specific data type and can be addressed by its name. Let's consider the following example:

```
x = np.array([('John', 12, 89.5), ('Michael', 12, 76.2)],
             dtype=[('name', '<U15'), ('class', 'i'),
                    ('score', 'f')])
x
```

```
array([('John', 12, 89.5), ('Michael', 12, 76.2)],
      dtype=[('name', '<U15'), ('class', '<i4'), ('score', '<f4')])
```

Structured arrays can be created by invoking `np.array()`, just like regular *arrays*. In contrast to those, you need to provide a *list* of *tuples*, where each *tuple* stands for one data element (row in the data table), and a format definition provided to `dtype`. The format definition is a *list* of *tuples*, where each *tuple* consists of two *strings*: the *identifier* of the field and its *type*. In this case, the fields are named name, class, and score, with corresponding data types *string* (with 15 characters or fewer), an *integer*, and a *float*, respectively.

The advantage of *structured arrays* is that reading code becomes very intuitive as you can address fields by name:

```
x['name']
```

```
array(['John', 'Michael'], dtype='<U15')
```

or by row index:

```
x[1]
```

```
('Michael', 12, 76.2)
```

The disadvantage of *structured arrays* is that their elements are immutable and modifying them takes some effort. We thus end our brief discussion of *structured arrays* here and point to Section 8.2 in which we will discuss Pandas *DataFrames* that provide the same (and even higher) level of user-friendliness and much more flexibility.

4.10   References

Online resources

☐ General NumPy resources

NumPy project website
https://numpy.org/

NumPy documentation
https://numpy.org/doc/stable/

NumPy user guide
https://numpy.org/doc/stable/user/

NumPy API reference
https://numpy.org/doc/stable/reference/index.html#reference

NumPy tutorials
https://numpy.org/numpy-tutorials/features.html

NumPy glossary
https://numpy.org/doc/stable/glossary.html

Guide to NumPy book
https://docs.scipy.org/doc/_static/numpybook.pdf

☐ Arrays/Working with arrays

NumPy fundamentals
https://numpy.org/doc/stable/user/basics.html

Array object
https://numpy.org/doc/stable/reference/arrays.html

np.ndarray reference
https://numpy.org/doc/stable/reference/arrays.ndarray.html

Array routines
https://numpy.org/doc/stable/reference/routines.html

Data types
https://numpy.org/devdocs/user/basics.types.html

☐ Constants

Constants reference
https://numpy.org/doc/stable/reference/constants.html

☐ Random numbers

np.random reference
https://numpy.org/doc/stable/reference/random/index.html

☐ Simple statistics

> Statistics reference
>> https://numpy.org/doc/stable/reference/routines.statistics.html

☐ Polynomials

> Polynomials reference
>> https://numpy.org/doc/stable/reference/routines.polynomials.html

☐ Linear Algebra

> `np.linalg` reference
>> https://numpy.org/doc/stable/reference/routines.linalg.html

☐ File input/output

> Input and Output
>> https://numpy.org/doc/stable/reference/routines.io.html

> `pickle` module reference
>> https://docs.python.org/3/library/pickle.html

☐ Special *array* types

> Masked *arrays*
>> https://numpy.org/doc/stable/reference/maskedarray.html

> np.ma reference
>> https://numpy.org/doc/stable/reference/routines.ma.html

> Structured *arrays*
>> https://numpy.org/doc/stable/user/basics.rec.html

Print resources

Harris, Charles R., et al. "Array programming with NumPy." *Nature*, vol. 585, no. 7825, Sept. 2020, pp. 357–362. doi:10.1038/s41586-020-2649-2.

Oliphant, Travis E. *A Guide to NumPy*. 2nd ed., CreateSpace Independent Publishing Platform, 2015.

5   SciPy: Numerical Methods

As we learned in Chapter 2, the term "SciPy" refers to different things in the Python universe. In general, SciPy is an open-source software stack for scientific computing in Python with a focus on numerical methods. This SciPy ecosystem includes a number of popular packages, such as NumPy (Chapter 4), Matplotlib (Chapter 6), and Pandas (Chapter 8), as well as the SciPy package itself, which is the topic of this chapter.

The SciPy package provides a number of computationally efficient numerical methods, such as routines for numerical integration, interpolation, optimization, linear algebra, and statistics that are easy to use and feature a common interface that is compatible with other libraries in the SciPy ecosystem. All this functionality is based on the use of NumPy *arrays* (see Section 4.1), enabling high computational performance. Given the wide range of functionality implemented in the SciPy package, we focus in this introduction and in the accompanying Notebook (cambridge.org/9781009029728/ch5) on some common functionality that the reader might find useful.

We saw in Chapter 4 that it is customary to import the NumPy package as a whole and to name its *namespace* np. This is typically not the case for SciPy. NumPy is usually imported as a whole as it provides some basic numerical functionality (e.g., in the form of *arrays*, Section 4.1), whereas SciPy contains a variety of highly specialized functions and methods. Therefore, one would only import those functions or modules from the package that is actually being used. This also minimizes confusion, as some objects in SciPy carry similar or even identical *identifiers* to those available in NumPy. In the following, we will only import those functions that we will actually use, but we assume that NumPy has been imported as np.

5.1   Special Functions

The module **scipy.special** contains a wide variety of special functions that are implemented in SciPy for your convenience. The set of functions includes elliptical functions, Bessel and Legendre functions, different polynomials, and hypergeometric functions, as well as error functions, functions related to information theory, combinatorics, statistics, and many others.

To keep this book reasonably short and since most of these functions can be utilized in the same simple way, we restrict ourselves to a very short example use case involving the **factorial** function, implemented as **scipy.special.factorial()**:

```
from scipy.special import factorial

factorial(5)
```

```
120.0
```

Since SciPy builds upon NumPy, all special functions are vectorized, meaning that you can apply them to *arrays* in a component-wise fashion:

```
factorial(np.array([1, 2, 3, 4, 5]))
```

```
array([  1.,    2.,    6.,   24.,  120.])
```

5.2   Constants

As a scientist, you are probably working with mathematical or physical constants all the time. **scipy.constants** helps you with that: instead of having to remember long and complicated numbers, you simply have to remember to import scipy.constants.

For instance, the speed of light in a vacuum in units of m/s can be accessed as follows:

```
from scipy import constants as const

const.c
```

```
299792458.0
```

It is just as easy to access as a wide range of other constants, units, and prefixes. For instance, did you know that a light year can be comfortably expressed in terms of peta inches?

```
const.light_year / (const.peta * const.inch)
```

```
372.4697036449134
```

Please refer to the scipy.constants reference for a full list of constants and their definitions. In case your favorite physical constant is missing from this list, make sure to check the **physical_constants** dictionary, which contains physical constants recommended by CODATA 2018 (Tiesinga et al., 2011), including their units and uncertainties. For instance, the mass of a proton can be accessed as:

```
const.physical_constants['proton mass']
```

```
(1.67262192369e-27, 'kg', 5.1e-37)
```

where the returned *tuple* contains the constant's value, unit, and uncertainty, in that order. For a list of all physical constants contained in this *dictionary*, you can access a list of all *dictionary* keys using `const.physical_constants.keys()`.

5.3   Numerical Integration

The module **scipy.integrate** contains a number of numerical integrators to integrate over functions, fixed numerical data, as well as ordinary differential equations (ODEs). In this section, we will discuss the former two cases, while ODEs are discussed in detail in Section 5.8.

5.3.1   Integrating over Functions

As a first example, we will integrate the sine function from $x = 0$ to $x = \pi/2$. This integral is simple, so we can derive the exact solution analytically:

$$\int_0^{\pi/2} \sin(x)\, dx = [-\cos(x)]_0^{\pi/2} = -(0 - 1) = 1. \tag{5.1}$$

We will use the **Quadrature** method, implemented as **scipy.integrate.quad()**, to numerically solve this integral. This function is a numerical integrator that uses a Fortran 77 implementation (QUADPACK) of this algorithm as a backbone, and requires an integrator function object that is to be integrated over, as well as the lower and upper limits of the integration. Optional arguments include absolute (`epsabs`) and relative error limits (`epsrel`) to define when computation is stopped. As an integrator function we can simply pass `np.sin`, since Python functions are objects:

```
from scipy.integrate import quad

quad(np.sin, 0, np.pi/2)
```

```
(0.9999999999999999, 1.1102230246251564e-14)
```

`quad()` returns a *tuple* containing the integration result and the corresponding uncertainty; as you can see, the result almost perfectly matches our analytical solution. Note that we passed `np.sin` (without brackets); this means that we provide the function as an object and leave the evaluation of the function to the quadrature method.

Now consider the following Gaussian integral:

$$\int_{-\infty}^{+\infty} e^{-ax^2}\, dx = \sqrt{\frac{\pi}{a}}. \tag{5.2}$$

We can define this mathematical function simply as a Python function. This example differs from the previous example in that the integration is not just over a finite range, but over all real numbers. Furthermore, this Gaussian integral contains a yet-undefined factor a. However, NumPy is not able to deal with symbolic math (but SymPy is; see Chapter 7) and therefore we have to provide a value for a to solve the integral numerically. We choose $a = 2$:

```python
def gauss(x, a):
    """A simple Gaussian function."""
    return np.exp(-a*x**2)


quad(gauss, -np.inf, np.inf, args=2)
```

```
(1.2533141373155017, 4.467450311842062e-09)
```

(Please note that $\sqrt{\pi/2} = 1.253314$, so the result is correct.) We can express the limits of the integral ($[-\infty, \infty]$) using `np.inf` (see Section 4.3); also note that we can provide arguments to our function `gauss()` using the optional argument `args`. Since `gauss()` only has a single argument besides `x`, we can pass a scalar value here. If `gauss()` had more arguments (e.g., `gauss(x, a, b, c)`), we would need to provide those as a *list* or *tuple* (e.g., `quad(gauss,..., args=(a,b,c))`). In any case the first argument of `quad()` must be the variable that is integrated over.

Finally, SciPy provides multivariate versions of `quad()`:

☐ `scipy.integrate.dblquad()` for integrations in two dimensions,

☐ `scipy.integrate.tplquad()` for three dimensions, and

☐ `scipy.integrate.nquad()` for n dimensions,

all of which work very similarly. In this final example, we will calculate the three-dimensional integral over a volume element using `tplquad()`. In this case, the function that we integrate over is the volume element expressed in spherical coordinates, $r^2 \sin(\theta)\, dr\, d\phi\, d\theta$, which we implement as a Python function:

```python
from scipy.integrate import tplquad


def spherical_volume_element(theta, phi, r):
    """Volume element in spherical coordinates."""
    return r**2*np.sin(theta)


tplquad(spherical_volume_element,
        0, 1,         # limits in r
        0, 2*np.pi,   # limits in phi
        0, np.pi)     # limits in theta
```

```
(4.1887902047863905, 1.3890950796949933e-13)
```

Of course, the result is $4\pi/3$. In this case – as in all multivariate implementations of quad() – please note that the order of the three variables (r, phi, theta) in the call of tplquad() is reversed from the order in the definition of the integrand function.

5.3.2   Integrating over Sampled Values

There might be cases in which you need to integrate over a distribution of sampled values since the underlying function is not known. In this case, SciPy offers a number of numerical integrators that work very similarly. We will showcase their application based on **scipy.integrate.simps()**, which implements **Simpson's rule** for numerical integration. In this example, we will sample the sine function in the interval $[0, \pi/2]$ and integrate the resulting distribution; the result should be very similar to the result we obtained with scipy.integrate.quad() based on the actual sine function in the above example:

```
from scipy.integrate import simps

x = np.linspace(0, np.pi/2, 100)
y = np.sin(x)

simps(y, x)   # note the order of the arguments: y, x
```

```
0.9999998326009374
```

In contrast to the function integrators introduced above, integrations over samples will not provide uncertainty measures. However, keep in mind that the number of samples (i.e., the sampling interval) will significantly affect the accuracy of your computation.

5.4   **Optimization and Root Search**

A number of different optimization algorithms for finding extreme function values are available in **scipy.optimize** for both univariate and multivariate problems.

5.4.1   Local Univariate Optimization

The function **scipy.optimize.minimize_scalar()** serves as a wrapper for a number of different solvers to find the minimum value of a function of a single variable. Consider the function $f(x) = (x-3)^2$, which has its global minimum value at $x = 3$. We can use **Brent's algorithm** to find this value numerically:

```
from scipy.optimize import minimize_scalar

def func(x):
    """A simple function."""
    return (x-3)**2

minimize_scalar(func)
```

```
     fun: 0.0
    nfev: 10
     nit: 4
 success: True
       x: 3.0
```

The function returns an **OptimizeResult** object that contains all you need to know about the procedure. For instance, the attribute success tells you whether the algorithm did succeed in finding a minimum or not, fun returns the function value at the solution x, and nit contains the number of iterations that were necessary.

In case you are dealing with a function with multiple minima, you can use the bracket parameter to define a starting range with which you would like to initialize Brent's algorithm:

```
minimize_scalar(np.sin, bracket=(3, 5))
```

```
     fun: -0.9999999999999999
    nfev: 12
     nit: 8
 success: True
       x: 4.712388992568656
```

However, please keep in mind that the solution does not necessarily have to end up within this bracket.

5.4.2 Local Multivariate Optimization

scipy.optimize.minimize() is the multivariate equivalent of minimize_scalar(). As such, it can be used to solve our univariate problem from above with only minor modifications:

```
from scipy.optimize import minimize

def func(x):
    """A simple function."""
    return (x-3)**2
```

```
minimize(func, 0)

     fun: 2.5388963550532293e-16
hess_inv: array([[0.5]])
     jac: array([-1.69666681e-08])
 message: 'Optimization terminated successfully.'
    nfev: 6
     nit: 2
    njev: 3
  status: 0
 success: True
       x: array([2.99999998])
```

First of all, the function call of `minimize()` includes one additional positional argument, `x0`, which is the initial guess for the solver. Note that `x0` must have the same dimensionality as your function. Since our function `func` is only univariate, we can use a simple *integer* value here. Also, note the additional attributes in the `OptimizeResult` object that is returned to you, including the Jacobian matrix (`jac`) and the inverse of the objective function's Hessian (`hess_inv`), and the fact that `x` is now being returned as an *array*.

Let us now consider a real multivariate problem. We define a function with two variables, x and y, as well as parameters a, b, and c: $f(x, y) = (x - a)^2 + (y - b)^2 + c$. This function has a minimum at $(x, y) = (a, b)$.

There are two things you must consider when turning this function into a Python function (`func2d()`) to be used with `minimize()`. First, the function to be minimized is expected to have only a single input variable `x`, which can be an *array*, so we have to pack both x and y into `x` (`x=(x, y)`). Second, we need to provide values for the parameters a, b, c as arguments of `func2d()` – this is taken care of in `minimize()` using the `args` parameter. When invoking `minimize()`, the function will vary `x` in search of minima, while keeping the parameters passed by `args` constant. Parametric functions are useful, if, for instance, you want to explore the behavior of your function over a given parameter space, expressed by your function arguments:

```
def func2d(x, a, b, c):
    """A two-dimensional surface."""
    return (x[0]-a)**2 + (x[1]-b)**2 + c
```

To find the minimum of function `func2d()` numerically, we need to assign values to its three parameters; we choose some random *integer* values for this example:

```
minimize(func2d, (0, 0), args=(4, 5, 2))
```

```
      fun: 2.000000000000098
 hess_inv: array([[ 0.80487808, -0.24390243],
                  [-0.24390243,  0.69512192]])
      jac: array([ 5.36441803e-07, -3.27825546e-07])
  message: 'Optimization terminated successfully.'
     nfev: 12
      nit: 3
     njev: 4
   status: 0
  success: True
        x: array([4.00000026, 4.99999983])
```

The result, x, now contains a pair of coordinates that correspond to x and y.

The above examples all used the same optimization algorithm. However, both methods offer alternatives using the method keyword argument: minimize_scalar() supports 3 different minimization algorithms, while minimize() offers a total of 14 different methods (see the corresponding reference for a list). In most cases, it should not matter which method is used. But there may be exceptions to this rule, especially with respect to computational performance, so it might be worth experimenting with the optimization method.

5.4.3   Function Fitting

scipy.optimize.lsq_linear() represents a linear method for fitting parametric functions to data; the nonlinear equivalents are **scipy.optimize.least_squares()** and **scipy.optimize.curve_fit()**. Since all of these methods work similarly, we introduce here only one of these functions, curve_fit().

A typical use case for curve_fit() is to find a set of parameters Θ for a function $f(x, \Theta)$ by minimizing the residuals $y - f(x, \Theta)$ for given sets of x and corresponding y. Consider the polynomial function $f(x, a, b, c, d) = ax^3 + bx^2 + cx + d$ with parameters $\Theta = (a, b, c, d) = (5, -2, 1, 0)$. In the following code cell we generate a set $y = f(x, \Theta)$ values (ys) for equidistant x (xs) and then use curve_fit() to fit $f(x, a, b, c, d)$ to the data to recover the parameters a, b, c, and d:

```python
from scipy.optimize import curve_fit

def fun(x, a, b, c, d):
    """A polynomial function."""
    return a*x**3 + b*x**2 + c*x + d

xs = np.linspace(-5, 5, 5)
ys = fun(xs, 5, -2, 1, 0)
```

```
popt, pcov = curve_fit(fun, xs, ys)

print(popt)
print(fun(0, *popt))
```

```
[ 5.00000000e+00 −2.00000000e+00  1.00000000e+00  4.76557815e−24]
4.765578148199792e−24
```

The parameters and the function value at $x = 0$ are recovered with high accuracy (see Figure 5.1, left panel, for a plot of the results). Using curve_fit() is straightforward; all it requires is the function to be fitted to the data (fun), x values (xs), and corresponding y values (ys). The function returns two *arrays*: popt, which is a one-dimensional *array* holding the best-fit solutions for our parameters (in this case $\Theta = [a, b, c, d]$), and pcov, which is the covariance of the parameters listed in popt. The covariance matrix is useful to investigate interrelations between the parameters and one can easily derive uncertainties (1σ) on the estimated parameters as np.sqrt(np.diag(pcov)).

By default, curve_fit() utilizes the **Levenberg–Marquardt** algorithm to fit the function, but other algorithms can be selected using the function's method parameter. To restrict the search in parameter space, the bounds parameter can be invoked to provide upper and lower bounds on each parameter. Also, a sequence of first-guess parameters can be provided using p0.

Real-world measurements are affected by uncertainties. curve_fit() can account for such uncertainties and derive that set of parameters Θ that will minimize the residuals $y - f(x, \Theta)$ while properly weighting the individual data points based on their uncertainties. We simulate measurement uncertainties by adding random noise to our y values, ys: we draw measurement uncertainties (errs) for each measurement from a Gaussian distribution and then add these uncertainties to our ys and rerun the fitting:

```
np.random.seed(43)  # fix random seed

errs = np.random.normal(loc=0, scale=300, size=len(ys))
ys_err = fun(xs, 5, −2, 1, 0) + errs

popt, pcov = curve_fit(fun, xs, ys_err, sigma=errs,
                       absolute_sigma=True)

print(popt)
print(fun(0, *popt))
```

```
[  5.92810004   2.11598822 −20.54940534 −46.53133151]
−46.5313315110218
```

The best-fit parameters (popt) now clearly differ from the set of parameters from which our data set (xs and ys) has been generated, as does the value at $x = 0$. Figure 5.1 (right

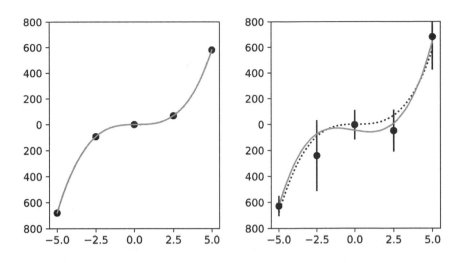

Figure 5.1 Fitting results obtained with scipy.optimize.curve_fit() (gray line) based on five data points (black dots) following a third-order polynomial function (black dotted line). **Left:** Using the exact function values as input data points, curve_fit() is able to reproduce the function parameters of the polynomial and its course with high accuracy. **Right:** curve_fit() is able to account for uncertainties assigned to the data points (displayed here as error bars); the resulting fitted function (gray line) differs from the original function (dotted line) and follows more closely those data points with low uncertainties while putting less weight on those data points with high uncertainties.

panel) visualizes the fit and shows how data points with smaller uncertainties clearly have a higher weight in defining the best-fit parameters. curve_fit() accounts for the uncertainties using the sigma parameter, which in this case holds an uncertainty value for each value in xs; please note that in order to utilize these uncertainties as absolute values, i.e., in the same units as the function, you have to set absolute_sigma=True.

5.4.4 Root Search

For the task of root finding, **scipy.optimize.root_scalar()** for univariate or scalar functions and **scipy.optimize.root()** for multivariate or vector functions are available. Since both functions work very similarly, we will present here only the univariate case.

Consider the function $f(x) = (x + a)(x + b)$, which has two roots at $x = -a$ and $x = -b$ (see Figure 5.2). We will use root_scalar() to find the roots of this function for parameters $a = -2$ and $b = 4$:

In order to use this function correctly, there should be some understanding of the different methods that are available for root finding. The default root search method is the **bisection method**, which requires the user to provide two locations that serve as brackets for the iterative search algorithm. The key here is that the corresponding function values have opposite signs (and that the function is continuous, obviously). In the case of our function, the latter requirement means that we cannot simply provide a bracket that is

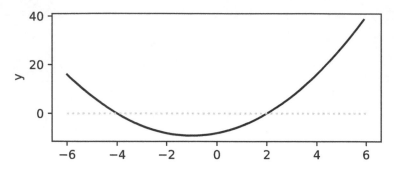

Figure 5.2 Example function for univariate root search: $f(x) = (x - 2)(x + 4)$ with roots at $x = -4$ and $x = 2$.

wide enough to include both roots. Hence, `root_scalar()` will only find one root at a time. Looking at the graph (Figure 5.2), a good choice for a bracket around the root at $x = -4$ would be $[-5, -2]$ (or most other choices). Now we can run `root_scalar()` to find this root:

```
from scipy.optimize import root_scalar

def fun(x, a, b):
    """A simple function."""
    return (x+a)*(x+b)

root_scalar(fun, args=(-2, 4), method='bisect', bracket=(-5,-2))
```

```
      converged: True
           flag: 'converged'
 function_calls: 43
     iterations: 41
           root: -3.9999999999995453
```

The resulting **RootResults** object has a number of attributes, including a binary flag (`converged`) indicating whether the method has converged to a solution, the number of times the function has been evaluated (`function_calls`), the number of iterations (`iterations`), and the actual result of the root search (`root`). Note that the solution is not exactly -4. This is due to the fact that the method stops iterating when a certain termination tolerance has been reached; the default tolerance can be modified using the `rtol` and `xtol` (see Section 5.8.1) parameters of `root_scalar()`.

Another common root search algorithm is **Newton's method**, which requires a first guess for the location of a root and the first derivative of our function:

```
def fun_deriv(x, a, b):
    """The derivative of our simple function."""
    return 2*x + a + b

root_scalar(fun, args=(-2, 4), method='newton', fprime=fun_deriv,
            x0=3)
```

```
     converged: True
          flag: 'converged'
function_calls: 10
    iterations: 5
          root: 2.0
```

Note how Newton's method converges much faster in this particular case.

5.5 Numerical Interpolation

Interpolation means the approximation of a function inbetween locations for which the exact function values are known. In contrast to function fitting, interpolation makes no assumptions on the global behavior of the function to be interpolated; instead, it only makes assumptions on the behavior of the function between these locations. As a result, it is only able to estimate function values in between the known function behavior, but not beyond (this is referred to as extrapolation).

One of the easiest forms of interpolation assumes a linear behavior of the function and simply approximates the function value based on a linear function that is anchored to the two closest locations that bracket the location to be interpolated. Other interpolation algorithms utilize nearest-neighbor approximation (the same function value as the nearest-neighbor location with a known function value) or polynomials of higher order. Support for interpolation problems is provided by **scipy.interpolate**.

5.5.1 Univariate Interpolation

In the case of univariate interpolation, the **scipy.interpolate.interp1d()** class creates a callable function that will interpolate function values y for any x provided. Consider the case in which we try to interpolate the function $f(x) = x^4$ between the locations $x \in [-3, -1.5, 0, 1.5, 3]$. First, we generate values on the x-axis, xs, and the corresponding values on the y-axis, ys=f(xs):

```
xs = np.linspace(-3, 3, 5)

def fun(x):
    """A simple 4-th order polynomial."""
    return x**4

ys = fun(xs)
```

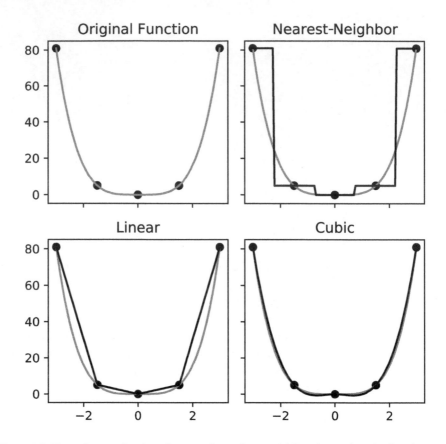

Figure 5.3 Example use of `scipy.interpolate.interp1d()` to interpolate the function $f(x) = x^4$. Black points indicate the locations of known function values. The top left panel shows the original function as shown by a gray line. The other panels interpolate the function based on the known locations using different methods (black lines).

We can now use the `interp1d()` function to create a function object that can be called directly with x values at which to interpolate:

```python
from scipy.interpolate import interp1d

interp = interp1d(xs, ys)
interp(0.32)
```

```
array(1.08)
```

The result is a NumPy *array* with the interpolated function values. In the example shown above, the default interpolation kind is used, which is **linear interpolation**. Different kinds of interpolation can be chosen using the `kind` argument, leading to different results as shown in Figure 5.3.

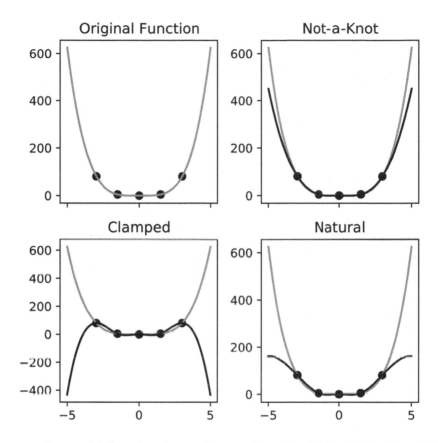

Figure 5.4 Impact of different boundary conditions on the results of CubicSpline() applied to interpolate the function $f(x) = x^4$. Black points indicate the locations of known function values; the gray line indicates the original function, black lines correspond to cubic spline interpolations.

For well-behaved functions, third-order polynomials (kind='cubic' in interp1d()) provide good interpolation results that are twice continuously differentiable. This method is typically referred to as a *Cubic Spline*, which is also separately implemented as **scipy.interpolate.CubicSpline**. The advantage of this class over interp1d() is the higher degree of customizability. For instance, CubicSpline objects are able to extrapolate beyond the range of known data. Furthermore, the user can pick between different boundary conditions as shown in Figure 5.4 (please refer to the corresponding Notebook for some example code).

5.5.2 Multivariate Interpolation

For the case of multivariate interpolation, scipy.interpolate contains a number of options for both unstructured data and grid data. We will introduce only one of these functions, **scipy.integrate.griddata()**, which provides sufficient flexibility to be applicable in most situations: the function can be applied to *n*-dimensional data (i.e., it is not restricted to two-dimensional data) and it has the most common interpolations routines built in.

A typical use case for `griddata()` involves the interpolation of a (potentially unknown) multivariate function from a sparse sample of locations at which the function value is known. In the following example, we simulate this situation by synthesizing function values z at random locations (x, y) within a small area ($x \in [0, 1)$, $y \in [0, 1)$) in the x-y plane; the underlying function we use is $f(x, y) = \cos(20x)\sin(30(1 - \sqrt{y}))$, but this is only relevant for the generation of the synthetic data:

```python
def fun(x, y):
    """A more complex 2d surface function."""
    return np.cos(20*x)*np.sin(30*(1-np.sqrt(y)))


x = np.random.rand(1000)
y = np.random.rand(1000)


z = fun(x, y)
```

Based on these randomly sampled data points, as well as a predefined grid, `griddata()` will interpolate the underlying function $f(x, y)$ with different methods. The most convenient way to generate the grid on which to interpolate the function is to use `np.mgrid` (see Section 4.1.3). We generate the grid and fit the data with `griddata()` using different methods:

```python
from scipy.interpolate import griddata

xgrid, ygrid = np.mgrid[0:1:100j, 0:1:100j]

pred_near = griddata((x, y), z, (xgrid, ygrid), method='nearest')
pred_lin = griddata((x, y), z, (xgrid, ygrid), method='linear')
pred_cub = griddata((x, y), z, (xgrid, ygrid), method='cubic')
```

Figure 5.5 shows the plotted predictions from the different interpolation methods. While **nearest-neighbor interpolation** provides a rather spotted appearance, **linear** and especially **cubic interpolation** lead to much smoother results. Please note that only the nearest-neighbor method fills the entire area with interpolated function values. In the case of linear or cubic interpolation, areas close to the edges of the interpolation ranges may be left empty due to a lack of data points, which are randomly distributed in this example. Those areas for which no interpolation is possible can be filled with a constant value using `griddata()`'s `fill_value` parameter.

5.6   Linear Algebra

We saw in Chapter 4 that NumPy *arrays* can be used as vectors and matrices, providing perfect data types for linear algebra use cases. `scipy.linalg` provides a wide range of

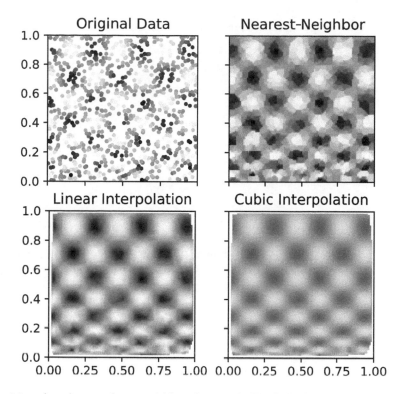

Figure 5.5 `scipy.interpolate.griddata()` example. **Top Left:** Original data based on which the interpolations are performed. **Other Panels:** Interpolation results using different interpolation methods.

functionality for such applications. Many of the functions in this submodule use BLAS or LAPACK routines in the background for efficient computations. Please note that `scipy.linalg` imports most of the functionality from `np.linalg`; identically named functions might differ in their functionality.

5.6.1 Matrix Operations

Please refer to Section 4.7 for a discussion of basic matrix operations. We mainly focus here on the discussion of functionality that is unique to `scipy.linalg`.

Consider the following matrix:

$$A = \begin{pmatrix} 4 & 3 \\ 3 & 2 \end{pmatrix},$$

which we implement in Python as

```
A = np.array([[4, 3], [3, 2]])
```

With `scipy.linalg.det()`, we can calculate the determinant of this matrix:

```
from scipy import linalg

linalg.det(A)
```

```
-1.0
```

or its norm with `scipy.linalg.norm()`:

```
linalg.norm(A)
```

```
6.164414002968976
```

or its inverse matrix, A^{-1}, with `scipy.linalg.inv()` (if available):

```
linalg.inv(A)
```

```
array([[-2.,  3.],
       [ 3., -4.]])
```

We can easily check whether the inverse matrix is correct by evaluating the matrix product $A \cdot A^{-1}$:

```
np.matmul(linalg.inv(A), A)
```

```
array([[1., 0.],
       [0., 1.]])
```

the result of which is, of course, the identity matrix.

`scipy.linalg.eig()` is a function to derive eigenvalues and eigenvectors. While this sounds very similar to `np.linalg.eig()`, the SciPy version enables the computation of both the left and the right eigenvectors, and it solves the generalized eigenvalue problem of a square matrix. Additional functions are available to solve eigenvalue problems for Hermitian, tridiagonal, and banded matrices. Since they all work in a somewhat similar fashion, we refer to Section 4.7 for an example.

Finally, `scipy.linalg` contains a wide range of functionality for the **decomposition** of matrices and for solving linear equation systems. Let's have a look at the latter first.

Consider the following system of linear equations:

$$
\begin{aligned}
2x_1 + x_2 + 3x_3 &= 9 \\
x_1 - 2x_2 + x_3 &= -2 \\
3x_1 + 2x_2 + 2x_3 &= 7
\end{aligned}
$$

which can be displayed in matrix notation ($A \cdot \mathbf{x} = \mathbf{b}$) as

$$\begin{pmatrix} 2 & 1 & 3 \\ 1 & -2 & 1 \\ 3 & 2 & 2 \end{pmatrix} \cdot \begin{pmatrix} x_1 \\ x_2 \\ x_3 \end{pmatrix} = \begin{pmatrix} 9 \\ -2 \\ 7 \end{pmatrix}$$

This system of linear equations can be expressed by a square matrix A and vector $\mathbf{b}$ and can thus be easily solved with the **scipy.linalg.solve()** function, which is rather similar to the same function provided through np.linalg (see Section 4.7.3). This function requires only A and $\mathbf{b}$ and the solution vector $\mathbf{x}$ will be output:

```
A = np.array([[2, 1, 3], [1, -2, 1], [3, 2, 2]])
b = np.array([9, -2, 7])
```

```
linalg.solve(A, b)
```

```
array([-1.,  2.,  3.])
```

If A is of a special matrix type, this information can be provided to solve() with the assume_a parameter to support the solution finding: "sym" if A is symmetric, "her" is A is hermitian, "pos" if A is positive definite, and "gen" for a generic matrix (default).

scipy.linalg also provides special functions for solving systems involving specific matrix types. In case A is a triangular matrix, **scipy.linalg.solve_triangular()** should be used; **scipy.linalg.solve_banded()** in case A is a banded matrix (note that A is not required to be of square shape), as well as other special cases.

The algorithm utilized by solve() to solve a system of linear equations is based on **LU decomposition** with partial pivoting, which is available in the form of two separate functions: **scipy.linalg.lu()** and **scipy.linalg.lu_factor()**. Both functions decompose a matrix A into a lower triangular matrix, L, and an upper triangular matrix, U. The difference between the two functions is that, in addition to L and U, lu() returns a binary permutation matrix P indicating the permutations necessary to satisfy $PA = LU$:

```
linalg.lu(A)  # returns (P, L, U)
```

```
(array([[0., 0., 1.],
        [0., 1., 0.],
        [1., 0., 0.]]),
 array([[1.        , 0.        , 0.        ],
        [0.33333333, 1.        , 0.        ],
        [0.66666667, 0.125     , 1.        ]]),
 array([[ 3.        ,  2.        ,  2.        ],
        [ 0.        , -2.66666667,  0.33333333],
        [ 0.        ,  0.        ,  1.625     ]]))
```

lu_factor(), on the other hand, returns only a NumPy *array* named lu that merges L and U by containing the off-diagonal nonzero elements of L in its lower triangle (unit diagonal elements of L are omitted) and the nonzero elements of U in its upper triangle. In a similarly memory-efficient fashion, instead of the permutation matrix P the function returns a pivot *array*, piv, for each row of A, holds the corresponding row with which this row was interchanged:

```
linalg.lu_factor(A)   # returns lu, piv
```

```
(array([[ 3.         ,  2.         ,  2.         ],
        [ 0.33333333, -2.66666667,  0.33333333],
        [ 0.66666667,  0.125      ,  1.625      ]]),
 array([2, 1, 2], dtype=int32))
```

The advantage of lu_factor() is that, in addition to the very efficient storage of information, both lu and piv can be directly used as input parameters for the function **scipy.linalg.lu_solve()**, which solves a system of linear equations based on LU decomposition and provides the same result as solve():

```
linalg.lu_solve(linalg.lu_factor(A), b)
```

```
array([-1.,  2.,  3.])
```

In addition to LU decomposition, scipy.linalg contains a wide range of other decomposition algorithms, such as

☐ **Cholesky decomposition (scipy.linalg.cholesky()**, which also comes with a linear equation solver, **scipy.linalg.cho_solve()**),

☐ **QR decomposition (scipy.linalg.qr())**, and

☐ **Singular value decomposition (scipy.linalg.svd())**.

Finally, we would like to point out the SciPy module **scipy.sparse**, which has its own library for linear algebra, **scipy.sparse.linalg**, to deal with sparse two-dimensional matrices and their efficient implementation and processing. We omit the discussion of sparsity for the sake of keeping this book short, but we strongly believe that the functionality discussed in this section will help the user to deal with those modules.

5.7   Statistics

The NumPy package contains some of the most basic functions for descriptive statistics: mean(), median(), std(), etc. (See Section 4.5 for an overview). **scipy.stats** goes a few steps further, comprising a wide range of univariate, multivariate, and discrete probability distributions, as well as more functions for descriptive statistics, correlation functions, statistical tests, and much more.

The Swiss-army knife (or *Sackmesser*, as they say in Switzerland) of `scipy.stats` is the **`scipy.stats.describe()`** function, which simply derives a number of useful descriptive statistics for any NumPy *array*:

```python
from scipy import stats

a = np.random.normal(size=10000)
s = stats.describe(a)
s
```

```
DescribeResult(nobs=10000, minmax=(-3.856375329240597,
    4.479084251025757),
    mean=0.013534053064887258, variance=1.0020215237320191,
    skewness=-0.0080664682066731, kurtosis=0.07645608593476849)
```

The results, including measures like sample size, mean, and variance, are provided in the form of a **DescribeResult** object. Individual metrics from this object can be extracted as attributes:

```python
s.mean
```

```
0.013534053064887258
```

5.7.1 Univariate Continuous Probability Distributions

`scipy.stats` provides a unified interface to comfortably deal with a wide range of **probability distributions**, allowing you to easily access probability density functions and cumulative density functions, and to draw random samples from these distributions. The following example should provide you with a sense of how to use these probability distribution classes. Please be aware that in order to produce reproducible results, you will need to set the seed value for your random number generators. Since SciPy builds upon NumPy, you can set the seed value with `np.random.seed()` as described in Section 4.4.

Consider a **Normal distribution**, implemented as **`scipy.stats.norm()`**, from which we draw ten random numbers:

```python
from scipy.stats import norm

norm.rvs(size=10)
```

```
array([-1.38593767,  0.89270951,  0.04557416,  0.69261578,
        0.3576738 , -0.14233488, -0.40889239,  0.22063606,
        1.56021517,  1.32031721])
```

The method `rvs` allows you to draw random variates from a given distribution (in this case `norm`). The parameter `size` specifies the number of samples to be drawn. Note that this function call is very similar to **numpy.random.normal()** (see Section 4.4).

You can also specify the properties of your distribution using the location (`loc`; mean value in the case of `norm`) and scale (`scale`; standard deviation in the case of `norm`) parameters:

```
gauss = norm(loc=5, scale=2)
gauss.mean(), gauss.std()
```

```
(5.0, 2.0)
```

We can draw random numbers from this distribution using the same method as before:

```
gauss.rvs(size=5)
```

```
array([4.16030601, 5.04342604, 3.81770634, 5.6573647 , 3.92527482])
```

A wide range of descriptive statistics methods is implemented for each probability distribution as class methods:

```
print('mean:', gauss.mean())
print('median:', gauss.median())
print('standard deviation:', gauss.std())
print('variance:', gauss.var())
print('1-st moment = mean:', gauss.moment(1))
print('2 sigma bracket:', gauss.interval(0.9545))
print('expectation value = mean:', gauss.expect(lambda x: x))
```

```
mean: 5.0
median: 5.0
standard deviation: 2.0
variance: 4.0
1-st moment = mean: 5.0
2 sigma bracket: (0.9999951122007928, 9.000004887799205)
expectation value = mean: 5.0
```

While most of these methods are easily explained, others are slightly more complicated. For instance, `moment(n)` derives the nth order noncentral moment ($n = 1$ is identical to the mean) of the underlying distribution, `interval(alpha)` derives the α confidence interval with equal areas around the median (the 95.45% range brackets the 2-sigma confidence interval), and `expect(fun)` derives the expectation value of a function `fun` over the underlying probability distribution. Note that it is possible to modify those

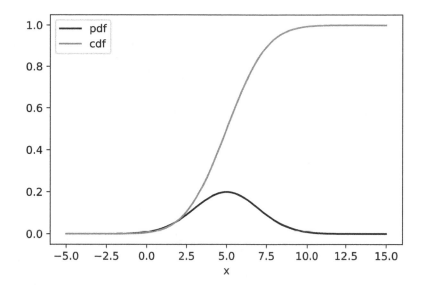

Figure 5.6 Comparison of the probability density function (pdf) and the cumulative distribution function (cdf) for our modified Normal distribution gauss.

parameters defining a probability distribution (in the case of norm() this is scale and loc) in either of these methods, too (e.g., norm.mean(loc=2, scale=0.1)).

You can also directly access the distribution's underlying **probability density function** (pdf) and its **cumulative distribution function** (cdf) as shown in Figure 5.6, which is generated by the following script (we learn about plotting with Matplotlib in Chapter 6):

```python
import matplotlib.pyplot as plt

x = np.linspace(-5, 15, 100)
plt.plot(x, gauss.pdf(x), label='pdf', color='black')
plt.plot(x, gauss.cdf(x), label='cdf', color='grey')
plt.xlabel('x')
plt.legend()
```

So far, we have only considered a simple univariate Normal distribution. scipy.stats contains almost 100 different continuous univariate probability density functions that can all be accessed using the same API. For instance, Figure 5.7 shows the χ^2 distribution for different degrees of freedom (df). This is possible since all of these classes are derived from a generic parent class, which even enables you to implement your own probability density distribution to utilize this common API and functionality.

5.7.2   Multivariate and Discrete Probability Distributions

Both multivariate and discrete probability distributions share APIs that are similar to that of the univariate case.

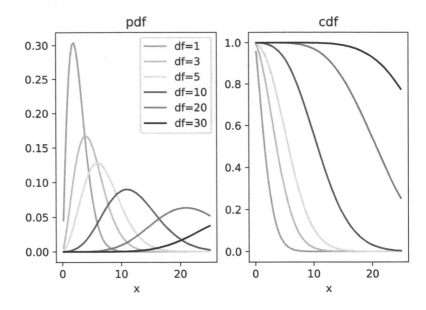

Figure 5.7 The probability density function (left) and the cumulative distribution function (right) of the χ^2 distribution for different degrees of freedom (df).

We start with the multivariate case and show how to utilize a multivariate Normal distribution. For the sake of simplicity and easier plotting, we focus here on the two-dimensional case, but it should be clear that higher-dimensional applications work very similarly.

As a first example, we plot the probability density function of a Normal distribution in two dimensions (see Figure 5.8), utilizing **scipy.stats.multivariate_normal()** :

```
from scipy.stats import multivariate_normal

xgrid, ygrid = np.mgrid[-1:1:.01, -1:1:.01]
norm2d = multivariate_normal(mean=[0.1, 0.2],
                             cov=[[2, 0.3], [0.3, 1]])
z = norm2d.pdf(np.dstack((xgrid, ygrid)))

plt.imshow(z, origin='lower', cmap='Greys_r')
plt.contour(z, colors='white')
```

Note how our 2d-Normal distribution is defined by two parameters: mean, which is the location of the mean of the distribution in two dimensions, and cov, which is a positive semi-definite covariance matrix.

Generating random variates from this distribution works in the exact same way as in the univariate case:

```
norm2d.rvs(size=3)
```

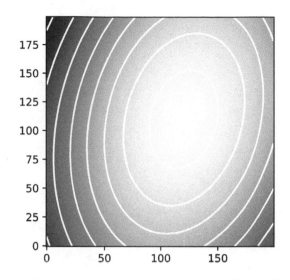

Figure 5.8 The probability density function of a two-dimensional Normal distribution with contour lines.

```
array([[-0.13538416, -0.15443739],
       [-2.14191249,  0.51744353],
       [ 0.70846622,  0.21360603]])
```

Note how each of the three random samples is two-dimensional.

Finally, we will have a look at discrete probability distributions. For instance, consider the case of a **binomial distribution** (**scipy.stats.binom()**) with parameters $n = 10$ and $p = 0.5$. The **probability mass function** (pmf, the discrete equivalent of the pdf) of this distribution over the *integer* variable k describes the probability of, e.g., obtaining "heads" k times in 10 perfectly fair coin tosses ($p = 0.5$). This probability, for instance for the case $k = 3$, can easily be calculated:

```
from scipy.stats import binom
binom(n=10, p=0.5).pmf(3)
```

```
0.11718750000000014
```

We can also plot the probability mass function (pmf) over a range of values k (see Figure 5.9):

```
from scipy.stats import binom
k = range(11)
plt.bar(k, binom(n=10, p=0.5).pmf(k), color='grey')
plt.xlabel('k')
plt.ylabel('pmf')
```

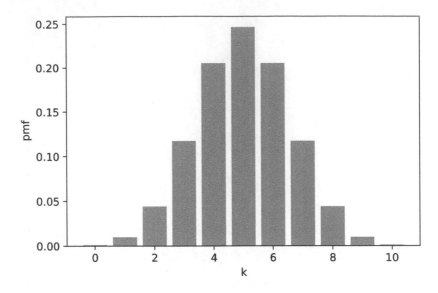

Figure 5.9 The probability mass function (pmf) of a Binomial distribution with $n = 10$ and $p = 0.5$ over the range $k \in [0, 1, ..., 9, 10]$.

5.7.3   Correlation Tests

Correlation functions provide a measure for the intensity of relationship or association between two data sets. The most important correlation measure is the Pearson correlation coefficient, which is implemented as **scipy.stats.pearsonr()**. The Pearson correlation coefficient, r, measures the linear relationship between two data sets and, by assuming that each data set is drawn from a Gaussian distribution, can be used to test for noncorrelations in the data sets. A wide range of other correlation tests are implemented as part of **scipy.stats**, like Spearman rank correlation and Kendall's τ, but these can be used exactly like Pearson's r.

pearsonr(), like most other implemented correlation tests, returns a correlation coefficient – a number between -1 and 1 with 0 indicating the absence of association and 1 (-1) indicating a maximum (negative) relationship – and a two-sided p-value for a hypothesis test with the null hypothesis that the two data sets are not associated, which can be loosely interpreted as the probability that an uncorrelated system produces data sets that have at least the same correlation measure as computed for these data sets.

To showcase the use of **pearsonr()** and most other correlation functions, we test for a linear correlation between an equidistant set of x values and values y that were generated from x using three different functions – a linear function, a combination of a linear and a sine function, and a point cloud – to which we add noise:

```
n = 100
x = np.linspace(0, 10, n)
```

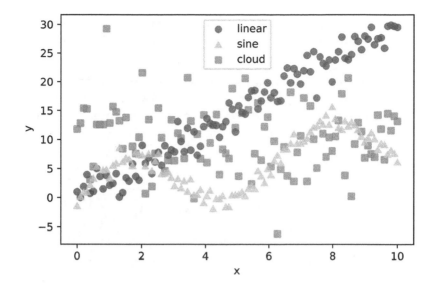

Figure 5.10 Scatter plots of the data distributions utilized in our correlation analysis.

```
linear = 3 * x + np.random.normal(loc=0, scale=2, size=n)
sine = x + 5*np.sin(x) + np.random.normal(loc=0, scale=1, size=n)
cloud = np.random.normal(loc=10, scale=5, size=n)
```

The three data samples are visualized in Figure 5.10. We run `pearsonr` on these data sets using:

```
print('linear', stats.pearsonr(x, linear))
print('sine', stats.pearsonr(x, sine))
print('cloud', stats.pearsonr(x, cloud))
```

```
linear (0.9797199554204509, 3.118145385863985e-70)
sine (0.6002567712191895, 4.0930717838548105e-11)
cloud (-0.089519560313744, 0.3757679885553531)
```

As one would expect, r is highest for the linear data set and lowest (in absolute terms) for the cloud data set. The p-values for the linear and the sine data sets are small enough to rule out the null hypothesis that an uncorrelated system ends up with the same correlation coefficient. Please note that the square of r is generally defined as the coefficient of determination, r^2, another useful measure for the comparison of data sets.

5.7.4   Distribution Tests

In addition to correlation tests, `scipy.stats` also contains a wide range of other statistical tests, including distribution tests. Distribution tests test the null hypothesis that a data sample, x, is drawn from a population following a given probability distribution. Here, we focus on two such tests: the Anderson–Darling test and the Kolmogorov–Smirnov test.

The **Anderson–Darling test** is implemented as **scipy.stats.anderson()**. We showcase the use of anderson() by checking whether a sample of 10^4 random variates drawn from a Normal distribution (*array* a) or a lognormal distribution (*array* b) are drawn from a Normal distribution:

```
from scipy import stats


a = stats.norm.rvs(loc=3, scale=5, size=int(1e4))
b = stats.lognorm.rvs(s=1, size=int(1e4))


print('a:', stats.anderson(a, dist='norm'))
print('b:', stats.anderson(b, dist='norm'))
```

```
a: AndersonResult(statistic=0.09327630706502532, critical_values=
    array([0.576, 0.656, 0.787, 0.918, 1.092]), significance_level=
    array([15. , 10. ,  5. ,  2.5,  1. ]))
b: AndersonResult(statistic=1019.0929522524693, critical_values=array
    ([0.576, 0.656, 0.787, 0.918, 1.092]), significance_level=array
    ([15. , 10. ,  5. ,  2.5,  1. ]))
```

Calling anderson() returns an **AndersonResult** object with attributes statistic, critical_values, and significance_level, which we will discuss in the following. The statistic, the actual result calculated by the function, has to be compared against the critical values that refer to different significance levels. The critical values are precalculated for different significance levels and depend on the distribution for which they are tested. If the derived statistic is larger than a critical value, the null hypothesis that the data is drawn from a population following a Normal distribution can be rejected at the corresponding significance level. In the case of sample a, the null hypothesis cannot be rejected at either significance level; sample a is likely to be drawn from a Normal distribution, which is indeed true. For b, the statistic is much larger than either critical value, meaning that at any significance level we can reject the null hypothesis, so sample b is likely not to be drawn from a Normal distribution, which is also correct. Note how this test is able to properly account for nonstandard distribution parameters for the Normal distribution. The Anderson–Darling test implementation is able to test for a number of distributions including Normal, exponential, logistic, and Gumbel.

More flexibility for distribution testing is provided by the **Kolmogorov–Smirnov test** (**scipy.stats.kstest()**, which allows the user to test against any probability distribution implemented within scipy.stats, or even their own distribution.

However, we would like to focus here on a different implementation of the KS-test, which is the two-sample KS-test, **scipy.stats.ks_2samp()**. This implementation allows you to test the null hypothesis that two samples, x and y, are drawn from the same probability distribution. We can easily check this hypothesis for the two samples that we generated for the Anderson–Darling test:

```
stats.ks_2samp(a, b)
```

```
KstestResult(statistic=0.3627, pvalue=0.0)
```

The result of the function call is a `KstestResult` object with two attributes: `statistic` and `pvalue`. If the derived statistic is small or the p-value is high, we cannot reject the null hypothesis that both samples were drawn from the same distribution, which is not the case here.

For the sake of completeness, we now consider two samples that are indeed drawn from the same distribution:

```
c = stats.norm.rvs(loc=3, scale=5, size=int(1e4))
stats.ks_2samp(a, c)
```

```
KstestResult(statistic=0.013, pvalue=0.3667356837968788)
```

In this case, the p-value is very high and the statistic is low, meaning that we cannot reject the null hypothesis. Keep in mind that this result does not prove that both samples are drawn from the same distribution – we simply cannot rule out the possibility that they might be drawn from the same distribution.

Also, note that the two-sample KS-test will reject the null hypothesis if two samples are drawn from distributions following the same functional behavior but have different parameters:

```
d = stats.norm.rvs(loc=0, scale=1, size=int(1e4))
stats.ks_2samp(a, d)
```

```
KstestResult(statistic=0.558, pvalue=0.0)
```

5.8 Ordinary Differential Equations

Differential equations are very common in many scientific areas. The reason for this popularity is that, quite often, it is easier to describe the changes in the state of a system than to describe the actual state directly. One distinguishes between ordinary differential equations (ODEs) and partial differential equations (PDEs): the former deals with functions of only a single independent variable and its derivatives and the latter deals with multivariate functions and their partial derivatives. Some differential equations can be integrated analytically (see Section 7.6.4 to learn how SymPy can help you with that) or numerically if an analytical solution is unfeasible or simply not necessary. In this section, we will introduce SciPy methods for numerically integrating ODEs that are implemented as part of the `scipy.integrate` module. There are different tools for solving initial value problems and boundary value problems, which we will introduce in the following.

5.8.1　Initial Value Problems

A very wide range of ODEs can be written in the following standard form:

$$\dot{y}(t) = f(y(t), t), \quad t \geq t_0, \quad y(t_0) = y_0. \tag{5.3}$$

Because we specify sufficient conditions at an initial time $t = t_0$ to fix the solution, this is called an *initial value problem*. A great deal of research has been devoted to the initial value problem shown in Equation (5.3). **scipy.integrate.solve_ivp()** is able to integrate initial value problem ODEs. A number of different numerical integrators are available, allowing you to choose a method that is suitable to your problem.

As a first simple example, we consider **exponential decay** of the form

$$\dot{y}(t) = -y(t), \qquad y(t_0 = 0) = 1,$$

and suppose we want the solution at $t = 1$. The following code solves this problem numerically:

```python
from scipy.integrate import solve_ivp

def fun(t, y):
    """Exponential decay ODE."""
    return -y

solve_ivp(fun, [0,1], [1], t_eval=[0,1])
```

```
  message: 'The solver successfully reached the end of the
           integration interval.'
     nfev: 14
     njev: 0
      nlu: 0
      sol: None
   status: 0
  success: True
        t: array([0, 1])
 t_events: None
        y: array([[1.        , 0.36809008]])
 y_events: None
```

`solve_ivp()` returns an **OdeResult** object that contains a lot of information. The representation shown above is nicely formatted, and most items are easy to understand and can be accessed as attributes. The solutions (y) provided are $y(t=0) = 1$, which is in fact our initial condition, and $y(t=1) = e^{-1}$, which is, of course, the correct solution. Calling `solve_ivp()` and its output seems complicated, so let us go through it step by step. The required input for `solve_ivp()` consists of the function to be integrated (`fun` in this case), the interval of integration (`[0, 1]`), and the initial data (`[1]`). In this example, we also provide the keyword argument `t_eval` (see below). The Python function `fun(t, y)` returns the right-hand side of the exponential decay ODE as an *array* of the same shape as y. Note the order of the arguments in `fun`: the first argument is `t`, which is scalar, and the second argument is y, which is also scalar in this case, but could be *n*-dimensional if a system of *n* equations is provided. Similarly, we will need an *array* y0 that contains the initial data; again, in this case, y0 is one-dimensional, but could be *n*-dimensional. Finally, we can supply `t_eval` an *array* of *t*-values for which we would like the corresponding y-values returned; if omitted, `t_eval` will be automatically picked, covering a logarithmic scale over the interval of integration.

In this case, `solve_ivp()` utilizes an explicit **Runge–Kutta** method of order 5(4), which is the default ODE solver. If a different solver is wished for, it can be set with the `method` keyword argument (please refer to the References for a list of available solvers). Most solvers use adaptive step sizes in the integration process to minimize error tolerances. These error tolerances can be controlled via the keyword arguments `atol` (absolute error tolerance) and `rtol` (relative error tolerance); the solver tries to keep the local error estimates below the threshold `atol + rtol*abs(y)`. We should recognize that `atol` and `rtol` refer to local one-step errors, and that the global error may be much larger. For this reason, it is unwise to choose these parameters to be so large that the details of the problem are poorly approximated. If they are chosen so small that the solver can satisfy neither of the criteria, a run time error will be reported.

Finally, we briefly discuss other useful features of `solve_ivp()`. Suppose the function `fun` depends on parameters, e.g., `f(t, y, alpha, beta)`. The function `solve_ivp()` needs to be told this as a keyword argument specifying a *tuple*, e.g., `args=(alpha, beta)`. Furthermore, `solve_ivp()` can cope automatically with equations or systems that are or become stiff. If this is a possibility, then it is strongly recommended to supply the Jacobian of $f(y, t)$ as a function, say `jac(y, t)`, and to include it with the keyword argument `jac`. If it is not supplied, then `solve_ivp()` will try to construct one by numerical differentiation, which can be potentially dangerous in critical cases.

Here is another simple example of a system of equations, the **harmonic oscillator**:

$$\ddot{y}(t) + \omega^2 y(t) = 0, \qquad y(0) = 1, \ \dot{y}(0) = 0,$$

which we will solve and plot for $\omega = 2$ and $0 \leq t \leq 2\pi$. We first rewrite the equation as a system:

$$\mathbf{y} = (y, \dot{y})^T, \quad \ddot{y}(t) = (\dot{y}, -\omega^2 y)^T,$$

and plug the system into `solve_ivp()`, resulting in Figure 5.11:

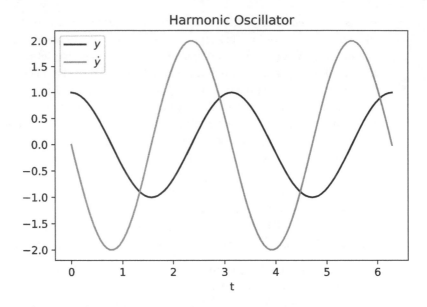

Figure 5.11 The solutions we achieved by numerically integrating the harmonic oscillator equation with `solve_ivp()`.

```python
def fun(t, Y, omega):
    """Harmonic oscillator as first-order system."""
    y, ydot = Y
    return ydot, -omega**2*y

sol = solve_ivp(fun, [0, 2*np.pi], [1, 0],
                t_eval=np.linspace(0, 2*np.pi, 101), args=(2,))

fig, ax = plt.subplots()
ax.plot(sol.t, sol.y[0], label=r'$y$', color='black')
ax.plot(sol.t, sol.y[1], label=r'$\dot{y}$', color='grey')
ax.set_xlabel('t')
ax.set_title('Harmonic Oscillator')
ax.legend()
fig.show()
```

A few things should be noted here. The first is that in the definition of function fun, we have "unwrapped" the vector argument for the sake of clarity in the return values. Secondly, in the call of function `solve_ivp()`, the argument args must be a *tuple*, even if there is only one value.

Finally, we point out that there is an older function, **scipy.integrate.odeint()**, that is capable of performing integration of ODEs. While providing reliable results, the interface of this particular function is not as flexible as that of `solve_ivp()` and offers fewer options. Therefore, it is suggested to use the newer function, `solve_ivp()`, instead.

5.8.2 Boundary Value Problems

Boundary value problems are much harder to solve than initial value problems as they pose global problems instead of local problems. Therefore, the existence and uniqueness of solutions for boundary value problems is far less clear than for initial value problems, and depends in an intrinsic way on the behavior of the solution throughout the integration interval.

We utilize the **scipy.integrate.solve_bvp()** function, which is designed to solve first-order boundary value problems subject to two-point boundary conditions of the following standard form:

$$\frac{d\mathbf{y}}{dx} = f(x, \mathbf{y}, \mathbf{p})$$

$$g(\mathbf{y}(a), \mathbf{y}(b), \mathbf{p}) = 0$$

where x is an independent scalar variable, $\mathbf{y}(x)$ is a function returning an n-dimensional vector, and $\mathbf{p}$ is a k-dimensional vector of parameters that are unknown and will be found together with $\mathbf{y}(x)$. The boundary conditions are defined as a function $g(\mathbf{y}(a), \mathbf{y}(b), \mathbf{p})$ over the range $a \geq x \geq b$. In order to solve this problem, $n + k$ boundary conditions are required, which implies that g must be an $(n+k)$-dimensional function. To introduce the use of the function `solve_bvp()`, we solve the **Sturm–Liouville problem**, for which $y - A * sin(k * x)$ is a solution for $k = n\pi$ with $n \in \mathbb{N}$:

$$\Delta y + k^2 \cdot y = 0$$

with the boundary conditions

$$y(0) = y(1) = 0 \text{ and } y'(0) = k.$$

(The latter condition enforced $A = 1$.) We rewrite the problem as a first-order system:

$$\frac{d\mathbf{y}}{dx} = \begin{bmatrix} y_1' \\ y_2' \end{bmatrix} = \begin{bmatrix} y_2 \\ -k^2 \cdot y_1 \end{bmatrix}$$

and implement the system as function `fun()`:

```python
def fun(x, y, p):
    """Sturm—Liouville problem implementation as first—order system,
    rhs evaluation"""
    k = p[0]
    return np.vstack((y[1], -k**2 * y[0]))
```

in which p is implemented as a *list* or *array* with a single element. We implement the boundary condition as function `g()`:

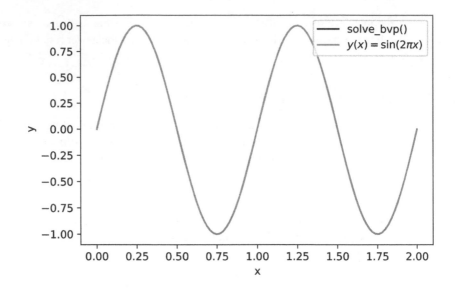

Figure 5.12 Our numerical integration of the Sturm–Liouville problem with `solve_bvp()` compared to the analytical solution (both lines are on top of each other).

```
def g(ya, yb, p):
    """Boundary condition"""
    k = p[0]
    return np.array([ya[0], yb[0], ya[1] - k])
```

In order to use the solver function, we have to provide an initial mesh for vector x (x) and an initial guess for **y** (y_init), which are then provided to the function together with the function fun() and the boundary condition function g():

```
x = np.linspace(0, 2, 10)
y_init = np.zeros((2, x.size))
y_init[0, 1] = 1
y_init[0, 3] = -1
sol = solve_bvp(fun, g, x, y_init, p=[6])
```

y_init is chosen in such a way as to guide the solver to find a solution for $k = 2\pi$ by setting the values of y to roughly follow $\sin(2\pi x)$ and initializing p with an initial guess that is somewhat close to the expected result. The value of p found by the solver is

```
sol.p[0]
```

```
6.283294600464725
```

which agrees very well with our expectation (2π). We compare the numerical solution found by `solve_bvp()` to the actual solution, $y(x) = \sin(2\pi x)$ in Figure 5.12. Indeed, the numerical solution approximates the analytical solution very well over the given range. However, this example also showcases that numerically solving boundary value problems for systems of ODEs is rather complex and requires some rough guesses for the expected solution and, thus, some parameter tuning to find the correct solution.

5.9 SciKits: A Whole New World

We hope this chapter gave you an impression of the capabilities behind SciPy – even if we are only able to present a tiny fraction of the entire package here. But wait... there's even more!

The SciPy universe includes a number of supplemental scientific packages that are much more focused on specific research tasks: the **SciKits**. There is a huge (and ever-growing) variety of these SciKits, so we would like to point out only a rather small selection for different purposes:

☐ **scikit-learn** is a highly popular machine learning package and the de facto standard library for "traditional" machine learning methods (Pedregosa et al., 2011).

☐ **scikit-image** is a large library for image processing (Walt et al., 2011).

☐ **scikit-bio** is a package for bioinformatics.

☐ **scikit-video** provides support for video processing in Python.

☐ **scikit-hep** provides tools and methods for particle physicists.

☐ **scikit-cuda** provides a Python interface to the Cuda programming language to run code on Graphics Processing Units (GPUs).

While providing merely a glimpse, we hope that this list motivates you to look out for interesting SciKit packages that may support you in your research. For a full list of all available and registered SciKits, please refer to the References.

5.10 References

Online resources

☐ General SciPy resources

SciPy project website
`https://scipy.org/`

SciPy documentation
`https://docs.scipy.org/doc//scipy/index.html`

"Scipy Cookbook"
`https://scipy-cookbook.readthedocs.io/`

SciPy user guide

`https://docs.scipy.org/doc//scipy/tutorial/index.html#user-guide`

SciPy API reference

`https://docs.scipy.org/doc//scipy/reference/index.html#scipy-api`

☐ Special functions

Tutorial

`https://docs.scipy.org/doc/scipy/tutorial/special.html`

Reference

`https://docs.scipy.org/doc/scipy/reference/special.html`

☐ Constants

Reference

`https://docs.scipy.org/doc/scipy/reference/constants.html#module-scipy.`
`constants`

☐ Numerical integration/Ordinary differential equations

Tutorial

`https://docs.scipy.org/doc/scipy/tutorial/integrate.html`

Reference

`https://docs.scipy.org/doc/scipy/reference/integrate.html#module-scipy.`
`integrate`

☐ Optimization and root search

Tutorial

`https://docs.scipy.org/doc/scipy/tutorial/optimize.html`

Reference

`https://docs.scipy.org/doc/scipy/reference/optimize.html#module-scipy.`
`optimize`

☐ Numerical interpolation

Tutorial

`https://docs.scipy.org/doc/scipy/tutorial/interpolate.html`

Reference

`https://docs.scipy.org/doc/scipy/reference/interpolate.html#module-scip`
`y.interpolate`

☐ Linear algebra

Tutorial

`https://docs.scipy.org/doc/scipy/tutorial/linalg.html`

Reference

```
https://docs.scipy.org/doc/scipy/reference/linalg.html#module-scipy.li
nalg
```

☐ Statistics

Tutorial

```
https://docs.scipy.org/doc/scipy/tutorial/stats.html
```

Reference

```
https://docs.scipy.org/doc/scipy/reference/stats.html#module-scipy.
stats
```

☐ SciKits

SciKits project page

```
https://projects.scipy.org/scikits.html
```

List of all SciKits available

```
https://pypi.org/search/?q=scikit
```

scikit-learn

```
https://scikit-learn.org/
```

scikit-image

```
https://scikit-image.org/
```

scikit-bio

```
http://scikit-bio.org/
```

scikit-video

```
http://www.scikit-video.org/
```

scikit-hep

```
https://scikit-hep.org/
```

scikit-cuda

```
https://scikit-cuda.readthedocs.io/en/latest/
```

Print Resources

Pedregosa, Fabian, et al. "Scikit-learn: Machine Learning in Python." *Journal of Machine Learning Research*, vol. 12, 2011, pp. 2825–2830.

Tiesinga, Eite, et al. "CODATA recommended values of the fundamental physical constants: 2018." *Reviews of Modern Physics*, vol. 93, 2 June 2021, p. 025010. doi:`10.1103/RevModPhys.93.025010`.

Walt, Stéfan van der, et al. "scikit-image: image processing in Python." *PeerJ*, vol. 2, June 2014, e453. doi:`10.7717/peerj.453`.

6 Matplotlib: Plotting

The Matplotlib package provides plotting capabilities that are fully compatible with the greater SciPy and NumPy environment. The development of Matplotlib was initially inspired by MATLAB's plotting capabilities (hence the name), but the project has been for a long time entirely independent of MATLAB and is fully implemented in Python and NumPy.

For an overview of Matplotlib's capabilities, the reader is strongly urged to peruse the Matplotlib Gallery, where a large collection of publication quality figures, and the code to generate them, is displayed. This is an excellent way (a) to explore the visual capabilities of Matplotlib and (b) to learn ways to implement well-designed figures. Because Matplotlib contains hundreds of functions, we can include here only a small subset. Note that almost all of the figures in this book were generated using Matplotlib, and the source code for each figure and all examples in this chapter are contained in the Jupyter Notebooks available with this book (cambridge.org/9781009029728/ch6).

6.1 Getting Started: Simple Figures

Converting theoretical wishes into actual figures involves two distinct processes, *frontends* and *backends*, and the reader needs to know a little about both.

6.1.1 Frontends

The *frontend* is the user interface. Matplotlib offers two different interfaces: the procedural **pylab** interface imitates MATLAB's syntax, but is limited in its functionality and thus we discourage using it; and the more *pythonic* **pyplot** interface that provides an object-oriented API and full generality. In this book, we will only discuss the use of *pyplot*.

The recommended way to access *pyplot* is to import its functionality as follows:

```
import matplotlib.pyplot as plt
```

We will follow this convention in this book and import most functionality discussed in this chapter from *pyplot* (the **plt** module). Note that this approach is different from how we use other packages, such as the NumPy package (Chapter 4), where we import functionality directly from the package level (`import numpy as np`). In Matplotlib, low-level settings are being performed on the package level, one of which is discussed in the following subsection.

6.1.2   Backends

The *frontend* supplies Python with user-requests. But how should Python turn them into visible results? Should they be output to a screen (which screen?), to paper (which printer?), to another application? These questions are obviously hardware-dependent and it is the job of the software *backend* to answer them. The Matplotlib package contains a wide range of *backends*, but which one should be used? Fortunately, your Python installer will most likely have recognized your hardware configuration and chosen the optimal general purpose *backend* for it. **plt@.get_backend()** will reveal which *backend* is actually being used, in case you are interested. In many instances there should be no need to change this, but there are exceptions: for instance, you might want to be able to generate plots in scripts that are not rendered on the screen first. A good choice in this case is typically the **Agg** backend. If you want to change your backend to **Agg**, you can do so by invoking

```
import matplotlib
matplotlib.use('Agg')
```

Now, any plots that are generated will not be displayed to you, so make sure to use `plt.savefig()` (see Section 6.1.3) to write your plots to file.

6.1.3   A Simple Figure

Provided you only want to draw a simple figure, you can get by with just a few lines of code. The following code cell, for instance, produces the plot shown in Figure 6.1:

```
x = np.linspace(-np.pi, np.pi, 101)
y = np.sin(x) + np.sin(3*x)/3.0

plt.plot(x, y)
plt.xlabel('x')
plt.ylabel('y')
plt.title('A simple plot')
plt.show()
```

The first lines of the cell should be clear: we define two NumPy *arrays* as the data to be plotted: x is a sequence of equidistant values ranging from $-\pi$ to π and y is the outcome of a sum of sine functions applied to each of the values from x.

Matplotlib commands are called in the following lines. The most important call here is **plt.plot(x, y)**, which does most of the hard work by plotting a line that is defined

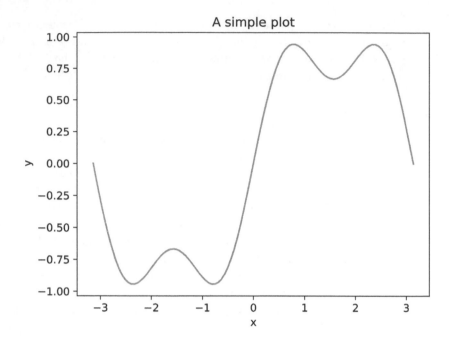

Figure 6.1 A minimalistic plot generated with Matplotlib.

by values of **x** on the abscissa and corresponding values of **y** on the ordinate (see Section 6.4.1 for more details on line plots). The following commands, **plt.xlabel()**, **plt.ylabel()**, and **plt.title()** provide axis labels on the abscissa and ordinate, and set the title of the plot, respectively. None of these three commands is required to display the plot on the screen, but providing proper labeling of axes and the plot in general should be good custom. Technically, all the lines discussed so far create a plot – but they display nothing on the screen.[1] This is typically done by invoking **plt.show()**, which tells the chosen *backend* (see Section 6.1.2) to create the corresponding output. What exactly happens when you invoke plt.show() depends on the backend and Python interface you are using. When running a script or code in the Python interpreter, most likely a window will open that shows the plot and provides some control over the display. If you run your code in a Jupyter Notebook, the plot appears below the corresponding code cell.

It is also possible to **display plots interactively** in combination with plt.show(). Running your code in the Python interpreter, you will not need to do anything: if your *backend* supports interactive plotting, it will open an interactive plot window. In Jupyter Notebooks, it requires some line magic (see Section 2.4.2) to open interactive plots. First, be aware that the ipympl package must be installed (if it is not there, you can install it by typing "pip install ipympl" into your console). In any cell that is

---

[1] This is not really the case for Jupyter Notebooks: Notebooks will always try to display Matplotlib plots when a cell is executed, even without explicitly invoking plt.show().

supposed to open a plot interactively, the first line must be `%matplotlib widget`. An example is provided in the Jupyter Notebook corresponding to this chapter. Interactive plotting allows you to modify axis ranges on the fly and has some other neat tricks. The nicest feature of interactive plotting is introduced in Section 6.9.2.

If, instead of displaying the plot, you prefer to **save the plot to a file**, you can replace `plt.show()` with **`plt.savefig()`**:

```
plt.savefig('simple_plot.pdf')
```

which saves the plot as `simple_plot.pdf` using the *pdf* file format.

The types of files that can be written depend on the implementation and *backend*, but most support `png`, `pdf`, `ps`, `eps` and `svg` files. A useful keyword argument to know for `savefig()` is `dpi`, which allows you to define the resolution in *dots per inch* to be used in creating a **raster image** files such as `png` and `jpg`. Note that **vector file** formats such as `svg`, `ps`, `eps` and `pdf` are not affected by this argument. Another useful keyword argument is `transparent`, which, if `True` (default is `False`), turns the background of the resulting plot transparent.

This example merely scratches on the surface of what is possible with Matplotlib. The following sections will dive deeper into the possibilities and API, starting with a discussion of the object-oriented nature of Matplotlib.

6.2   Object-Oriented Matplotlib

Matplotlib is capable of very much more than the simple plot discussed previously. This is implemented in object-oriented fashion using classes, as reviewed briefly in Section 3.11. However, while that section was concerned with the actual construction of classes, the scientist user will be using predefined ones, and so needs only to assimilate two pieces of jargon.

A *figure* class instance is what an artist would call his "canvas;" see Figure 6.2. A Matplotlib session might include several *figures*. Within a *figure* there may be one or more class *axes* instances. Note that "*axes*" is a plural noun. It refers to, e.g., the set of coordinate axes, not merely a single coordinate axis. For example, Figure 6.2 contains two *axes* instances. Each instance contains an *x-axis* and a *y-axis*. In order to master plotting, we need to be able to access both classes.

Fortunately it is very easy to construct *figure* and *axes* instances. Distinct *figure* instances can be instantiated by calling `plt.figure()`:

```
fig1 = plt.figure()
fig2 = plt.figure()
```

Clearly an *axes* instance belongs to a *figure*. However, a *figure* may contain many *axes*, a configuration we refer to as a *compound figure* (see Section 6.8 for an in-depth

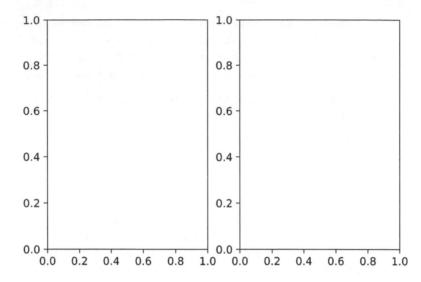

Figure 6.2 A schematic figure produced by Matplotlib. The totality of what is shown here is a *Figure* class instance. It contains two *Axes* class instances (left and right panel). Each *axes* instance contains an *x-axis* and a *y-axis*.

discussion). For example, Figure 6.2 contains two *axes* arranged in one row with two columns. In order to add *axes* to *figures*, we can use `plt.add_subplot()`:

```
ax1 = fig1.add_subplot(121)
ax2 = fig1.add_subplot(122)
```

In this case, both *axes* are now part of `fig1`, creating the same setup as shown in Figure 6.2. The arguments to `plt.add_subplot()` consist in this case of three *integers* that define, in this order, the number of rows, the number of columns, and the index of the current *axis* in the compound figure with index 1 starting in the upper left corner of the *figure* increasing to the right. *axes* are typically named **ax** (or some variation thereof) to make clear that you are dealing with an *axes* object. In this book, we stick to this convention, as you will see. The same setup can also be achieved with a one-liner:

```
fig, ax = plt.subplots(1, 2)
```

which will return a *figure* instance, `fig`, and an *array* of *axes*, `ax`, as shown in Figure 6.2. **`plt.subplots()`** takes as arguments the number of rows and the number of columns of the resulting compound figure; this shape is reflected by the shape of `ax`:

```
ax.shape
```

```
(2,)
```

Please note that `plt.subplots()` is not only useful for creating *compound figure*. For instance, `plt.subplots(1, 1)`, or in fact even `plt.subplots()`, is a perfectly legitimate function call for creating a single-*axes figure* (one *figure* object and one *axes* object). As an example, let us consider the simplest plot shown in Section 6.1.3, and rewrite the code in object-oriented form. Those lines dealing with Matplotlib functionality could be replaced by:

```
fig, ax = plt.subplots())
ax.plot(x, y)
ax.set_xlabel('x')
ax.set_ylabel('y')
ax.set_title('A simple plot')
fig.show()
```

"Why should I?" the tyro will exclaim. "Why should I replace four valid lines of code (to define the plot) with five, and use longer function names?" We need to examine carefully what is going on here.

In fact, the code used in Section 6.1.3 to generate Figure 6.1, which is based on functionality directly drawn from `plt`, serves as a wrapper. In practice, Matplotlib does the following: Matplotlib internally converts the `plt`-based instructions to the equivalent of the object-oriented code shown here. However, the private names for the *figures* and *axes* objects are not available to the ordinary user, strictly limiting the flexibility of this approach.

For simple figures, the `plt`-based approach, implemented early on to ensure MATLAB consistency, is harmless until one tries to construct more complicated figures. Using `plt`-based functionality will come with a range of restrictions, preventing you from designing good-looking plots. It is for this reason that we highly recommend using the object-oriented procedure for anything other than quick, simple figures.

Therefore, the advantages of the object-oriented approach (full control over what is going to happen) clearly outweigh its disadvantages (slightly longer code). For users who are already used to the `plt`-based functionality, here is a quick summary of what to expect. First of all, pretty much all functions to create plots such as `plt.scatter()` (see Section 6.4.2) can be called directly on an *axes* object: `ax.scatter()`. For some functionality, such as `plt.xlabel()`, `plt.ylabel()`, and `plt.title()`, equivalents operating on *axes* objects exist that have slightly different names: these functions use the prefix "set_" (`ax.set_xlabel()`, `ax.set_ylabel()`, `ax.set_title()`). Admittedly, this is a rather minor difference – and it is actually also more *pythonic* by being more explicit than the `plt`-based approach. Nevertheless, it might take some time to get used to the object-oriented approach, but it is well worth the time, as we will see in the following sections.

6.3   Customizing Plots

The object-oriented nature of Matplotlib may feel unnecessarily complicated to a beginner, but it offers a great deal of flexibility and customizability. In this section, we will introduce some of the basic elements that will allow you to generate plots in publication quality. More importantly, mastering the concepts presented here will enable you to try out some more complex concepts on your own. In the following, we will provide only a few code examples (a few more examples are provided in the corresponding Jupyter Notebook), as it is best to apply these concepts yourself and see how they work.

Finally, please be aware that most of the concepts introduced in this section are also available for the simpler `plt` interface, but, as we discussed in the previous section, they might have slightly different names (e.g., `plt.title()` instead of `ax.set_title()`) and might provide less modularity and flexibility. In the following code examples, we assume that `ax` is a single *axes* object.

6.3.1   Figure Size

The physical size of any visualization is important to enable readability – and the same applies to the size of a *figure* object. Naturally, all *axes* objects defined for a given *figure* must be able to fit inside that *figure*. Therefore, the *figure size* should be chosen carefully to fit all *axes*, as well as their labels, titles, etc. The size of a *figure* must be defined at instantiation, using the `figsize` keyword argument, which requires a *tuple* of *float* or *integer* values corresponding to the width and height of the *figure* in units of inches. Therefore, the *figsize* keyword argument is available for `plt.figure()` and for `plt.subplots()`, as those return *figure* objects. For instance, the following line of code creates a *figure* object containing a panel of 4 (2×2) *axes* objects of physical extent 10 cm×10 cm (using a conversion factor of 2.54 cm/inch):

```
fig, ax = plt.subplots(2, 2, figsize=(10/2.54, 10/2.54))
```

6.3.2   Axis Range and Scaling

By default, Matplotlib will create plots with linear scaling and display a range of values on each axis (i.e., *x*-axis and *y*-axis) that is based on the minimum and maximum values of the data points provided. Although Matplotlib usually makes an excellent choice of axis extents, they are easily changed for the *x*-axis with:

```
ax.set_xlim(xmin, xmax)
```

and similarly for the *y*-axis with `ax.set_ylim(ymin, ymax)`.

Sometimes, however, one or more logarithmic axes are desired. The scaling of the *x*-axis can be easily changed to a logarithmic scale by invoking

```
ax.set_xscale('log')
```

and similarly for the *y*-axis.

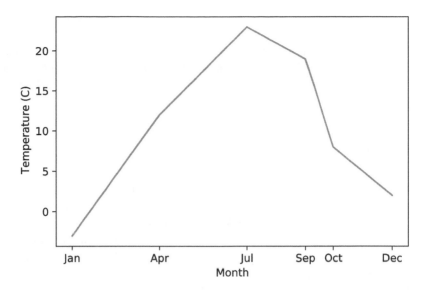

Figure 6.3 An example plot with manually set, nonequidistant ticks on the *x*-axis defined with `ax.set_xticks()` and corresponding *string* labels provided with `ax.set_xticklabels()`.

6.3.3   Ticks

The location of ticks on the *x*-axis and *y*-axis is also selected by Matplotlib in a typically smart way, but, of course, there is a way to override this automatic choice. The methods **ax.set_xticks()** and **ax.set_yticks()** control the ticks along both axes and each take a *list* or NumPy *array* as input that indicates the tick locations. It is also useful to know that providing an empty *list* will remove ticks entirely. Now that we are able to select ticks manually, can we also label them manually? Of course! **ax.set_xticklabels()** and **set_yticklabels()** does exactly that; you simply provide a *list* of labels that has the same length as the *list* of ticks. Consider the following example resulting in Figure 6.3:

```
months = [1, 4, 7, 9, 10, 12]
temp = [-3, 12, 23, 19, 8, 2]

fig, ax = plt.subplots()
ax.plot(months, temp)
ax.set_xticks(months)
ax.set_xticklabels(['Jan', 'Apr', 'Jul', 'Sep', 'Oct', 'Dec'])
ax.set_xlabel('Month')
ax.set_ylabel('Temperature (C)')
plt.show()
```

6.3.4   Grid

By default, Matplotlib does not display a grid. It can be added manually by invoking **ax.grid()**. This function supports many of the keyword arguments discussed in Section 6.4.1, including `linestyle`, `linewidth`, and `color`; the distribution of the grid lines follows that of the ticks on each axis.

6.3.5   Legend

Suppose we are producing a figure with two or more curves. We may attach a label to each curve, by including the parameter `label='string'` in the call to `ax.plot()`. After all of the curves have been plotted, the function **ax.legend()** draws a legend that contains a line for each labeled curve showing its style and label. This function provides a wide range of keyword arguments, the most important of which, `loc`, defines the position of the legend; while `'best'` tries to find the most suitable location by itself, you can name a corner (e.g., `'upper right'`) or an edge (e.g., `'lower center'`). There are a number of other options: e.g., `title` allows you to provide a title label, with `ncol` you can set the number of columns of your legend, `framealpha` provides transparency support of the legend background, and this is just some of the other tweaks available.

6.3.6   Transparency

Most Matplotlib functions support transparency for lines, surfaces, and markers, which is typically provided with the `alpha` keyword argument to which a *float* value is assigned; 1 means solid, whereas 0 means fully transparent. To create a transparent background, review Section 6.1.3.

6.3.7   Text and Annotations

Suppose we wish to place a plain text *string* in a *figure* starting at (x, y) in data coordinates, i.e., those defined by the *x*-axis and *y*-axis of an *axes* object. The extremely versatile Matplotlib function **ax.text()** does precisely that:

```
ax.text(x, y, 'this is a text label')
```

There are various ways of enhancing it by changing its `color` (red, blue, ...), `fontsize` (as a *float* in pt), `fontstyle` (normal, italic, ...) and many other properties as detailed by the function's *docstring*. There follows an example for the use of this function.

Sometimes we wish to refer to a particular feature on the figure, and this is the purpose of **ax.annotate()**, which has a slightly idiosyncratic syntax. It allows you to place a label at location `xytext` (in data coordinates) from which an arrow points to a different location (`xy`) on the plot. Consider the following example, the result of which is shown in Figure 6.4:

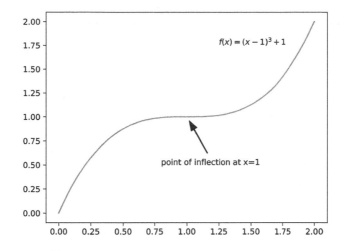

Figure 6.4 A simple example that showcases the use of `text()`, `annotate()` and the generation of mathematical formulae with *mathtext* (see Sections 6.3.7 and 6.3.8).

```
x = np.linspace(0, 2, 101)
y = (x-1)**3 + 1

fig, ax = plt.subplots()
ax.plot(x, y)
ax.text(1.25, 1.75, r'$f(x)=(x-1)^3+1$')
ax.annotate('point of inflection at x=1', xy=(1,1),
            xytext=(0.8,0.5), horizontalalignment='center',
            arrowprops=dict(facecolor='black',width=1,
            shrink=0.05))
plt.show()
```

6.3.8   Mathematical Formulae

This is an opportune moment to discuss the Achilles heel of all plotting software. How do we display decently formatted mathematical formulae? Most word processors offer add-on tools to display mathematical formulae but quite often, and especially for intricate formulae, they look ugly. Matplotlib provides a way to generate properly formatted mathematical formulae by taking advantage of TeX functionality.

Matplotlib includes a primitive engine called ***mathtext*** to provide TeX-style expressions. This is far from a complete LaTeX installation, but it is self-contained, and the Matplotlib documentation features a succinct review of the main TeX commands. The engine can be accessed from plot functions that expect to receive a *string* argument, e.g., `ax.title()`, `ax.text()`, `ax.set_xlabel()`, `ax.set_ylabel()`, or `ax.annotate()`. As a concrete real-life example, consider the following line of code, which we used in the generation of Figure 6.4:

```
ax.text(1.25, 1.75, r'$f(x)=(x−1)^3+1$')
```

To understand this line, consider first the *string* itself. You need to know that mathematics is defined in TeX between a pair of dollar ($) signs. Then TeX strips the dollar signs and sets the mathematics in italic font with the font size determined by the (TeX) context. The r prepended to the *string* indicates that this is a **raw** *string*, so that Matplotlib will call up its *mathtext* engine. (Without it, the dollar signs would be rendered verbatim.)

6.3.9   Colors

In most cases, the readability of plots increases significantly by plotting data in different colors. This capability is implemented in most plotting functions discussed here, such as `plt.plot()` (Section 6.4.1), `plt.scatter()` (Section 6.4.2), `plt.imshow()` (Section 6.6), and others with the **color** keyword argument. Changing the color of a specific feature such as a plot line is as simple as assigning the name of the color to this keyword argument. For instance, the following sample creates a green plot line:

```
ax.plot(x, y, color='green')
```

Be aware that Matplotlib is not limited to standard colors such as "red," "green," and "blue." Instead, it provides a huge variety of colors, including somewhat exotic varieties such as "lightgoldenrodyellow," "mediumvioletred," and "lightsteelblue." See the "List of named colors" in Section 6.10. If you require an even wider selection of colors, or if you are interested in defining your own colors, please review the "Specifying colors" document (see Section 6.10). One more comment on colors: you might have noticed that assigning colors explicitly is not required to generate plots using colors. If none are defined, Matplotlib will use colors that follow a specific sequence. Of course, the sequence underlying this cycle can be altered, but we leave the details to the interested reader at this point.

Sometimes it is beneficial to the visual presentation of data to **color-code the individual data points**, which allows for representing a third dimension on an otherwise two-dimensional plot. Such color-coding is implemented in Matplotlib with the concept of *colormaps*. The idea is that the user provides a *list* or NumPy *array* of numerical values to the c keyword argument (note that it is not `color` in this case) of the respective plotting function, which has to be of the same length as the input data (x and y). Such functionality is available for a number of functions, including `plt.plot()` (Section 6.4.1), `plt.scatter()` (Section 6.4.2), `plt.imshow()` (Section 6.6), and others. In the following example, which makes use of the scatter plot function `plt.scatter()`, we plot points that follow the function $f(x) = x^3$ and encode the distance of the individual points from the origin in the points' color as shown in Figure 6.5:

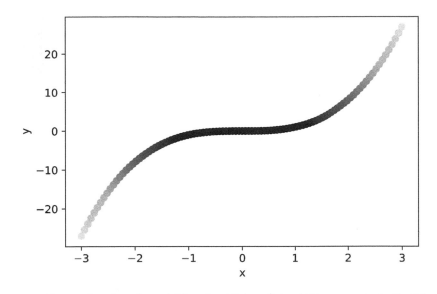

Figure 6.5 Scatter plot of a polynomial function ($f(x) = x^3$) in which we encode the Euclidean distance to the origin in the color of the markers.

```
x = np.linspace(-3, 3, 101)
y = x**3
r = np.sqrt(x**2 + y**2)   # Euclidean distance

fig, ax = plt.subplots()
ax.scatter(x, y, c=r)
ax.set_xlabel('x')
ax.set_ylabel('y')
fig.show()
```

Note how we compute the Euclidean distance to the origin as r and provide this *array* to the `color` keyword argument of the plotting function. The actual color encoding, i.e., identifying the range of values and assigning a specific color to each value over this range, is done internally. By default, a *min-max* scaling is used. If you prefer to set the range manually, you can do so by setting the minimum and maximum values via `vmin` and `vmax`, respectively.

The choice of color is performed by the *colormap* and the corresponding **cmap** keyword argument. The default *colormap* in NumPy is *viridis*, which shows low values in purple, high values in yellow and intermediate values in shades of blue and green.[2] A wide range of *colormaps* is available as part of Matplotlib, which can be easily imported with

---

[2] While not immediately obvious, *viridis* was selected as default due to its being seen as unbiased and its accessibility to people with deficiencies in perceiving colors.

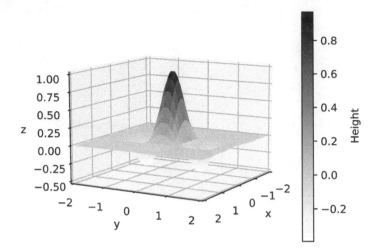

Figure 6.6 Plot of a 3d surface generated with `plot_surface()` using color-encoding and a colorbar.

the function **plt.get_cmap()** (see the following example and the reference table of available *colormaps*, Section 6.10).

So far, we used color encodings only to provide qualitative information on the data plotted in color. In order to be able to interpret the color data quantitatively, we can add a **colorbar** that indicates which colors are assigned to which values. The following code cell plots a 3d surface using `plt.plot_surface()`, which we will elaborate on in Section 6.9.2, with a color encoding that indicates the height (*z* value) of the surface and a color bar (using **ax.colorbar()**) for reference (see Figure 6.6):

```python
xx, yy = np.mgrid[-2:2:101j, -2:2:101j]
zz = np.exp(-2*xx**2-yy**2)*np.cos(2*xx)*np.cos(3*yy)

fig, ax = plt.subplots(subplot_kw={'projection':'3d'})
surf = ax.plot_surface(xx, yy, zz, cmap=plt.get_cmap('Greys'),
                       linewidth=0)
cbar = plt.colorbar(surf, label='Height')
ax.set_xlim3d(-2.0, 2.0)
ax.set_ylim3d(-2.0, 2.0)
ax.set_zlim3d(-0.5, 1.0)
ax.set_xlabel('x')
ax.set_ylabel('y')
ax.set_zlabel('z')
ax.elev, ax.azim = 10, 30
fig.show()
```

Note that we use the *Greys* colormap in this case and we remove the wireframe structure from the surface plot with `linewidth=0`. A color bar has to be generated for a specific object, which is in this case the instance of `plt.plot_surface()`, which weve named `surf` here. We add a `label` to the color bar and point out that many other options exist to customize the color bar.

6.4   Cartesian Plots

In the following, we will introduce some plotting functions based on cartesian coordinate systems. Be aware that we will limit our introduction to their application to *axes* objects (i.e., function call: `ax.<function>`) but we would like to point out that the same functions can also be directly invoked from `plt` (i.e., `plt.<function>`; see Section 6.2 for a discussion).

6.4.1   Line Plots

`ax.plot()` is a very powerful and versatile function that allows you to create line plots. The simplest call – see, e.g., the example code shown in Section 6.1.3 and the example plot shown in Figure 6.1 – would be `ax.plot(x,y)`, where x and y are one-dimensional NumPy *arrays* of the same length that refer to the abscissa and ordinate values, respectively, of the nodes of the linear segments to be plotted. This would generate a curve linking the points $(x[0], y[0])$, $(x[1], y[1])$, ..., using the default style options. It is worth keeping in mind that `plot()` is only able to draw line segments without any curvature. However, as shown in Figure 6.1 and the corresponding code presented in Section 6.1.3, one is able to approximate smooth curvature by utilizing high resolution input data, i.e., *arrays* with a dense coverage of the range to be plotted.

The most concise call would be `ax.plot(y)`, where y is a *NumPy* vector of length n. Then a default x vector is created with *integer* spacing to enable the curve to be drawn. The syntax allows many curves to be drawn with one call. Suppose y and z are ordinate values for abscissa values x of the same length, then the following code would plot both curves on the same *axes*:

```
ax.plot(x, y)
ax.plot(x, z)
```

In order to be able to distinguish different curves (and to create visually appealing plots), there is a wide range of style options available, which we will discuss in the following.

By the style of a curve, we mean its color, nature, and thickness. Matplotlib allows for a variety of line colors, which have to be provided to the `color` keyword argument: `ax.plot(x, y, color='red')`. Please see Section 6.3.9 for a general discussion of colors in Matplotlib. Curves are by default solid lines, but other **line styles** are possible. To change the line style, utilize the `linestyle` keyword argument in combination with

Table 6.1 The 12 most commonly used marker styles.

character	marker style
.	point (default)
o	circle
*	star
+	plus
x	x
v	triangle down
^	triangle up
<	triangle left
>	triangle right
n	square
p	pentagon
h	hexagon

one of the following self-describing *string* values: solid, dashed, dotted, dashdot, or None (for no curve at all). Finally, we can modify the **line width** of our curve by providing a *float* value to the linewidth keyword argument. The value refers to the width of the curve in measures of printer's points. Thus to draw a magenta dash-dotted curve of width four points, we would use:

```
ax.plot(x, y, color='magenta', linestyle='dashdot', linewidth=4)
```

6.4.2   Scatter Plots

To plot point clouds, **ax.scatter()** would be the function of choice. It also requires two input *arrays*, holding the x and y coordinates of the data points to be plotted. ax.scatter() provides a number of keyword arguments: marker to set the marker style, s to set the marker size, linestyle for line segments connecting the markers (if desired), as well as color to set the marker and line color. Matplotlib offers a bouquet of marker styles, and the 12 most commonly used ones are given in Table 6.1. The following complete example code produces a simple scatter plot using different clusters with different colors and symbols (see Figure 6.7):

```
fig, ax = plt.subplots()

for i in range(3):
    x = np.random.normal(loc=[3, 0, 1][i],
                         scale=[0.5, 1, 0.2][i], size=20)
    y = np.random.normal(loc=[2, 1, 3][i],
                         scale=[0.5, 1, 0.2][i], size=20)
    ax.scatter(x, y, marker=['o', 's', '^'][i], s=20,
               color=['black', 'grey', 'lightgrey'][i],
               label=i)
```

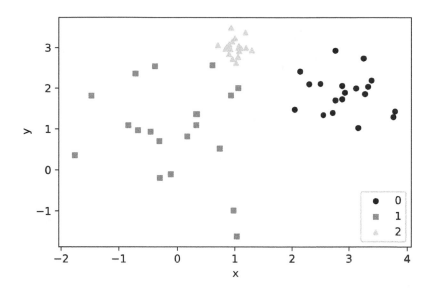

Figure 6.7 A scatter plot example generated with scatter(), showing the effect of using different marker types.

```
ax.set_xlabel('x')
ax.set_ylabel('y')
ax.legend(loc=4)
plt.show()
```

It is also possible to specify different colors for the marker face (markerfacecolor) and the marker edge (markeredgecolor). In combination with markeredgewidth, which specifies the width of the edge, there are many many possibilities, not all of them aesthetically pleasant.

6.4.3 Error Bars

When measurements are involved, we often need to display error bars. Matplotlib handles these efficiently, using the function **ax.errorbar()**. This function behaves like ax.plot(), but with extra parameters. Consider first, errors in the y-variable, which we specify with the yerr argument. If yerr is a scalar (homoscedastic errors) or an *array* of values (heteroscedastic errors) that has the same dimension as y, then symmetric error bars are drawn. In the latter case, each element of yerr is the error of that element of y with the same index. Thus for the kth point at y[k], the error bar extends from y[k]-yerr[k] to y[k]+yerr[k]. If the errors are not symmetric, then yerr should be a $2 \times n$ *array*, and the kth error bar extends from y[k]-yerr[0,k] to y[k]+yerr[1,k]. Analogous remarks apply to x-errors and the keyword argument xerr. By default, the color and line width are derived from the main curve. Consider

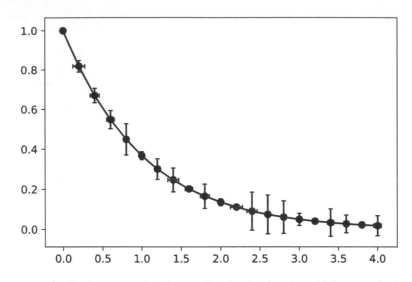

Figure 6.8 A simple plot generated with `errorbar()`, showing data with heteroscedastic error bars.

the following example with heteroscedastic symmetric errors in both x and y, resulting in Figure 6.8:

```
x = np.linspace(0, 4, 21)
y = np.exp(-x)
xe = 0.08*np.random.rand(len(x))
ye = 0.1*np.random.rand(len(y))

fig, ax = plt.subplots()
ax.errorbar(x, y, xerr=xe, yerr=ye, marker='o', capsize=2,
            color='black')
plt.show()
```

Note that `marker` defines the marker type (see Section 6.4.2) and `capsize` defines the width of the caps, which defaults to zero otherwise.

6.4.4   Plotting Filled Areas

`ax.fill_between()` provides a way to plot lines and fill the area between them. The outcome of this function depends crucially on its arguments. Generally, you need to provide three *lists* or NumPy *arrays* that all must have the same length: the first one containing x-values, the second and third containing corresponding y-values that describe the range of values to be filled. Strictly speaking, the second sequence of y-values is not required; if omitted, all those values default to zero, meaning that the area between the y-values provided and the x-axis are filled. Let's consider the data plotted in

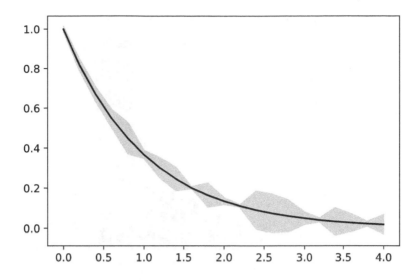

Figure 6.9 Displaying uncertainties as filled areas with `ax.fill_between()`.

Figure 6.8 and plot the uncertainties as a filled range around the actual values as shown in Figure 6.9:

```
fig, ax = plt.subplots()
ax.fill_between(x, y+ye, y-ye, color='lightgrey')
ax.plot(x, y, color='black')
plt.show()
```

Although nontrivial, it is possible to use this function to draw somewhat arbitrary shapes by providing hand-crafted *arrays* containing the corners of the shapes. Be aware that shapes generally need to be closed, which means that the final pair of (x, y) values must be identical to the first pair.

6.4.5 Bar Plots

Another common type of plot are bar plots, which can be realized with **ax.bar()** and are commonly used to visualize histograms and other data. The arguments required by this function include a *list* or NumPy *array* of x-values (`x`) that correspond to the bar centers or edges (make sure to use `align='edge'` in the latter case) and the corresponding bar heights (`height`). Both `x` and `height` must have the same length, if `x` provides bar center locations. In addition to typical keyword arguments like `color`, `alpha`, etc., `ax.bar()` features some unique arguments that allow you to control the width of the bars (`width`) and the y-coordinate of their bottoms (`bottom`, which defaults to zero). The latter allows you to stack bar plots on top of each other. Consider the following example in which we draw numbers from two different Gaussian distributions,

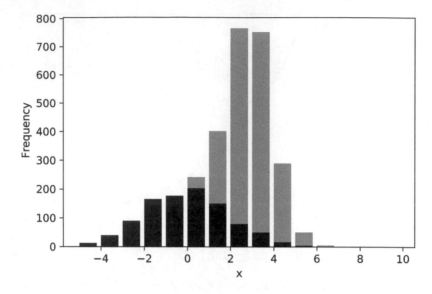

Figure 6.10 A stacked bar plot visualizing histograms of two Gaussians, generated with `ax.bars()`.

create histograms with `np.histogram()` and plot the stacked histograms as shown in Figure 6.10:

```
x1 = np.random.normal(loc=0, scale=2, size=1000)
x2 = np.random.normal(loc=3, scale=1, size=2000)
hist1, bins = np.histogram(x1, bins=np.linspace(-5, 10, 16))
hist2, bins = np.histogram(x2, bins=np.linspace(-5, 10, 16))

fig, ax = plt.subplots()
ax.bar(bins[:-1], hist1, align='edge', width=0,
       color='black')
ax.bar(bins[:-1], hist2, bottom=hist1, align='edge',
       width=0.8, color='grey')
ax.set_xlabel('x')
ax.set_ylabel('Frequency')
plt.show()
```

6.5   Polar Plots

Suppose we use polar coordinates (r, θ) and define a curve by $r = f(\theta)$. It is straightforward to plot this curve using **`ax.polar()`** (or `plt.polar()`), which behaves rather like `ax.plot()`. Figure 6.11 was created with the following code cell:

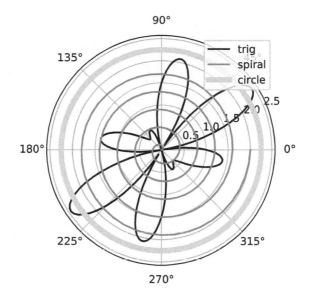

Figure 6.11 A simple polar plot generated with Matplotlib.

```
theta = np.linspace(0, 2*np.pi, 201)
r1 = np.abs(np.cos(5.0*theta) - 1.5*np.sin(3.0*theta))
r2 = theta/np.pi
r3 = 2.25*np.ones_like(theta)

fig, ax = plt.subplots(subplot_kw={'projection': 'polar'})
ax.plot(theta, r1, label='trig', color='black')
ax.plot(5*theta, r2, label='spiral', color='grey')
ax.plot(theta, r3, label='circle', color='lightgrey',
        linewidth=5)
ax.legend(loc='upper right')
plt.show()
```

6.6   Plotting Images

Matplotlib can be used to plot image data via the function **ax.imshow()** (or
plt.imshow()). Image data can be provided in the form of a NumPy *array*. For a
simple *grayscale image*, only a single value per pixel (typically *float* values between 0
and 1, or 0 and 255 in the case of 8-bit encoding) is required, so the *array* must have
two dimensions, which are the height and width in units of pixels. In the following code
cell we load a grayscale image (gray=True) that is stored within SciPy (see Chapter 5)
as an *array*:

Figure 6.12　A simple grayscale image plot generated with `plt.imshow()`.

```
from scipy.misc import face

im = face(gray=True)
print(im.shape)
print(np.min(im), np.max(im))
```

```
(768, 1024)
0 250
```

Internalize the properties of this *array*: it has a shape of (768, 1024), and thus only two dimensions, and it consists of values ranging from 0 to 250 (obviously using an 8-bit encoding with a potential maximum value of 255).

To display the data contained in `im` as an image, we can use `plt.imshow()` to generate the output shown in Figure 6.12:

```
fig, ax = plt.subplots()
ax.imshow(im, cmap='Greys_r')
fig.show()
```

In its simplest use case, `imshow()` is called with the image data *array* as its sole argument. In this case, however, we also select a specific *colormap* (to prevent Matplotlib from using *viridis* in this case): `Greys_r` displays low values in dark shades and high values in bright shades (see Section 6.5 for more on *colormaps*). Although the image appears in the correct up-right **orientation**, a look at the *y*-axis reveals something unexpected: the coordinate origin of the image is in the top left corner and not the bottom left corner as is typically the case in plots. This is nothing to worry about. The image stored in `im` is stored in matrix coordinates (rows, columns) instead of typical image coordinates (x, y); therefore, the image appears upright although the coordinate origin is in the upper left corner. If your image is stored in pairs of (x, y)-coordinates, you can use the keyword argument `origin='lower'` to set the coordinate origin in the bottom left corner. To switch between the matrix and image coordinate conventions you can use the transposed *array*, `im.transpose()` or `img.T`, and adapt the y-axis origin (`origin='upper'` or `origin='lower'`), where necessary.

The situation becomes slightly more complicated for *color images*. Color data are typically provided in the form of *RGB* values, a *tuple* containing values for the red, green, and blue content of a pixel, each represented by a *float* in the range [0, 1] or *integers* in the range [0, 255]. We can load the same image as a color image:

```
im = face()
print(im.shape)
print(np.min(im), np.max(im))
```

```
(768, 1024, 3)
0 255
```

Note the different *shape* of `im`: although the image still has the same height (768) and width (1024), every single pixel now consists of three numbers that refer to the three color channels (`r`, `g`, and `b`; in this order). We extract the color information for a single pixel (x=330, y=600) that is part of a green plant:

```
im[600,330]
```

```
array([153, 195, 132], dtype=uint8)
```

Indeed, interpreting the resulting *array* as RGB-triplet, the green value is significantly higher than the others. Note that since the image *array* is provided in coordinates of rows and columns, we have to query a specific location as (y, x) coordinate pair. In order to extract a single color channel, one can simply use:

```
r = im[:,:,0]
g = im[:,:,1]
b = im[:,:,2]
```

and in order to combine them again into a format that will be interpreted as an RGB image by `imshow()`, we can take advantage of `np.dstack()` (see Section 4.1.5):

```
im2 = np.dstack([r, g, b])
im2.shape
```

```
(768, 1024, 3)
```

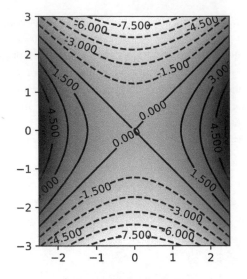

Figure 6.13 A plain contour plot generated with contour(). Note the different line styles that are used for the different contour levels, as well as the labels that were automatically generated by clabel().

Of course, this results in the same image that we had before. One final note: plotting the color version of im would, of course, display the same image as shown in Figure 6.12 with proper colors.

6.7   Contour Plots

Suppose we have a relation $F(x, y) = z$, and let z_0 be a fixed value for z. Subject to the conditions of the implicit function theorem, we can, after possibly interchanging the roles of x and y, solve this relation, at least locally, for $y = f(x, z_0)$. These are the "contour curves" or "contours" of z. What do they look like as z_0 varies? In principle, we need to specify two-dimensional *arrays* of equal shape for each of x, y, and z, and a vector of values for z_0. Matplotlib allows for a number of short-cuts in this process using the **ax.contour()** function. For example, according to the documentation, we can omit the x- and y-arrays. However, Matplotlib then creates the missing *arrays* as *integer*-spaced grids using np.meshgrid(), which creates the transpose of what is usually needed, and so we should be careful if using this option! If we do not specify the z_0 vector, we can give instead the number of contour curves that should be drawn, or accept the default value. By default, the z_0 values are not shown on the plot; the **ax.clabel()** function can be used to generate them, using as argument the values returned by **ax.contour()**. Figure 6.13 was produced by the following code cell:

```
[X, Y] = np.mgrid[-2.5:2.5:51j, -3:3:61j]
Z = X**2 - Y**2

fig, ax = plt.subplots()
ax.imshow(Z, extent=[-2.5, 2.5, -3, 3], cmap='Greys_r')
curves = ax.contour(X, Y, Z, 12, colors='black')
ax.clabel(curves)
fig.show()
```

X, Y and Z are 51×61 *arrays* of *floats*. We plot Z with the proper `extent` *tuple* and over-lay the outcome of the function `ax.contour`, which draws 12 contour curves and returns their values. The Z-value labels are then attached to the curves with `ax.clabel()`.

6.8   Compound Figures

We saw in Section 6.4.1 that it is possible to draw several curves into a single *axes* object by invoking `ax.plot()` several times for different data sets. Sometimes it is useful to present data in a panel consisting of several *axes* for better readability.

As we already saw in Section 6.2, this task is performed easily thanks to Matplotlib's object-oriented framework. Consider the following example in which we plot four different decay rates in the same *figure* that contains a 2×2 grid of *axes* (see Figure 6.14).

```
t = np.linspace(0,5,101)
y1 = 1.0/(t+1.0)
y2 = np.exp(-t)
y3 = np.exp(-5*t**2)
y4 = np.exp(-0.5*t**3)

fig, ax = plt.subplots(2, 2, sharex=True, sharey=True)
# top left axes:
ax[0, 0].plot(t, y1, color='grey')
ax[0, 0].set_ylabel(r'$f(t)$')
ax[0, 0].set_title(r'$1/(t+1)$', y=0.8)
# top right axes:
ax[0, 1].plot(t, y2, color='grey')
ax[0, 1].set_title(r'$\exp(-t)$', y=0.8)
# bottom left axes:
ax[1, 0].plot(t, y3, color='grey')
ax[1, 0].set_xlabel(r'$t$')
ax[1, 0].set_ylabel(r'$f(t)$')
ax[1, 0].set_title(r'$\exp(-5t^2)$', y=0.8)
```

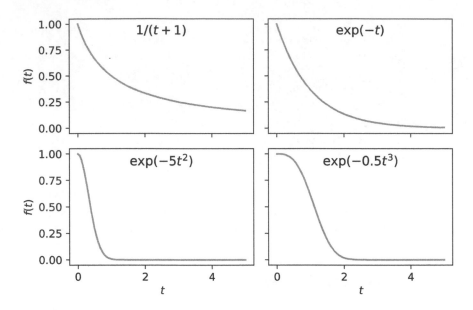

Figure 6.14 An example of a compound plot showing different decay functions. Note that all plots (*axes*) share the same *x* and *y* values, which is a result of setting `sharex=True` and `sharey=True` in `subplots()`.

```
# bottom right axes:
ax[1, 1].plot(t, y4, color='grey')
ax[1, 1].set_xlabel(r'$t$')
ax[1, 1].set_title(r'$\exp(-0.5t^3)$', y=0.8)
fig.subplots_adjust(hspace=0.1, wspace=0.1)
fig.tight_layout()
fig.show()
```

The first five lines of this code cell generate data to be plotted; the following lines generate a *figure* with a 2 × 2 *array* of *axes*. Note that `plt.subplots()` is called with the keyword arguments `sharex=True` and `sharey=True`, which means that all four *axes* share the same value ranges on their *x*-axis and *y*-axis. We then populate each *axes* with a curve, assign some axis labels where appropriate and titles utilizing *mathtext* (see Section 6.3.8). After all plots are generated, we adjust the horizontal and vertical spaces between the *axes* with **plt.subplots_adjust()** and we call **plt.tight_layout()** to minimize the margins around the *axes*.

Of course, there are no requirements that all *axes* in a *figure* must be of the same plot type, or of the same size. While Matplotlib offers a huge degree of flexibility here, generating flawless compound plots often requires a lot of hard work. We encourage the reader to play with the settings presented here to gain some experience, which will help to understand more complex features of Matplotlib.

6.9 Multidimensional Visualization

In many scientific problems, one does not just work in a two-dimensional setting but in a much higher dimensional space. This poses a problem for the visualization of measured and modeled data. In this section, we will investigate how we can utilize Matplotlib functionality for this task.

6.9.1 The Reduction to Two Dimensions

The screen and a paper page are both two dimensional, and so any representation of a three- or higher-dimensional object must ultimately be reduced to two dimensions.

A common approach is often called the **"cut plane" technique**, which imposes some arbitrary condition or conditions on the coordinates so as to reduce their dimensionality. The simplest and most common approach is to assume constant values for all but two of the coordinates, e.g., $z = z_0$, $w = w_0$, $\ldots$, thus giving a restricted but two-dimensional view of the object. Hopefully, by doing this several times for a (not too large) set of choices for z_0, w_0, $\ldots$, we will be able to recover valuable information about the object. An example of this approach is the contour curve procedure in Matplotlib mentioned in Section 6.7.

Other approaches exist, but we refer the interested reader to the literature in order to identify suitable methods to visualize highly dimensional data.

6.9.2 3D Plots

If your visualization problem is restricted to three dimensions (or you can find a three-dimensional representation for a subset of your problem), Matplotlib provides you some functionality to visualize your data. The crucial detail is that for 3d plots, `ax` must be an instance of the `Axes3d` class instead of `Axes`, which is achieved by instantiating with

```
fig, ax = plt.subplots(subplot_kw={'projection':'3d'})
```

or alternatively

```
fig = plt.figure()
ax = fig.add_subplot(projection='3d')
```

In this section, we shall consider three cases, with a concrete example for each. Our examples are artificial in the sense that they are predefined analytically. However, in setting them up we need to construct finite sets of discrete data. In the real world, we would instead use our own finite sets of discrete data, derived either from experiment or a complicated numerical simulation.

The first case we consider is that of a **parametrized curve** $\mathbf{x}(t) = (x(t), y(t), z(t))$, and as a specific example we consider the curve $C_{nm}(a)$:

$$x = (1 + a\cos(nt))\cos(mt), \quad y = (1 + a\cos(nt))\sin(mt), \quad z = a\sin(nt),$$

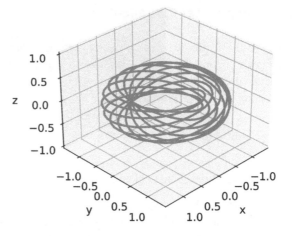

Figure 6.15 A 3d-plot of a parametrized curve plotted with `mplot3d()`.

where $t \in [0, 2\pi]$, n and m are *integers*, and $0 < a < 1$. This is a spiral wrapped around a circular torus, with major and minor radii 1 and a, respectively, a three-dimensional generalization of the well-known **Lissajous figures**. We visualize this parametrized curve with the next code cell using the **ax.mplot3d()** function and show the result in Figure 6.15:

```
theta = np.linspace(0, 2*np.pi, 401)
a, m, n = 0.3, 11, 9    # arbitrary parameters
x = (1 + a*np.cos(n*theta)) * np.cos(m*theta)
y = (1 + a*np.cos(n*theta)) * np.sin(m*theta)
z = a*np.sin(n*theta)

fig, ax = plt.subplots(subplot_kw={'projection':'3d'})
ax.plot(x, y, z, linewidth=2, color='grey')
ax.set_zlim3d(-1.0, 1.0)
ax.set_xlabel('x')
ax.set_ylabel('y')
ax.set_zlabel('z')
ax.elev, ax.azim = 30, 45
fig.show()
```

Note that since `ax` is here an `Axes3D` object, `ax.plot()` now takes three positional arguments. As you can probably guess, **ax.set_zlim3d()** sets the range in the z dimension and `ax.elev` and `ax.azim` set the initial viewing angle for the scene. When viewed interactively, it is possible to rotate and zoom the scene to get a better picture of it.

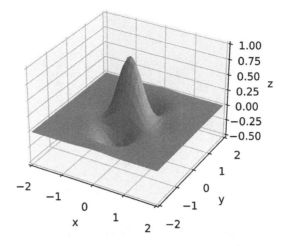

Figure 6.16 An example of a simple surface generated with plot_surface().

The second case we consider is that of a **surface** of the form $z = z(x, y)$. Here we consider the artificial but specific example:

$$z = e^{-2x^2-y^2} \cos(2x) \cos(3y) \quad \text{where } -2 \leqslant x \leqslant 2, -3 \leqslant y \leqslant 3.$$

We can plot this surface with the function **plt.plot_surface()** as shown in the following example code, the result of which is shown in Figure 6.16:

```
xx, yy = np.mgrid[-2:2:101j, -2:2:101j]
zz = np.exp(-2*xx**2-yy**2)*np.cos(2*xx)*np.cos(3*yy)

fig, ax = plt.subplots(subplot_kw={'projection':'3d'})
ax.plot_surface(xx, yy, zz, color='lightgrey')
ax.set_xlim3d(-2.0,2.0)
ax.set_ylim3d(-2.0,2.0)
ax.set_zlim3d(-0.5,1.0)
ax.set_xlabel('x')
ax.set_ylabel('y')
ax.set_zlabel('z')
fig.show()
```

If a "wire frame" representation of the surface is preferred, it can be obtained by simply replacing the call to ax.plot_surface() with **ax.plot_wireframe()**.

For the third and final case we consider here, we shall treat the more general case of a **parametrized surface** $x = x(u, v)$, $y = y(u, v)$, $z = z(u, v)$, which reduces to the case

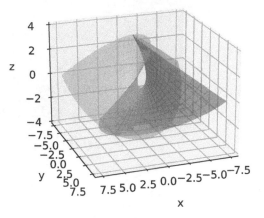

Figure 6.17 Enneper's surface visualized using `plot_surface()`, taking advantage of the concept of transparency.

if we choose $x = u$, $y = v$. As a concrete example, we consider the self-intersecting minimal surface discovered by Enneper:

$$x = u(1 - u^2/3 + v^2), \quad y = v(1 - v^2/3 + u^2), \quad z = u^2 - v^2 \quad \text{where } -2 \leqslant u, v \leqslant 2.$$

A code snippet to draw Figure 6.17 is:

```
[u,v] = np.mgrid[-2:2:51j, -2:2:61j]
x, y, z = u*(1-u**2/3+v**2), v*(1-v**2/3+u**2), u**2-v**2

fig, ax = plt.subplots(subplot_kw={'projection':'3d'})
ax.plot_surface(x.T, y.T, z.T, alpha=0.5, color='lightgrey')
ax.elev, ax.azim = 20, 70
ax.set_xlabel('x')
ax.set_ylabel('y')
ax.set_zlabel('z')
fig.show()
```

Notice first that the underlying code is based on image-processing conventions, and so the Matplotlib commands expect two-dimensional *arrays* to be supplied in image form. Thus we need to supply the transpose of the *x*-, *y*-, and *z-arrays*. It should be noted that this is a nontrivial self-intersecting surface, and its visualization requires a judicious choice of parameters. Further, the optimal choice may well depend on the viewing angle. There is a great deal of computation going on here, but rendering should be smooth even on older laptops.

This is a great time to remind the reader that Matplotlib supports interactive plotting (see Section 6.1.3). Using the corresponding line magic (`%matplotlib widget`) allows you to change the viewing angle on the fly and rotate the surface. It therefore helps you to find the best projection, which makes interactive plotting very useful for 3d visualizations. Please see the Jupyter Notebook for this chapter for an example.

6.10   References

Online resources

☐ General Matplotlib resources

   Project website
   https://matplotlib.org/

   Documentation
   https://matplotlib.org/stable/index.html

   User guide
   https://matplotlib.org/stable/users/index

   API reference
   https://matplotlib.org/stable/api/index

   Tutorials
   https://matplotlib.org/stable/tutorials/index.html

   Examples
   https://matplotlib.org/stable/plot_types/index.html

   Cheat sheet
   https://matplotlib.org/cheatsheets/

   Gallery
   https://matplotlib.org/stable/gallery/index.html

☐ Getting started: simple figures

   Quickstart
   https://matplotlib.org/stable/tutorials/introductory/usage.html

   Backends
   https://matplotlib.org/stable/users/explain/backends.html

☐ Object-oriented Matplotlib/Customizing plots

   Basic usage
   https://matplotlib.org/stable/tutorials/introductory/usage.html

   Pyplot reference
   https://matplotlib.org/stable/api/_as_gen/matplotlib.pyplot.html

   Legend reference
   https://matplotlib.org/stable/api/_as_gen/matplotlib.pyplot.legend.html

   Annotations
   https://matplotlib.org/stable/tutorials/text/annotations.html

Text in Matplotlib figures
`https://matplotlib.org/stable/tutorials/text/text_intro.html`

Writing mathematical expressions
`https://matplotlib.org/stable/tutorials/text/mathtext.html`

List of named colors
`https://matplotlib.org/stable/gallery/color/named_colors.html`

Specifying colors
`https://matplotlib.org/stable/tutorials/colors/colors.html`

Colormap reference
`https://matplotlib.org/stable/gallery/color/colormap_reference.html`

☐ Cartesian plots/Polar plots/Plotting images/Contour plots

Pyplot function reference
`https://matplotlib.org/stable/api/_as_gen/matplotlib.pyplot.html`

☐ Compound figures

Arranging multiple axes in a figure
`https://matplotlib.org/stable/tutorials/intermediate/arranging_axes.ht`
`ml`

☐ Multi-dimensional visualization

3d plotting
`https://matplotlib.org/stable/gallery/index.html#d-plotting`

7   SymPy: Symbolic Math

A *computer algebra system* (CAS) is a computer program designed to manipulate mathematical expressions in symbolic rather than numeric form, a task carried out routinely by theoretical scientists. There are a number of specialist programs, and some general purpose systems applicable to a wide range of problems, and it is the latter that we consider here. Perhaps the best known commercial systems are *Maple* and *Mathematica*. In this chapter, we introduce SymPy, which is a Python package for symbolic math applications that is written entirely in Python and can thus be used within a Python environment.

In this book and the accompanying Jupyter Notebook (cambridge.org/9781009029728/ch7), we follow the convention introduced by the SymPy documentation and import functionality from the package as needed. As a result, later code cells of this chapter rely upon imports performed in earlier code cells.

7.1   Symbols and Functions

When writing down algebra, one often uses expressions like

```
D = (x+y)*exp(x)*cos(y)
```

This will not work in SymPy, principally because SymPy is a Python library and so its syntax must conform to that of Python. The snippet fails, first because the *identifier* x is not defined. We have to associate x with a definite value, e.g., x = 4, and this defeats the purpose – we want to leave x and y to take unknown arbitrary values. SymPy gets around this by defining a new entity: a *symbol*, actually a Python class. There are several ways to create *symbol* instances, and perhaps the easiest way to define the *symbols* x and y is to use

```
from sympy import symbols

x, y = symbols('x y')
```

If we try to run the equation code cell now, Python will still complain because `exp(x)` and `cos(x)` are undefined. It recognizes a function, of course, but has no definition for the exponential of a *symbol*. SymPy contains such definitions. Let us combine everything in the following code cell:

```
from sympy import exp, cos

x, y = symbols("x y")
D = (x+y)*exp(x)*cos(y)
D
```

```
(x + y)*exp(x)*cos(y)
```

Before we talk about what happens here mathematically, we need to spend a few words on what is displayed here. Running this code cell in a Jupyter Notebook, you are likely to see a much prettier version of this output, which looks more like this:

$$(x + y)\, e^x\, cos(y)$$

The reason for this is that SymPy will check the environment you are working on (e.g., a Jupyter Notebook, the Python interpreter, etc.) and it selects a means of output that gives you the most visually appealing results. In the case of Jupyter Notebooks, *MathJax* is utilized to render your output in a very appealing way. You can invoke this "check" for rendering capabilities manually by calling the **sympy.init_printing()** function. Naturally, you can also use this function to select an output that suits you: please refer to the documentation for details. In the following, we make use of the `print()` function to obtain compact ASCII representations of the outputs, which are more print-friendly than fancier representations.

Now we get back to what is actually going on here. Notice that we never declared D as a *symbol*, because it was unnecessary. By definition it inherits all of the properties of the right-hand side of the declaration; see Section 3.2. The class `Symbol` contains definitions of all of the standard operations, e.g., addition, multiplication, exponentiation, etc., and so the right-hand side of the *D*-declaration is itself a *symbol*. All Python has to do is to associate the *identifier* D with it. In its simplest form, the *symbols* creation operator takes a *string* of one or more comma- or space-separated labels and returns a *tuple* of identifiers to the corresponding *symbols*. You could assign b, c, a = symbols("a b c"), but not if you valued your sanity. Note that these labels/*identifiers* can be of arbitrary length, and if it is a "standard" symbol with, e.g., a greek letter, then that should be shown on output. For example, if we were to declare `theta` to be a *symbol*, then the output should look like θ. SymPy knows about the standard labels. The *docstring* for `symbols()` offers several ways of mass-producing *symbols*, and careful study is highly recommended. It is important to realize early on that *symbols* must be immutable; see Section 3.5.4.

D is a known *function* of x and y. We usually also need unknown *functions*, e.g., $f(x, y)$ as well. They can be created by giving an additional keyword, identifying those new symbols as *functions*:

```
from sympy import Function

f, g = symbols("f g", cls=Function)
print(f(x), f(x, y), g(x))
```

```
f(x) f(x, y) g(x)
```

Notice that SymPy neither knows nor cares about the number of function arguments. It is the user's responsibility to check consistency of argument values.

Especially when considering simplification, it is helpful to know that certain *symbols* are always of a specific **type**. For a real-life example consider the equation, ubiquitous in complex variable courses, $z = x + iy$. It is tacitly assumed that both x and y take real values only. Otherwise the splitting into real and imaginary parts does not make sense. Within SymPy, suppose that i and j take integer values, while u and v are always real. This is indicated by

```
i, j = symbols("i j", integer=True)
u, v = symbols("u v", real=True)
i.is_integer, j*j,  (j*j).is_integer, u.is_real
```

```
(True, j**2, True, True)
```

Note how we check for integer types with **is_integer** and real types with **is_real**, both of which are attributes (see Section 3.11).

As can be seen from the output of this code cell, neither i nor j represent $\sqrt{-1}$ in SymPy. It is catered for as **sympy.I**. Also very useful are e, π, and ∞, available as **sympy.E**, **sympy.pi**, and **sympy.oo**, respectively.

As we have said, expressions are immutable. So how does one find out the result of **substituting specific values** for, say, x and y in D? This is done with the substitution operator, which is available either as a function **sympy.subs()**, or more commonly, as a class method (**sympy.symbols.subs()**). For instance, to find D when **x=0**:

```
D0 = D.subs(x, 0)
D0pi = D0.subs(y, sympy.pi)
print(D0, D0pi, D.subs([(x, 0), (y, sympy.pi)]))
```

```
y*cos(y) −pi −pi
```

Here, the third element shows how to make many substitutions at once using a *list* of (old, new) *tuples*. We repeat: *symbols* such as D are immutable, and so D is not changed by the substitution operation in the first line.

7.2   Conversions from Python to SymPy and Vice Versa

Suppose x and y are *symbols*. So are x+1 and 0.5*y. The *integer* and *float* are widened to *symbols*. Fractions need a little care. Consider this line:

```
x + 1/3
```

```
x + 0.333333333333333
```

Python parses "1/3" as *float*, which is correct, but probably not really charming to the eye. **sympy.Rational()** provides a means to represent rational numbers:

```
from sympy import Rational

print(x + Rational(1, 3))
print(Rational('0.5')*y)
```

```
x + 1/3
y/2
```

Although Rational() is extremely useful, there are other more user-friendly ways to achieve the same effect.

sympy.S() converts singleton expressions, given as strings, to their *SymPy* equivalents. Compare the code cell above with this:

```
from sympy import S

print(x + S('1/3'))
print(S("1/2")*y)
```

```
x + 1/3
y/2
```

Similarly, the function **sympy.sympify() converts arbitrary expressions**, given as *strings*, to their SymPy equivalents. It is assumed that all relevant *symbols* have already been declared as such. Two examples are explored here:

```
from sympy import sympify

D_s = sympify('(x+y)*exp(x)*cos(y)')
cosdiff = sympify("cos(x)*cos(y) + sin(x)*sin(y)")
print(D_s)
print(cosdiff)
```

```
(x + y)*exp(x)*cos(y)
sin(x)*sin(y) + cos(x)*cos(y)
```

D_s should behave in an identical manner to the D defined earlier.

We saw that `sympy.subs()` provides symbolic function evaluations. If you prefer **numerical values** for function evaluations, you can obtain those with `sympy.evalf()`, which takes a single optional *integer* argument, the precision. Consider the following example:

```
cospi4 = cosdiff.subs([(x, sympy.pi/2), (y, sympy.pi/4)])
print((cospi4, cospi4.evalf(), cospi4.evalf(6)))
```

```
(sqrt(2)/2, 0.707106781186548, 0.707107).
```

After substituting x and y with corresponding values, we can see three different outputs: `subs()` returns the symbolic result, `evalf()` returns the numerical result with some default precision, and `evalf(6)` returns the same numerical result with a precision of six digits.

A different way to evaluate functions numerically is provided with `sympy.N()`. Be aware that N(`<expr>`, `<args>`) actually serves as a wrapper and is the equivalent of using `sympify(<expr>).evalf(<args>)`.

All of this is perfectly adequate for a few selected values of the arguments, but what if we want to use the expression as a function, preferably a *ufunc* in the sense of Section 4.2.1? The SymPy function `sympy.lambdify()` does precisely that. It takes as arguments a *tuple* of the function arguments, the name of the expression, and the Python base library to be used. In practice, it's extremely easy:

```
from sympy import lambdify

func = lambdify((x, y), cosdiff, 'numpy')
xn = np.linspace(0, 2*np.pi, 4)
func(xn, 0.0)
```

```
array([ 1. , −0.5, −0.5,  1. ])
```

7.3   Matrices and Vectors

For the sake of completeness, we introduce matrices and vectors at this point. SymPy implements matrices with the **Matrix** class, and an *n*-vector as an $n \times 1$ matrix. The constructor requires an ordered *list* of rows, where each row is an ordered *list* of elements. As an example, we create a matrix:

```
from sympy import Matrix

M = Matrix([[1, x], [y, 1]])
M
```

```
Matrix([[1, x], [y, 1]])
```

a vector:

```
V = Matrix([[u], [v]])
print(V)
```

```
Matrix([[u], [v]])
```

and compute the product of both:

```
print(M*V)
```

```
Matrix([[u + v*x], [u*y + v]])
```

which, of course, uses matrix multiplication in this case (unlike NumPy; see Section 4.7.1). A surprisingly large number of functions/methods can be applied to matrices. Unfortunately, we can only introduce a small subsample and will need to leave it to the reader to explore SymPy's full matrix capabilities.

One useful method of the `Matrix` class is **eigenvects()**, which returns a *list* of *tuples*, where each *tuple* contains an eigenvalue, multiplicity, and a basis for the eigenvectors. For square matrices, the transpose (**M.T**), determinant (**M.det()**), and inverse (**M.inv()**) are readily available as attributes or class methods.

Before we let the reader explore the matrix capabilities of SymPy, we would like to point out an important detail. We stated above that symbols were immutable. This assertion needs to be qualified, and at this point the beginner might like to review the same issue for *lists*; see Section 3.5.4. A matrix M is immutable, but its content may be changed freely:

```
M[0,1]= u
M
```

```
Matrix([[1, u], [y, 1]])
```

7.4 Some Elementary Calculus

7.4.1 Differentiation

Suppose D is defined as in Section 7.1. We can use **sympy.diff()** to derive the first-order derivative of D with respect to x:

```
from sympy import diff

print(diff(D, x))
```

```
(x + y)*exp(x)*cos(y) + exp(x)*cos(y)
```

Alternatively, we could also use D.diff(x) resulting in the same expression. This second version relies on the fact that D is a *symbol* object. Higher derivatives are computed by providing the order as additional argument, e.g.,

```
print(D.diff(x, 2))
```

```
(x + y + 2)*exp(x)*cos(y)
```

or simply by adding more variable identifiers,

```
print(D.diff(x, x))
```

```
(x + y + 2)*exp(x)*cos(y)
```

Sometimes we may not wish to compute the derivative explicitly, so-called **"lazy" differentiation**. This is accomplished by the **sympy.Derivative()** function: note the capital letter. If, later, we want to carry out the evaluation, then the class method doit() carries out the postponed calculation:

```
from sympy import Derivative

D_xyy = Derivative(D, x, y, 2)
print(D_xyy, D_xyy.doit())
```

```
Derivative((x + y)*exp(x)*cos(y), x, (y, 2)) -((x + y)*cos(y) + 2*sin
    (y) + cos(y))*exp(x)
```

7.4.2 Integration

Indefinite integration is the inverse of differentiation and SymPy treats it accordingly. As with all computer algebra systems, the "constant of integration" is never shown explicitly. The following code cell integrates function D indefinitely over y, utilizing the **sympy.integrate()** function and the **sympy.symbols.integrate()** method:

```
from sympy import integrate

print(integrate(D, y))
print(D.integrate(y))
```

```
(x*sin(y) + y*sin(y) + cos(y))*exp(x)
(x*sin(y) + y*sin(y) + cos(y))*exp(x)
```

Naturally, indefinite integration over x and y works just the same way:

```
print(integrate(D, x, y))
print(D.integrate(x, y))
```

```
(x*sin(y) + y*sin(y) - sin(y) + cos(y))*exp(x)
(x*sin(y) + y*sin(y) - sin(y) + cos(y))*exp(x)
```

"Lazy" integration is handled by the **sympy.Integral()** function:

```
from sympy import Integral

yD = Integral(D, y)
print(yD)
print(yD.doit())
```

```
Integral((x + y)*exp(x)*cos(y), y)
(x*sin(y) + y*sin(y) + cos(y))*exp(x)
```

Definite integration works very similarly. One simply provides integration parameters in the form of a *tuple* (<variable>, <lower limit>, <upper limit>):

```
print(integrate(D, (y, 0, sympy.pi)),
      D.integrate((y, 0, sympy.pi)))
```

```
-2*exp(x) -2*exp(x)
```

Multiple definite integrals are handled in the obvious way:

```
print(integrate(exp(-x**2-y**2), (x, 0, sympy.oo),
                (y, 0, sympy.oo)))
```

```
pi/4
```

Of course, there is also a "lazy" version:

```
dint = Integral(exp(-x**2-y**2), (x, 0, sympy.oo),
                (y, 0, sympy.oo))
```

```
print(dint)
print(dint.doit())
```

```
Integral(exp(-x**2 - y**2), (x, 0, oo), (y, 0, oo))
pi/4
```

As every practicing scientist knows, differentiation is a reasonably straightforward operation. One needs to know the derivatives of a few elementary functions, the "product" or "Leibniz" rule, and the rule for differentiating a function of a function. The rest is algebra, and is readily automated.

Integration can be very much harder. Certainly one needs to know plenty of standard integrals, including the definitions of many "special functions." For instance, the indefinite integral of the Gaussian function e^{-x^2} cannot be expressed in terms of elementary functions, and so mathematicians have defined it as an *error function*:

$$erf(z) = \frac{2}{\sqrt{\pi}} \int_0^z e^{-u^2}\, du.$$

These problems are amenable to automation. However, the Achilles heel of all integrators is the following: one may need several changes of independent variables in order to reduce a given integral to a standard one. Such changes are learned by experience, and offer a serious problem to computer scientists. Thus it is an ongoing challenge to developers to include enough algorithms to handle tricky cases. SymPy has no problems with the following two examples, although it might take some time to receive the results:

```
from sympy import sqrt

print(integrate(sqrt(x+sqrt(x**2+1))/x, x))
```

```
sqrt(x)*gamma(-1/4)**2*gamma(1/4)*
hyper((-1/4, -1/4, 1/4), (1/2, 3/4),
    exp_polar(I*pi)/x**2)/(8*pi*gamma(3/4))
```

```
from sympy import sin

print(integrate(exp(-x)*sin(x**2)/x, (x, 0, sympy.oo)))
```

```
sqrt(2)*(-gamma(-1/4)*gamma(1/4)*hyper((1/2, 1), (3/4, 5/4, 3/2),
    -1/64)/4 + pi*fresnelc(sqrt(2)/(2*sqrt(pi)))*gamma(-1/4)*gamma
    (1/4)/2 - 3*pi*fresnels(sqrt(2)/(2*sqrt(pi)))*gamma(-3/4)*gamma
    (-1/4)*gamma(5/4)/(2*gamma(1/4)) + pi*gamma(1/4)*gamma(3/4))/(8*
    pi)
```

If SymPy cannot integrate your expression, it will eventually, after trying all of its store of algorithms, return the "lazy" integral form, a mark of failure. This can be deceptive, so please be aware.

7.4.3 Series and Limits

Suppose we really wanted to know the value of that last integral, at least for moderate values of x. We first define

```
foo = exp(sin(x))
```

We could consider first expanding foo as a Taylor series in x. This ought to be uniformly convergent for arbitrary y. Then term-by-term integration should give a useful approximation. SymPy allows us to calculate, e.g., the first 10 terms in the **Taylor series expansion** with **sympy.symbols.series()** and integrate it:

```
foo_ser = foo.series(x, 0, 10)
foo_ser.integrate(x)
```

```
x + x**2/2 + x**3/6 - x**5/40 - x**6/90 - x**7/1680 + x**8/720 + 31*x
    **9/51840 + x**10/56700 + O(x**11)
```

As expected, we obtain the expansion up to order 10; the remainder term obeys the usual applied mathematicians' "big-Oh" rules. If it bothers you, then remove it via a class method, e.g.:

```
print(foo_ser.integrate(x).removeO())
```

```
x**10/56700 + 31*x**9/51840 + x**8/720 - x**7/1680 - x**6/90 - x
    **5/40 + x**3/6 + x**2/2 + x
```

(Note the reversed order of terms.)

Limits are handled in a straightforward way, e.g.:

```
from sympy import limits

print(limit((foo-1-x)/x**2, x, 0))
```

```
1/2
```

At points of discontinuity, limits from below and from above will differ. By default limit() takes the limit from above, but both limits are readily available:

```
goo = 1/(x - 1)
print(limit(goo, x, 1, dir="-"))
print(limit(goo, x, 1, dir='+'))
```

```
−oo
oo
```

7.5   Equality, Symbolic Equality and Simplification

As our snapshot of some of SymPy's capabilities has shown, it can create quite complicated expressions, which might not be immediately useful to the user. Can we simplify
them? How would we test two long expressions to see if they were the same?

Let us start from pure Python. As we have seen, the "equals" sign (=) has nothing to
do with equality; it is the Python assignment operator (e.g., a=3), and SymPy of course
respects this. **Numerical equality** is handled by the double equality sign ==, e.g.:

```
12/3 == 4
```

```
True
```

Unfortunately for the end user, the SymPy developers have reserved == for "**Symbolic
equality**", which is not what the user wants. As an example, consider the two expressions:

```
ex1 = (x+y)**2
ex2 = x**2 + 2*x*y + y**2
ex1 == ex2
```

```
False
```

They are not "symbolically equal," for one is a product of sums, while the other is a sum
of products. Fortunately, SymPy can resolve this impasse. We can expand expressions
with **sympy.expand()** or **sympy.symbols.expand()**:

```
from sympy import expand

print(expand(ex1))
print(ex1.expand())
```

```
x**2 + 2*x*y + y**2
x**2 + 2*x*y + y**2
```

and we can factor expressions with **sympy.factor()** or **sympy.symbols.factor()**:

```
from sympy import factor
```

```
print(factor(ex2))
print(ex2.factor())
```

```
(x + y)**2
(x + y)**2
```

Both methods do what we might expect and we can exploit them for our problem:

```
print(ex1.expand() == ex2)
print(ex1 == ex2.factor())
```

```
True
True
```

expand() is an extraordinarily versatile function and we refer to its documentation for details. In particular there are many ways to extend its scope to more specialized expressions, e.g., **sympy.expand_trig()** for trigonometric expressions:

```
from sympy import expand_trig

print(expand_trig(sin(x+y)))
print(expand(cos(x−y), trig=True))
```

```
sin(x)*cos(y) + sin(y)*cos(x)
sin(x)*sin(y) + cos(x)*cos(y)
```

One has to be particularly careful when treating powers, because a number of apparent identities are not true. For example it is not true that $(x^a)^b \equiv x^{ab}$ in general; e.g., $\sqrt{x^2} \neq x$, for a simple counterexample is $((-1)^2)^{1/2} = 1 \neq (-1)^{2\times1/2} = (-1)^1 = -1$. However, the identity is true if b is an *integer*. Similarly it is not true that $x^a y^a \equiv (xy)^a$, try $x = y = -1, a = 1/2$. This identity does hold if both x and y are positive real numbers and a is real. SymPy is well aware of these problems and will not use these identities unless the user defined the Symbols with the appropriate restrictions in sympy.symbols().

An extremely useful function is **sympy.cancel()** which will take any rational expression and try to reduce it to canonical form. As an example, consider the matrix M defined and altered in Section 7.3:

```
A = M*M.inv()
print(A)
```

```
Matrix([[−u*y/(−u*y + 1) + 1/(−u*y + 1), 0], [0, −u*y/(−u*y + 1) +
    1/(−u*y + 1)]])
```

This is hard to read, but the result is definitely not the identity matrix. We apply cancel() to get canonical forms of the nonzero elements of A:

```
A[1,0] = A[1,0].cancel()
A[1,1] = A[1,1].cancel()
print(A)
```

```
Matrix([[1, 0], [0, 1]])
```

Yes, this is now clearly the identity matrix.

To see why `cancel()` is not a default option, have a look at this simple example (we abstain from printing the entire result here as our modest contribution to forest conservation):

```
c = (x**256 - 1)/(x-1)
print(c)
print(c.cancel())
```

```
(x**256 - 1)/(x - 1)
x**255 + x**254 + x**253 + x**252 + x**251 + x**250 ...
... + x**4 + x**3 + x**2 + x + 1
```

7.6   Solving Equations

Readers of the last section could argue, with some justification, that there appears to be no way of defining an "equation," since = and == have both been used up. Traditionally, an equation has both a left hand side, *lhs*, and a right hand side, *rhs*. Using definitions from before, let us set:

```
lhs = D
rhs = cosdiff
```

There are two ways in SymPy to create an **equation**, both given in the following code cell:

```
from sympy import Eq

eqn1 = Eq(lhs, rhs)
eqn2 = lhs - rhs
print(eqn1)
print(eqn2)
```

```
Eq((x + y)*exp(x)*cos(y), sin(x)*sin(y) + cos(x)*cos(y))
(x + y)*exp(x)*cos(y) - sin(x)*sin(y) - cos(x)*cos(y)
```

The expression `eqn1` produces the traditional form of an equation as an instance of **sympy.Eq**. The second, `eqn2`, is equally valid in contexts where an equation is expected. SymPy implicitly adds the missing =0.

The universal workhorse to solve equations is **sympy.solvers.solve()** (see Section 7.6.3), but for equations in one variable, **sympy.solveset()** (see Section 7.6.1) is recommended, while one is asked to use **sympy.linsolve()** (see Section 7.6.2) for linear systems of equations.

7.6.1   Equations with One Independent Variable

Simple univariate equations, written as expressions, are straightforward. For example:

```
from sympy import solveset

print(solveset(4*x−3, x))
print(solveset(3*x**3−16*x**2+23*x−6, x))
```

```
{3/4}
{1/3, 2, 3}
```

As the name suggests, `solveset()` returns a set of solutions, and so multiplicities are ignored. However, **sympy.roots()** can supply these:

```
from sympy import roots

quad = x**2 − 2*x + 1
print(solveset(quad, x))
print(roots(quad))
```

```
{1}
{1: 2}
```

Simple transcendental equations are solved over the complex plane, by default:

```
solveset(exp(x)−1, x)
```

```
ImageSet(Lambda(_n, 2*_n*I*pi), Integers)
```

This output seems a little cryptic; the rendered version probably makes more sense:

$$\{2ni\pi|n \in \mathbb{Z}\}$$

.

If `solveset()` cannot solve an equation, it returns a cop-out:

```
print(solveset(cos(x) − x, x))
```

```
ConditionSet(x, Eq(-x + cos(x), 0), Complexes)
```

The output is mathematics jargon for the following: x is a complex number that is also a member of the set of numbers satisfying $\cos x = x$!

7.6.2   Linear Equations with More than One Independent Variable

This is not a straightforward topic, and it is hard to find a clear concise account. In the following paragraphs, we look, in an abstract way, at a system of n linear equations in n unknowns. For the remainder of this section, we look at the simplest case, $n = 2$. Readers unfamiliar with the ideas in the next paragraphs should skip forward and backward between here and the following paragraphs, which provide a real-life example.

Let A be a $n \times n$ matrix with constant components, and let b be a given n-vector. Our aim is to solve the nth order linear system:

$$A x = b$$

for an n-vector of unknowns, x. The general case is also the simplest. This is when A is nonsingular, i.e., $\det A \neq 0$. Then the inverse A^{-1} exists, and so there is a unique solution:

$$x = A^{-1}b.$$

Next, suppose A is singular. Consider first the set of vectors k such that $Ak = 0$. This is called the *kernel* of A. It is easy to see that the *kernel* is actually a vector space. (Note that in the previous case, A nonsingular, the *kernel* is an empty set.) There is another vector space associated with A, its *range*, which is the set of vectors r such that one can find an x such that $Ax = r$. As an aside, there is an important result that the sum of the dimensions of the *kernel* and *range* is n. We can now split the case A is singular into two subcases. Suppose first that the given vector b lies in the *range*. Then, by definition, we can find an x_0 such that $Ax_0 = b$. However, consider $x = x_0 + k$, where k is an arbitrary vector in the *kernel*. Then $Ax = A(x_0 + k) = Ax_0 + Ak = b + 0 = b$. Hence, we have solutions, but infinitely many of them! However, if b is not in the *range*, then there are no solutions at all – the equations are inconsistent.

Let us consider some concrete examples in two dimensions. Suppose

$$A = \begin{pmatrix} 1 & 2 \\ 3 & 4 \end{pmatrix}, \qquad b = \begin{pmatrix} 0 \\ 2 \end{pmatrix};$$

in other words, we are considering the linear system:

$$x + 2y = 0, \quad 3x + 4y = 2.$$

Computing the inverse of A is a highly inefficient approach to finding the solution. Elementary methods, or Gaussian elimination, quickly show $x = 2$, $y = -1$. Next, we consider a singular A and set, say,

$$A = \begin{pmatrix} 1 & 2 \\ 2 & 4 \end{pmatrix} \qquad A \begin{pmatrix} x \\ y \end{pmatrix} = \begin{pmatrix} x + 2y \\ 2x + 4y \end{pmatrix} = \begin{pmatrix} X \\ Y \end{pmatrix}.$$

We see that the *range* of A is the set of vectors $(X, Y)^T$ such that $Y = 2X$, while the *kernel* is the set of vectors $(x, y)^T$ such that $x = -2y$. Here both are one-dimensional. Suppose first that $b = (1, 2)^T$, i.e., we are considering the linear system:

$$x + 2y = 1, \quad 2x + 4y = 2.$$

Then by elementary methods we find

$$x = 1 - 2\lambda, \ y = \lambda, \quad \lambda \text{ arbitrary.}$$

It should be evident that the λ-contribution comes from the *kernel*. Finally, consider the case $b = (1, 1)^T$, which is not in the range. The linear system

$$x + 2y = 1, \quad 2x + 4y = 1$$

has no solutions!

We now examine how SymPy's `linsolve()` handles these three possibilities. Obviously this is gross overkill for such simple systems, but the examples generalize in the obvious way to much more complicated problems.

One approach is to specify the equations in scalar form within a list. For an explicit example we consider the nonsingular case. We also need to specify a list of the unknowns:

```
from sympy import linsolve

eqns = [x+2*y, 3*x+4*y-2]
print(linsolve(eqns, [x,y]))
```

```
{(2, -1)}
```

In many cases, it will be more convenient to specify the system matrix A and the right-hand-side vector b. We consider the many-valued solution case:

```
A = Matrix([[1, 2], [2, 4]])
b = Matrix([[1], [2]])
print(linsolve((A, b), [x, y]))
```

```
{(1 - 2*y, y)}
```

Here the solution is to be interpreted as follows: y can take arbitrary values, and then $x = 1 - 2y$ is determined.

If the equations are the output from some other function, they are frequently supplied in augmented matrix form, i.e., the b-vector is adjoined as an extra last column to the A-matrix. We illustrate this example with the final example discussed:

```
A_b = Matrix([[1, 2, 1], [2, 4, 2]])
print(linsolve(A_b, [x, y]))
```

```
{(1 − 2*y, y)}
```

7.6.3   More General Equations

The SymPy function `solve()` is the universal workhorse for nonlinear equations, or systems of such equations. As a first example, consider the following system of equations as we run it through `solve()`:

```
from sympy.solvers import solve

neq = [y**2 − x**2 − 2*x −1, 3*x − y −1]
print(solve(neq, [x, y]))
```

```
[(0, −1), (1, 2)]
```

Next consider some equations involving square roots:

```
print(solve([sqrt(x) − sqrt(y) −1, sqrt(x+y) − 2], [x ,y]))
```

```
[(sqrt(7)/2 + 2, 2 − sqrt(7)/2)]
```

However, problems arise when we consider nth roots, where n is an odd integer, i.e., $3, 5, \ldots$. As a concrete example consider the two equations

$$\sqrt[3]{3x + 1} = x + 1, \qquad \sqrt[3]{3x - 1} = x - 1.$$

By cubing each equation, one sees that the solutions are, respectively,

$$x = -3, 0, 0, \qquad x = 0, 0, 3.$$

On the other hand, `solve()` returns only parts of these solutions:

```
from sympy import root

eq1 = root(3*x+1, 3) − x − 1
eq2 = root(3*x−1, 3) − x + 1
print(solve(eq1, x), solve(eq2, x))
```

```
[0] [3]
```

What has gone wrong? In the first case, the root $x = -3$ is missing, for which $\sqrt[3]{3x + 1} = \sqrt[3]{-8} = -2$. In the second, the root $x = 0$ is missing, for which $\sqrt[3]{3x - 1} = \sqrt[3]{-1} = -1$.

The default version of `solve()` ignores the cube roots of negative numbers! However, setting the flag `check` to `False` corrects this errant behavior:

```
print(solve(eq1, x, check=False), solve(eq2, x, check=False))
```

```
[-3, 0] [0, 3]
```

Many equations have no known analytic solutions. If a **numerical solution** is acceptable, then SymPy offers a variant **sympy.solvers.nsolve()** which does that:

```
from sympy.solver import nsolve

print(nsolve(eq1, x, 0))
print(nsolve(eq2, x, 0))
```

```
0
3.0 + 6.34781618646896e-51*I
```

`nsolve()` requires an initial guess for the solution; we use zero in both cases. Although the second solution is a complex number, its imaginary part is negligible and thus the solution is 3.

7.6.4   Solving Ordinary Differential Equations

A surprisingly large gamut of theoretical science is ruled by ordinary differential equations, and unfortunately only a few of them can be solved analytically, the subject of this section. The overwhelming majority need numerical treatment, and this difficult topic was explored in Section 5.8.

Turning to analytical solutions, we remark first that the novice should not expect miracles. Note that solving the indefinite integral $y = \int f(x)\,dx$ is equivalent to solving the differential equation $dy/dx = f(x)$, and so the problems attendant on the first exercise carry over to the second. SymPy will be able to solve only a limited range of ordinary differential equations. In this discussion, we will introduce the tools provided by SymPy, which should enable the reader to approach more complex problems with the help of the corresponding documentation.

SymPy's main workhorse for solving ODEs is **sympy.solvers.ode.dsolve()**. We start with some examples of what `dsolve()` can do and what it cannot do. Let us start with a single linear equation with constant coefficients:

```
from sympy import Function
from sympy.solvers.ode import dsolve

f = Function('f')
ode = f(x).diff(x, 2) + 4*f(x)
```

```
sol = dsolve(ode, f(x))
print(sol)
```

```
Eq(f(x), C1*sin(2*x) + C2*cos(2*x))
```

As usual by default, " $= 0$" is missing from the differential equation. Alternatively, one could use `ode = Eq(f(x).diff(x, 2) + 4*f(x), 0)` for more clarity. The correct general solution is given, which includes two integration constants `C1`, `C2`, displayed as C_1, C_2. Now suppose we would like to impose initial conditions, say, $f(0) = 2$, $f'(0) = 0$. We can provide a *dictionary* of these initial conditions to the keyword argument `ics` in the following way:

```
print(dsolve(ode, f(x), ics={f(x).subs(x, 0): 2,
                             f(x).diff(x).subs(x, 0): 0}))
```

```
Eq(f(x), 2*cos(2*x))
```

As we see, $C_1 = 0$ and $C_2 = 2$ for this set of initial conditions and the particular solution is given by

```
psol = sol.subs([('C2', 2), ('C1', 0)])
psol
```

```
Eq(f(x), 2*cos(2*x))
```

Those first-order nonlinear equations that are "exact" are solved quickly:

```
ode2 = sin(f(x)) + (x*cos(f(x)) + f(x))*f(x).diff(x)
print(dsolve(ode2, f(x)))
```

```
Eq(C1 + x*sin(f(x)) + f(x)**2/2, 0)
```

First-order equations with quadratic terms are often of *Bernoulli* type and usually yield an exact solution:

```
from sympy import log

ode3 = x*f(x).diff(x) + f(x) − log(x)*f(x)**2
print(dsolve(ode3))
```

```
Eq(f(x), 1/(C1*x + log(x) + 1))
```

Notice that if there is only one dependent variable, as here, it is not necessary to specify it as an argument to `dsolve()`.

Certain linear equations with variable coefficients are also easy to solve, e.g., an inhomogeneous *Euler* equation:

```
ode4 = f(x).diff(x, 2)*x**2 − 4*f(x).diff(x)*x + 6*f(x) − x**3
print(dsolve(ode4))
```

```
Eq(f(x), x**2*(C1 + C2*x + x*log(x)))
```

Some equations yield only to the solution by series technique:

```
ode5 = x*(f(x).diff(x, 2)) + 2*(f(x).diff(x)) + x*f(x)
print(dsolve(ode5))
```

```
Eq(f(x), (C1*besselj(1/2, x) + C2*bessely(1/2, x))/sqrt(x))
```

Besides equations in one variable, we can also solve **equations with two or more variables**:

```
ode6 = [f(x).diff(x) − 2*f(x) − g(x), g(x).diff(x) −f(x) − 2*g(x)]
print(dsolve(ode6))
```

```
[Eq(f(x), −C1*exp(x) + C2*exp(3*x)),
 Eq(g(x), C1*exp(x) + C2*exp(3*x))]
```

However, there is a serious limitation for elementary solvers such as `dsolve()`. In many real-world examples the given equation is not of a standard form, but is related to one via a simple transformation. Alas, `dsolve()` cannot deal with this. A simple example suffices to illustrate the problem, viz., $f'(x) = (x + f)^2$:

```
print(dsolve(f(x).diff(x) − (x + f(x))**2))
```

```
Eq(f(x), (−C1*x + I*C1 + x*exp(2*I*x) + I*exp(2*I*x))/
        (C1 − exp(2*I*x)))
```

`dsolve()` returns as a default the power series expansion about $x = 0$. However, consider the simple transformation $g(x) = x + f(x)$. This transforms the differential equation into one with the independent variable absent, $g'(x) = 1 + g^2$:

```
print(dsolve(g(x).diff(x) −1 − (g(x))**2))
```

```
Eq(g(x), −tan(C1 − x))
```

Thus the solution of `dsolve(f(x).diff(x) − (x + f(x))**2)` is $f(x) = \tan(x - C_1) - x$, which `dsolve()` has failed to pick up.

7.6.5   Solving Partial Differential Equations

SymPy provides some limited functionality to solve partial differential equations (PDEs) as part of the `sympy.solvers.pde` module. Due to the rather specific nature of PDEs and to keep this book reasonably short, we simply refer the interested reader to the corresponding documentation.

7.7   Plotting from within SymPy

In Chapter 6, we already introduced Matplotlib as a graphics workhorse capable of producing top-quality plots, and most scientist users will need to gain familiarity with it. Its input is numerical data, typically in NumPy *array* format. SymPy produces expressions, which are not quite the same thing. However, we saw in Section 7.2 that the `lambdify()` function can be used to transmogrify expressions into NumPy functions, exactly what is needed.

However, SymPy will often be used as an exploratory tool, and it would be very useful to provide a built in graphics facility without all of the cosmetic features of full Matplotlib. SymPy provides a `plotting` module, based, of course, on Matplotlib, for this purpose. It produces fully functional graphics functions in two and three dimensions, including some features not available in Matplotlib. In the following, we will only briefly introduce some limited plotting capabilities and leave it to the interested reader to explore other options.

For **line plots** we can utilize SymPy's version of Matplotlib's `plot()` (see Section 6.4.1), which is called **sympy.plotting.plot()**, but has a syntax that is rather different.

```
from sympy.plotting import plot
fig1 = plot(sin(x), x, x**2, (x, -4, 4),
            title='Plotting Sines with SymPy')
```

The output is shown in Figure 7.1; it is not ideal, but it is serviceable. In contrast to Matplotlib's `plot()` (see Section 6.4.1), the SymPy version takes as arguments an arbitrary number of functions, a *tuple* indicating the variable and ranges over which to plot, `(x, -4, 4)`, and you can directly assign a title label.

We turn next to **two-dimensional curves defined implicitly**. Matplotlib's `plot()` function required no modification to handle these. However, SymPy has a special function, **sympy.plotting.plot_parametric()**, for this purpose, which we illustrate with a simple case:

$$(x, y) = (\cos\theta + \tfrac{1}{2}\cos 7\theta + \tfrac{1}{3}\cos 17\theta, \ \sin\theta + \tfrac{1}{2}\sin 7\theta + \tfrac{1}{3}\sin 17\theta).$$

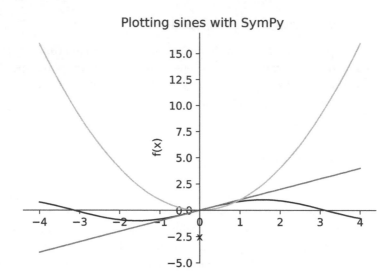

Figure 7.1 A simple line plot for different functions generated with SymPy's `plot()` function.

Notice in the code here, that we never need to specify the number of evaluation points. The SymPy function can determine what it thinks is needed. Of course, if it gets it wrong, there is always a manual override:

```
from sympy.plotting import plot_parametric
xc = cos(u) + cos(7*u)/2 + sin(17*u)/3
yc = sin(u) + sin(7*u)/2 + cos(17*u)/3
fig2 = plot_parametric(xc, yc, (u, 0, 2*sympy.pi))
```

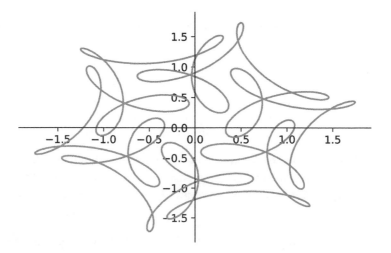

Figure 7.2 A parametrically defined curve using SymPy's `plot_parametric()` function.

The output is shown in Figure 7.2. Because Matplotlib is in control, by giving the plot object a name, here `fig2`, we can save it to a file, say `foo.pdf` via an extra line, using a class method:

```
fig2.save('foo.pdf')
```

SymPy plotting contains a functionality not present in Matplotlib, the ability to **plot one or more curves defined implicitly** in the plane. This feat can be accomplished with the function **sympy.plotting.plot_implicit()**. We consider the curve described by $x^2 + xy + y^2 = 1$, which is an ellipse, but it is not so easy to give it in explicit or parametric form. The input to `plot_implicit()` is the equation, and the ranges of the independent variables, resulting in Figure 7.3:

```
from sympy.plotting import plot_implicit
fig3 = plot_implicit(x**2+x*y+y**2 - 1, (x,-1.5,1.5),
                     (y,-1.5,1.5))
```

We now give an example with more complicated data. We are aiming to determine the curve in the complex plane given by $|\cos(z^2)| = 1$, where $z = x + iy$, and x and y are real. We first redefine x and y within SymPy, ensuring that they take only real values. We then define $z = x + iy$ and $w = \cos(z^2)$. We need to expand it in the form $w = X + iY$ for suitable X and Y, and that is what the next line does. Next we form $wa = |w|$ with the same expansion rules. (The reader may wish to review the relevant *docstrings* at this point.) Finally drawing it is straightforward:

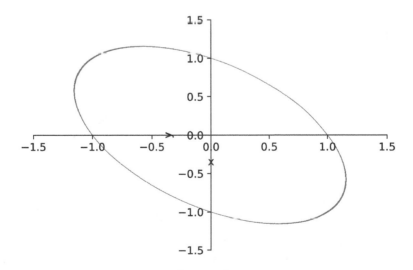

Figure 7.3 The implicitly defined curve $x^2 + xy + y^2 = 1$ generated with Sympy's `plot_implicit()` function.

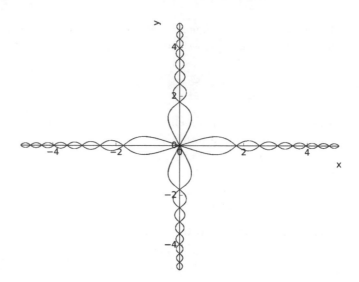

Figure 7.4 The implicitly defined curve $|\cos((x + iy)^2)| = 1$ generated with SymPy's `plot_implicit()` function.

```
from sympy import Abs

x, y = symbols("x y", real=True)
z = x + sympy.I*y
w = cos(z**2).expand(complex=True)
wa = Abs(w).expand(complex=True)
fig4 = plot_implicit(wa**2- 1)
```

The output is shown in Figure 7.4.

Our final example is to describe graphically the intersection in the positive quadrant of the two regions defined by $x^2 + y^2 < 4$ and $xy > 1$, respectively, i.e., the region within the circle that lies above the hyperbola branch. We need the function **sympy.And** to take both inequalities into account. The result is shown in Figure 7.5:

```
from sympy import And

fig5 = plot_implicit(And(x**2 + y**2 < 4, x*y > 1), (x,0,2),
                     (y, 0, 2), line_color='lightgrey')
```

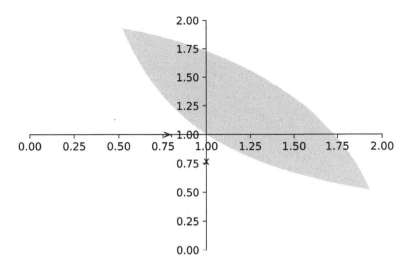

Figure 7.5 The region in the first quadrant defined by $x^2 + y^2 < 4$ and $xy > 1$, plotted using SymPy's `plot_implicit()` function.

The SymPy plotting function **`sympy.plotting.plot3d_parametric_line()`** allows you to plot **curves in three dimensions**. We illustrate this function with a single parametrically defined curve, a conical spiral, shown in Figure 7.6:

```
from sympy.plotting import plot3d_parametric_line
fig6 = plot3d_parametric_line(u*sympy.cos(4*u), u*sympy.sin(4*u),
                              u, (u, 0, 10))
```

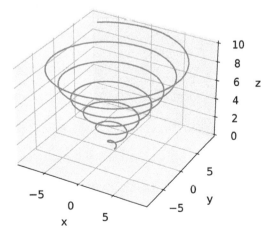

Figure 7.6 A conical spiral $(x, y, z) = (u \cos 4u, u \sin 4u, u)$ plotted with SymPy's `plot3d_parametric_line()`.

Finally, drawing surfaces based on Cartesian coordinates is straightforward. Here we show how to superimpose graphs of $z = x^2 + y^2$ and $z = xy$, drawn on different rectangular grids with **sympy.plotting.plot3d()**, the result of which is presented in Figure 7.7:

```
from sympy.plotting import plot3d
fig7 = plot3d((x**2 + y**2, (x, -3, 3), (y, -3, 3)),
              (x*y, (x, -5, 5), (y, -5, 5)))
```

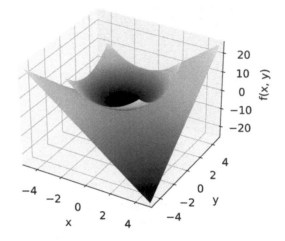

Figure 7.7 The surface $z = x^2 + y^2$ drawn for $-3 \leq x, y \leq 3$ and $z = xy$ drawn for $-5 \leq x, y \leq 5$ with SymPy's plot3d() function.

7.8   References

Online resources

☐ General SymPy resources

Project website
https://sympy.org

Documentation
https://docs.sympy.org

Features
https://sympy.org/en/features.html

API reference
https://docs.sympy.org/latest/reference/index.html

Tutorials
https://docs.sympy.org/latest/tutorials/index.html

How-to guides
https://docs.sympy.org/latest/guides/index.html

Explanations

`https://docs.sympy.org/latest/explanation/index.html`

☐ Symbols and functions/Matrices and vectors/Some elementary calculus

Introductory tutorial

`https://docs.sympy.org/latest/tutorials/intro-tutorial/index.html`

Basics

`https://docs.sympy.org/latest/reference/public/basics/index.html`

☐ Solving equations

Solvers

`https://docs.sympy.org/latest/modules/solvers/index.html`

☐ Plotting from within SymPy

Plotting

`https://docs.sympy.org/latest/modules/plotting.html`

8 Pandas: Data Handling

Pandas is a Python package for data analysis and manipulation. The development of the package started in 2008 and its name derives from *panel data*, a term that is common for multidimensional data sets as utilized in the fields of statistics and econometrics. The main idea behind Pandas was to fill a gap in the Python ecosystem that existed at that time: a lack of a comprehensive framework to deal with large amounts of – especially labeled – data sets and time-series data. Similarly to NumPy, Pandas is optimized for computational efficiency by implementing much of its functionality using C, while presenting a well-structured Python API to the user. Some concepts in Pandas lean on similar concepts in other data analysis tools, e.g., the *DataFrame* is closely modeled after *data.frame* objects available in the R programming language. In this chapter, we will introduce some basic functionality of Pandas to help readers interested in data analysis to get up to speed quickly. As usual, we will only scratch the surface of what is possible with Pandas, so we urge readers to explore Pandas in this chapter and the corresponding Jupyter Notebook (cambridge.org/9781009029728/ch8).

In the following, we will always assume that Pandas has been imported as **pd**:

```python
import pandas as pd
```

8.1 Series

Pandas provides two key concepts for storing data: *Series* and *DataFrame* objects. *Series* (**pd.Series**) can be used to store one-dimensional, and two-dimensional data. We can generate a *Series* easily from a *list* or *array*. Let us consider the case that you want to store some monthly average temperatures as a *Series*:

```python
s = pd.Series([-0.3, 0.4, 3.9, 7.4, 12.0, 15.0, 17.2, 16.8, 13.1,
               9.1, 3.7, 0.8], name='temp_C')
s
```

```
0    -0.3
1     0.4
2     3.9
3     7.4
4    12.0
```

```
5     15.0
6     17.2
7     16.8
8     13.1
9      9.1
10     3.7
11     0.8
Name: temp_C, dtype: float64
```

Similar to *arrays*, *Series* have specific data types; but by contrast, they also have a *name* attribute and each element of the *Series* has a unique *row label* or ***index label***. In this specific case, those are automatically generated ascending *integer* numbers. The row label can be used to address individual elements of the *Series*, e.g., the fourth element can be extracted with

```
s[3]
```

```
7.4
```

Note that this notation is very similar to the way indexing works in *lists* and *arrays*, but we will see later that indexing *Series* allows you to use all kinds of labels and not only *integer* indices. *Series* come with a wide range of methods for data analysis; we provide a few examples in the following code cell:

```
print('mean:', s.mean())
print('min:', s.min())
print('standard deviation:', s.std())
print('index of max element:', s.argmax())
print('values as list:', s.values)
print('indices of sorted Series:', s.argsort().values)
print('cumulative sum:', s.cumsum().values)
```

```
mean: 8.258333333333331
min: -0.3
standard deviation: 6.520242373260415
index of max element: 6
values as list: [-0.3  0.4  3.9  7.4 12.   15.   17.2 16.8 13.1  9.1
    3.7  0.8]
indices of sorted Series: [ 0  1 11 10  2  3  9  4  8  5  7  6]
cumulative sum: [-0.3  0.1  4.  11.4 23.4 38.4 55.6 72.4 85.5 94.6
   98.3 99.1]
```

Note that methods like `argsort()` or `cumsum()` return new *Series* objects; in the examples here, we convert those to *lists*, which take up less space when printed. For a more in-depth discussion of Pandas functions and methods, please refer to Section 8.4.

Let us have a closer look at *index labels*, which are called **indexes** in Pandas. Right now, our *index* consists simply of the *integer* position of each element, which is identical to indices utilized in *lists* and *arrays*. One advantage of *Series* over these *container* structures is that you can create your own *index*. In our temperature measurement example, we could, for instance, use the abbreviated month as a *string* as *index*:

```
s2 = s.set_axis(['jan', 'feb', 'mar', 'apr', 'may', 'jun',
                 'jul', 'aug', 'sep', 'oct', 'nov', 'dec'])
s2
```

```
jan   -0.3
feb    0.4
mar    3.9
apr    7.4
may   12.0
jun   15.0
jul   17.2
aug   16.8
sep   13.1
oct    9.1
nov    3.7
dec    0.8
Name: temp_C, dtype: float64
```

This representation certainly looks very nice, but, more importantly, it allows us to index the mean temperature of a given month in a very intuitive and readable way:

```
s2['oct']
```

```
9.1
```

As a result, the *index* may carry meaningful information and *Series* objects can therefore be considered to carry two-dimensional data. Playing devil's advocate, one might argue that this intuitive way to index *Series* objects is not a revolutionary advantage over other sequence containers such as *lists* or *arrays*. While there is a grain of truth in this thought, *Series* objects provide a huge range of useful methods (as shown) and there is at least one more useful property, as we will see in the following.

8.2   DataFrames

DataFrames are based on the *data.frame* concept of the R programming language and provide a handy way to deal with tabular data and therefore consist of rows and columns. As we will see in the following, individual columns of *DataFrames* are actually *Series* objects, building a bridge to the previous section. There are different ways to build *DataFrames* from scratch. Here, we focus on a method that is easy to understand and applicable to most problems: we will build a *DataFrame* from a *dictionary*. This happens in such a way that *dictionary* keys refer to column names and *dictionary* values are sequences of common length containing the actual column data. For illustration, we extend our example from Section 8.1 by adding more weather data: our *DataFrame* instance contains average temperatures (temp_C), average rain amounts (rain_mm), and labels corresponding to the month in which those measurements have been taken (mon):

```
df = pd.DataFrame({
    'mon': ['jan', 'feb', 'mar', 'apr', 'may', 'jun',
            'jul', 'aug', 'sep', 'oct', 'nov', 'dec'],
    'temp_C': [-0.3, 0.4, 3.9, 7.4, 12.0, 15.0, 17.2,
               16.8, 13.1, 9.1, 3.7, 0.8],
    'rain_mm': [59, 57, 84, 100, 143, 153, 172, 164,
                135, 89, 88, 80]})
df
```

	mon	temp_C	rain_mm
0	jan	-0.3	59
1	feb	0.4	57
2	mar	3.9	84
3	apr	7.4	100
4	may	12.0	143
5	jun	15.0	153
6	jul	17.2	172
7	aug	16.8	164
8	sep	13.1	135
9	oct	9.1	89
10	nov	3.7	88
11	dec	0.8	80

Similar to the *Series* objects introduced earlier, Pandas certainly knows how to represent the data contained in df in a visually appealing way. Note that **df** is a common *identifier* for a *DataFrame* object and we stick to this convention throughout this book. A different method to build *DataFrames* from scratch utilizes a *list* of *lists*, the latter of which represent the individual rows of the resulting *DataFrame*:

```
df2 = pd.DataFrame(
    [['jan', -0.3, 59], ['feb', 0.4, 57], ['mar', 3.9, 84],
     ['apr', 7.4, 100], ['may', 12.0, 143], ['jun', 15.0, 153],
     ['jul', 17.2, 172], ['aug', 16.8, 164], ['sep', 13.1, 135],
     ['oct', 9.1, 89], ['nov', 3.7, 88], ['dec', 0.8, 80]],
    columns=['mon', 'temp_C', 'rain_mm'])
```

This example generates the same *DataFrame* as before. Finally, Pandas also provides methods to read in data from a variety of file types, which we will discuss in detail in Section 8.6.

8.2.1   Axis Labels and Indexes

Every *DataFrame* has a **columns** attribute that provides you with a sequence of its column labels:

```
df.columns
```

```
Index(['mon', 'temp_C', 'rain_mm'], dtype='object')
```

Although the result is of type *Index*, it can be utilized like a *list*.

In general, an *index* is used in Pandas to store *axis* labels; in the case of df.columns, it returns the column labels. In order to retrieve the row labels, you can invoke the **df.index** attribute:

```
df.index
```

```
RangeIndex(start=0, stop=12, step=1)
```

The attribute returns a ***RangeIndex*** object, indicating that the row labels are a continuous sequence starting at 0 and ending just before 12 (the final element is 11) with a step size of one. This object can be easily turned into a *list*:

```
list(df.index)
```

```
[0, 1, 2, 3, 4, 5, 6, 7, 8, 9, 10, 11]
```

The row *index* labels are indeed the same labels that are shown in the first column (which does not carry a column label) in our representation of df. Every *DataFrame* has a row *index*; if none is provided in the generation of the *DataFrame* (as in our case), a simple *RangeIndex* starting at zero is generated. However, our *DataFrame* contains a column of month labels (mon) that would be perfectly suited as an *index*. Can we use this column as *index* instead of the *RangeIndex*? Yes, we can: by invoking the **df.set_index()** method on this column label:

```
df = df.set_index('mon')
df
```

```
     temp_C  rain_mm
mon
jan   -0.3      59
feb    0.4      57
mar    3.9      84
apr    7.4     100
may   12.0     143
jun   15.0     153
jul   17.2     172
```

aug	16.8	164
sep	13.1	135
oct	9.1	89
nov	3.7	88
dec	0.8	80

Note how the column of numerical row labels has disappeared and instead the column of months is used as *index* (indicated by the offset of the mon column label compared to the other column labels). Like most Pandas functions and methods, df.set_index() does not modify df; instead, it returns a modified copy.

As a shortcut, you can also define the row *index* column in the generation of a *DataFrame*:

```
df = pd.DataFrame({
    'temp_C': [-0.3, 0.4, 3.9, 7.4, 12.0, 15.0, 17.2, 16.8, 13.1,
               9.1, 3.7, 0.8],
    'rain_mm': [59, 57, 84, 100, 143, 153, 172, 164, 135, 89, 88,
                80]},
    index=['jan', 'feb', 'mar', 'apr', 'may', 'jun',
           'jul', 'aug', 'sep', 'oct', 'nov', 'dec'])
df
```

	temp_C	rain_mm
jan	-0.3	59
feb	0.4	57
mar	3.9	84
apr	7.4	100
may	12.0	143
jun	15.0	153
jul	17.2	172
aug	16.8	164
sep	13.1	135
oct	9.1	89
nov	3.7	88
dec	0.8	80

In this case, the row *index* has no specific label but this is also not necessary as it can always be accessed via df.index.

Before we close this introduction to Pandas *DataFrames*, we would like to mention three methods that will simplify your life, especially when dealing with large *DataFrames*. Sometimes, it is useful to inspect only the first *n* or final *n* rows of a *DataFrame*. This can be achieved with the methods **df.head()** and **df.tail()**, which are named after the infamous Unix commands. Both methods extract a specific number of rows (five by default; this may be overridden by providing an *integer* number when calling the method) from the *DataFrame* they are applied to:

```
df.head(3)
```

	temp_C	rain_mm
jan	−0.3	59
feb	0.4	57
mar	3.9	84

```
df.tail(2)
```

	temp_C	rain_mm
nov	3.7	88
dec	0.8	80

Please note that both methods do not simply display excerpts from *DataFrame* df, but actually return crops from this *DataFrame*, which in turn are *DataFrames*, as well. Finally, the **df.describe()** method provides a statistical overview of the *DataFrame* it is applied:

```
df.describe()
```

	temp_C	rain_mm
count	12.000000	12.000000
mean	8.258333	110.333333
std	6.520242	40.824087
min	−0.300000	57.000000
25%	2.975000	83.000000
50%	8.250000	94.500000
75%	13.575000	145.500000
max	17.200000	172.000000

For each column in the *DataFrame*, the method returns a bouquet of statistical information in a similar way as `scipy.stats.describe()` (see Section 5.7) does.

8.2.2   Accessing Data

Pandas provides different ways for accessing data stored in *DataFrames* and *Series*.[1] For instance, Pandas supports indexing through the same mechanisms that we have learned for *lists* and *arrays*. However, there are (admittedly rare) cases in which these mechanisms are ambiguous and therefore might not lead to the expected result. Therefore, as part of this book, we will only present the most explicit and preferred way for indexing

---

[1] While the following discussion focuses on *DataFrames*, you will see that the methods discussed in this section apply also to *Series* objects.

DataFrames (and *Series*), the `loc` and `iloc` properties. At first, using these properties might seem a bit ungainly in comparison to other methods, but they actually represent the most comprehensive way of indexing and are definitely worth learning. Before we introduce their use, what is a *property*? Python properties are a convenient way to deal with *get* and *set* methods of classes; they are not class methods and instead return *property* objects that enable you to access data in the underlying class object. Their use is straightforward, although it may seem unusual at first, as we will see in the following examples.

The first method to access rows in *DataFrames* uses the **df.iloc** property. Through this property, you can address individual rows through position-based *integer* values (ranging from 0 to `len(df)-1`); therefore, `iloc` ignores the *index* of.the *DataFrame* object and only operates on positions. To access row data, the most common use cases of `iloc` utilize single *integer* values to address single rows:

```
df.iloc[0]
```

```
temp_C      -0.3
rain_mm     59.0
Name: jan, dtype: float64
```

lists of *integer* values to address multiple rows:

```
df.iloc[[2,3,5]]
```

```
      temp_C  rain_mm
mar      3.9       84
apr      7.4      100
jun     15.0      153
```

or *slices* to address ranges of rows:

```
df.iloc[2:5]
```

```
temp_C  rain_mm
mar      3.9       84
apr      7.4      100
may     12.0      143
```

What might appear weird to you right now is that the `iloc` property uses square brackets instead of parentheses; this is due to the fact that it is a property and not a class method or function. Also, you might have noticed that the returned object types differ: indeed, when addressing a single row, a *Series* object is returned, whereas when addressing multiple rows, a *DataFrame* object is returned.

So now we can extract rows from a *DataFrame*, but what about **columns**? Single columns can be extracted easily as attributes:

```
df.rain_mm
```

```
jan     59
feb     57
mar     84
apr    100
may    143
jun    153
jul    172
aug    164
sep    135
oct     89
nov     88
dec     80
Name: rain_mm, dtype: int64
```

Just like in the case of single rows, single columns are extracted as *Series* objects. In order to extract multiple rows, resulting in a new *DataFrame* object, we suggest using the `loc` property, which we introduce next.

The **loc** property provides the most comprehensive way to access data in `DataFrames` as it enables the user to address a group of rows and columns at the same time, or either of those separately. This data access can be based on *index* labels or *logical arrays* (see Section 4.2.3); note that the latter is not available with `iloc`, which selects data only based on positions. The three examples that we showed for `iloc` look a little bit different when using `loc`, but they result in the same data, as shown in the following. We can select a single row based on its *index* label:

```
df.loc['jan']
```

```
temp_C    -0.3
rain_mm   59.0
Name: jan, dtype: float64
```

or multiple rows based on their *index* labels:

```
df.loc[['mar', 'apr', 'jun']]
```

```
     temp_C  rain_mm
mar     3.9       84
apr     7.4      100
jun    15.0      153
```

or a range of rows using slicing based on *index* labels:

```
df.loc['mar':'may']
```

```
     temp_C  rain_mm
mar     3.9       84
apr     7.4      100
may    12.0      143
```

Note how it is possible to slice even through nonnumerical indices and that the end point of the slice (may) is included in this case.

Using loc, column labels can be specified using the same logic, but keep in mind that it is mandatory to also specify the rows that you would like to extract in that case. The full notation of loc is df.loc[<rows>, <columns>]. Therefore, to extract all rows of the column rain_mm you can use the full slice (:) to address all row labels:

```
df.loc[:, 'rain_mm']
```

```
jan     59
feb     57
mar     84
apr    100
may    143
jun    153
jul    172
aug    164
sep    135
oct     89
nov     88
dec     80
Name: rain_mm, dtype: int64
```

Now, we can combine a selection of rows and columns and extract, for instance, the amount of rain that fell during the summer months from May to September:

```
df.loc['may':'sep', 'rain_mm']
```

```
may    143
jun    153
jul    172
aug    164
sep    135
Name: rain_mm, dtype: int64
```

But this is not all. We already saw in Section 8.1 that the *Series* class provides a wide range of methods, for instance, to aggregate elements of the *Series*. This allows us to derive the sum of rainfall over the summer months in a very concise and readable way:

```
df.loc['may':'sep', 'rain_mm'].sum()
```

```
767
```

It gets even better. `loc` also allows you to provide a **logical *array***, an *array* (or *list*) of *booleans*, to indicate those rows that you would like to extract. We can take advantage of this feature to create a powerful formalism to extract only those data points that meet certain conditions (compare to Section 4.2.3). The following example extracts the average temperatures during those months with rain amounts less than 100 mm:

```
df.loc[df.rain_mm < 100, 'temp_C']
```

```
jan    -0.3
feb     0.4
mar     3.9
oct     9.1
nov     3.7
dec     0.8
Name: temp_C, dtype: float64
```

What happens here is that the condition `df.rain_mm < 100` returns a *list* of *booleans* that are utilized by `loc` as a *boolean* mask or logical *array* to return only those rows for which the condition holds.

8.2.3   Modifying Data

The mechanisms that we learned to access data in *DataFrames* and *Series* (see previous section) also allow for modifying data as shown in the following example:

```
df2 = df.copy()
df2.loc[df2.rain_mm < 100, 'temp_C'] = 0
df2
```

```
      temp_C   rain_mm
jan      0.0        59
feb      0.0        57
mar      0.0        84
apr      7.4       100
may     12.0       143
jun     15.0       153
jul     17.2       172
```

aug	16.8	164
sep	13.1	135
oct	0.0	89
nov	0.0	88
dec	0.0	80

First, we create a copy of df, df2, so we do not alter df. After creating this copy, we modify the temperatures of those months in which the amount of rain is less than 100 mm to 0. We can therefore use the loc and iloc properties to identify data elements (rows, columns, or combinations thereof) to which we can assign new values. Naturally, the same mechanisms can be used to crop a selection of the current *DataFrame*:

```
df2 = df.copy()
df2 = df2.loc['may':'sep', :]
df2
```

	temp_C	rain_mm
may	12.0	143
jun	15.0	153
jul	17.2	172
aug	16.8	164
sep	13.1	135

Here we extract a *DataFrame* only containing the summer months from our original *DataFrame*, df.

Naturally, we can also **add data** to our *DataFrame*. Consider the case that we would like to add another column containing the temperature in units of Fahrenheit. The conversion of temperatures can be accomplished with the known relation $T_F = T_C \cdot 1.8 + 32$, which we will utilize in the following:

```
def temp_conversion(df):
    """Convert temperatures in a DataFrame from C to F"""
    return df.temp_C*1.8 + 32


df2 = df.assign(temp_F=temp_conversion)
df2
```

	temp_C	rain_mm	temp_F
jan	−0.3	59	31.46
feb	0.4	57	32.72
mar	3.9	84	39.02
apr	7.4	100	45.32
may	12.0	143	53.60
jun	15.0	153	59.00

```
jul    17.2    172    62.96
aug    16.8    164    62.24
sep    13.1    135    55.58
oct     9.1     89    48.38
nov     3.7     88    38.66
dec     0.8     80    33.44
```

The method **df.assign()** creates a new column from a functional relation based on data stored in the *DataFrame*.

If the data you would like to add is not related to the data present in the *DataFrame*, you can use the loc property that we introduced in Section 8.2.2 to define the new column's name and assign a sequence of the proper length (the number of rows in the *DataFrame*):

```
df2 = df.copy()
df2.loc[:, 'snowfall'] = [True, True, False, False, False, False,
                          False, False, False, False, True, True]
df2
```

```
       temp_C   rain_mm   snowfall
jan     -0.3        59       True
feb      0.4        57       True
mar      3.9        84      False
apr      7.4       100      False
may     12.0       143      False
jun     15.0       153      False
jul     17.2       172      False
aug     16.8       164      False
sep     13.1       135      False
oct      9.1        89      False
nov      3.7        88       True
dec      0.8        80       True
```

Please note the notation here (df2.loc[:, 'snowfall']): for each row in df2, we address a column ('snowfall') to which we assign a *list* of *booleans*. Since a column of this name does not yet exist, it is being added to the *DataFrame*. Similarly, single rows can be added to a *DataFrame*:

```
df2.loc['avg'] = [8.3, 110.3, False]
df2
```

```
       temp_C   rain_mm   snowfall
jan     -0.3      59.0       True
feb      0.4      57.0       True
```

mar	3.9	84.0	False
apr	7.4	100.0	False
may	12.0	143.0	False
jun	15.0	153.0	False
jul	17.2	172.0	False
aug	16.8	164.0	False
sep	13.1	135.0	False
oct	9.1	89.0	False
nov	3.7	88.0	True
dec	0.8	80.0	True
avg	8.3	110.3	False

However, this method cannot be used to add multiple rows. To add multiple new rows, the best way is to create a second *DataFrame* containing the new data but utilizing the same columns and then appending that *DataFrame* to the original *DataFrame*. Consider the following example in which we generate a new *DataFrame* that contains annual means for three years:

```
df2 = pd.DataFrame({'temp_C': [9.7, 9.5, 9.9],
                    'rain_mm': [1989.8, 1753.1, 1670.6]},
                   index=['2020', '2019', '2018'])
df2
```

	temp_C	rain_mm
2020	9.7	165.8
2019	9.5	146.1
2018	9.9	139.2

We would like to append this new *DataFrame* to our original *DataFrame* and use the **pd.concat()** function for this task:

```
pd.concat([df, df2])
```

	temp_C	rain_mm
jan	−0.3	59.0
feb	0.4	57.0
mar	3.9	84.0
apr	7.4	100.0
may	12.0	143.0
jun	15.0	153.0
jul	17.2	172.0
aug	16.8	164.0
sep	13.1	135.0
oct	9.1	89.0

```
nov      3.7     88.0
dec      0.8     80.0
2020     9.7    165.8
2019     9.5    146.1
2018     9.9    139.2
```

concat() does what its name suggests: it simply concatenates *DataFrames*. We can use this function to append the new data to the existing *DataFrame* preserving row order, and – more importantly – the row *index* from both *DataFrames*. If you find that the row *index* from both *DataFrames* is incompatible (which indeed it is) and therefore not that important, you can choose to ignore the *index* entirely and to replace it with a *RangeIndex*:

```
pd.concat([df, df2], ignore_index=True)
```

```
      temp_C   rain_mm
0      −0.3     59.0
1       0.4     57.0
2       3.9     84.0
3       7.4    100.0
4      12.0    143.0
5      15.0    153.0
6      17.2    172.0
7      16.8    164.0
8      13.1    135.0
9       9.1     89.0
10      3.7     88.0
11      0.8     80.0
12      9.7    165.8
13      9.5    146.1
14      9.9    139.2
```

As you can see, the row *index* from both *DataFrames* is removed and reset, but – of course – the order of the rows is preserved. The advantage of this approach is that you can append a *DataFrame* with an otherwise incompatible row *index*, as well as those that do not contain a meaningful row *index*.

concat() not only allows you to append rows, but you can also append columns. Consider the following case in which we generate a new *DataFrame* containing minimum and maximum temperatures for each month, which will then be appended as a new column to the original *DataFrame*. To showcase the power of concat(), the order of months in the new *DataFrame* will be reversed:

```
df3 = pd.DataFrame({'temp_min_C': [−1.9, 1.0, 6.2, 9.7, 13.0, 13.1,
                                   11.0, 7.8, 3.5, 0.6, −2.5, −3.0],
```

```
                    'temp_max_C': [3.5, 6.5, 12.3, 16.8, 20.9, 21.6,
                                   19.2, 16.3, 11.5, 7.3, 3.3, 2.5]},
                    index=['dec', 'nov', 'oct', 'sep', 'aug', 'jul' ,
                           'jun', 'may', 'apr', 'mar', 'feb', 'jan'])
pd.concat([df, df3], axis=1)
```

	temp_C	rain_mm	temp_min_C	temp_max_C
jan	−0.3	59	−3.0	2.5
feb	0.4	57	−2.5	3.3
mar	3.9	84	0.6	7.3
apr	7.4	100	3.5	11.5
may	12.0	143	7.8	16.3
jun	15.0	153	11.0	19.2
jul	17.2	172	13.1	21.6
aug	16.8	164	13.0	20.9
sep	13.1	135	9.7	16.8
oct	9.1	89	6.2	12.3
nov	3.7	88	1.0	6.5
dec	0.8	80	−1.9	3.5

The only difference to the function call is that we specified axis=1, which overrides the default axis=0. What does this mean? When we introduced the use of the loc property (Section 8.2.2), we learned that we can specify both rows and columns following the schema df.loc[<rows>, <columns>]. Pandas is very consistent about this schema and order: operations applied on axis=0 utilize rows, whereas operations applied to axis=1 utilize columns. Therefore, pd.concat([df, df3], axis=1) will concatenate two *DataFrames* column wise, whereas pd.concat([df, df3], axis=0) (or pd.concat([df, df3])) will concatenate two *DataFrames* row-wise. Now go ahead and check the numbers of the resulting *DataFrame*. You will see that concat() did not just paste the new columns next to the existing data, it actually accounted for the month label used as *index* and matched them properly.

So far in our examples, we made sure that both *DataFrames* that we concatenated had the same number of rows or columns, perpendicular to the *axis* on which we apply the concatenation operation. But what would happen if we were to concatenate two *DataFrames* along their rows with a different number of columns? If you expect Pandas to complain in this case, you underestimate its power:

```
df2 = pd.DataFrame({'temp_C': [9.7, 9.5, 9.9],
                    'rain_mm': [165.8, 146.1, 139.2],
                    'snowfall': [True, True, True]},
                   index=['2020', '2019', '2018'])
pd.concat([df, df2])
```

	temp_C	rain_mm	snowfall
jan	−0.3	59.0	nan
feb	0.4	57.0	nan
mar	3.9	84.0	nan
apr	7.4	100.0	nan
may	12.0	143.0	nan
jun	15.0	153.0	nan
jul	17.2	172.0	nan
aug	16.8	164.0	nan
sep	13.1	135.0	nan
oct	9.1	89.0	nan
nov	3.7	88.0	nan
dec	0.8	80.0	nan
2020	9.7	165.8	True
2019	9.5	146.1	True
2018	9.9	139.2	True

df2 has one more column than df, but concat() performs the concatenation without hesitation. The resulting *DataFrame* now contains all three columns. But what values will that third column contain for those rows that came from df, which did not contain this column? Pandas is smart about this issue and fills those rows with missing data with nans. In Section 8.2.4 we will learn some tools that Pandas provides to deal with such missing data. Here concat() utilizes a strategy that is called an ***outer join***, a term that originates from relational algebra and is often utilized in the context of relational databases like SQL and others. In an *outer join*, all rows and columns from df and df2 are considered in the concatenation operation ("*join*"); where data is missing, those values are filled with nans (see Section 4.3). The opposite of an *outer join* is an ***inner join***, in which only those subsets of rows and columns are considered that are complete and do not contain nans. Consider the following example:

```
pd.concat([df, df2], join='inner')
```

	temp_C	rain_mm
jan	−0.3	59.0
feb	0.4	57.0
mar	3.9	84.0
apr	7.4	100.0
may	12.0	143.0
jun	15.0	153.0
jul	17.2	172.0
aug	16.8	164.0
sep	13.1	135.0
oct	9.1	89.0

nov	3.7	88.0
dec	0.8	80.0
2020	9.7	165.8
2019	9.5	146.1
2018	9.9	139.2

By specifying the keyword argument join='inner' we can invoke an *inner join* with the result that only the two original columns are concatenated since only those are complete. The join keyword argument therefore allows you to shape the resulting *DataFrame* in a concatenation operation when some data is missing (if there is no data missing, both *inner* and *outer join* will lead to the same result).

For the sake of completeness, we will mention one more function that allows you to modify *DataFrames*. The **pd.merge()** function merges two *DataFrames* based on a common *index*. We briefly exemplify its use by reproducing one of our earlier results. We merge *DataFrames* df and df3 based on their common row *index*:

```
pd.merge(df, df3, left_index=True, right_index=True)
```

	temp_C	rain_mm	temp_min_C	temp_max_C
jan	−0.3	59	−3.0	2.5
feb	0.4	57	−2.5	3.3
mar	3.9	84	0.6	7.3
apr	7.4	100	3.5	11.5
may	12.0	143	7.8	16.3
jun	15.0	153	11.0	19.2
jul	17.2	172	13.1	21.6
aug	16.8	164	13.0	20.9
sep	13.1	135	9.7	16.8
oct	9.1	89	6.2	12.3
nov	3.7	88	1.0	6.5
dec	0.8	80	−1.9	3.5

As you see, the result is identical to the previous concatenation. merge() is highly customizable. In this example, we simply use the row *index* of the respective *DataFrame* (left_index=True and right_index=True) to perform the row matching on, but it is also possible to select any other column using the left_on and right_on keyword arguments. Furthermore, merge() provides even more options for *inner* and *outer joins*. Given its flexibility, we leave it to the interested reader to experiment with this function and others that are available.

8.2.4   Dealing with Missing Data

As we saw in Section 8.2.3, it is possible to have *DataFrame* (and, of course, also *Series*) objects that contain missing data. Such missing values are stored as np.nan values. Hence, to mark missing or erroneous values, we can assign `np.nan` to those values. Let us implant some missing data into our *DataFrame*:

```
df2 = df.copy()
df2.loc[['may', 'sep'], 'rain_mm'] = np.nan
df2.loc['feb', 'temp_C'] = np.nan
df2
```

```
     temp_C  rain_mm
jan    -0.3     59.0
feb     nan     57.0
mar     3.9     84.0
apr     7.4    100.0
may    12.0      nan
jun    15.0    153.0
jul    17.2    172.0
aug    16.8    164.0
sep    13.1      nan
oct     9.1     89.0
nov     3.7     88.0
dec     0.8     80.0
```

As you can see, all missing values appear as `nan`. Pandas provides you with tools to deal with missing data in your *DataFrames*. The two most common techniques might be to simply drop rows with missing data or to replace missing values with some predefined value. Let us have a look at both approaches.

First, we have to **identify missing values**: the **df.isna()** method returns a *DataFrame* of the same shape, with `True` values where data are missing and `False` otherwise:

```
df2.isna()
```

```
     temp_C  rain_mm
jan   False    False
feb    True    False
mar   False    False
apr   False    False
may   False     True
jun   False    False
jul   False    False
aug   False    False
sep   False     True
oct   False    False
nov   False    False
dec   False    False
```

The method **df.notna()** returns the exact opposite. Naturally, both methods can also be applied to *Series* objects.

To drop all rows with missing data, we can use the **df.dropna()** method:

```
df2.dropna()
```

```
      temp_C  rain_mm
jan    −0.3     59.0
mar     3.9     84.0
apr     7.4    100.0
jun    15.0    153.0
jul    17.2    172.0
aug    16.8    164.0
oct     9.1     89.0
nov     3.7     88.0
dec     0.8     80.0
```

By default, the method uses the keyword argument `axis=0`; in accordance with the behavior that we observed for other Pandas functions, changing its value to `axis=1` will drop all columns that contain missing data. Furthermore, you can use the keyword argument `how='all'` to only drop those rows or columns for which all elements are missing; the default value is `how='any'`.

Alternatively, you can **replace missing values** in your data with predefined values using the function **df.fillna()**. A zeroth order interpolation approach would be to replace missing data in each column with the respective mean value of that column:

```
df2.fillna(df2.mean(axis=0))
```

```
         temp_C  rain_mm
jan   −0.300000     59.0
feb    8.972727     57.0
mar    3.900000     84.0
apr    7.400000    100.0
may   12.000000    104.6
jun   15.000000    153.0
jul   17.200000    172.0
aug   16.800000    164.0
sep   13.100000    104.6
oct    9.100000     89.0
nov    3.700000     88.0
dec    0.800000     80.0
```

Here we calculate the mean values for each column (nan values are by default ignored in this computation) and store them in a *Series* object that is able to match the columns based on the column labels. Since the values in our two columns seem to roughly follow some functional behavior with added noise, you can also interpolate missing values using **df.interpolate()**:

```
df2.interpolate()
```

```
     temp_C  rain_mm
jan    -0.3     59.0
feb     1.8     57.0
mar     3.9     84.0
apr     7.4    100.0
may    12.0    126.5
jun    15.0    153.0
jul    17.2    172.0
aug    16.8    164.0
sep    13.1    126.5
oct     9.1     89.0
nov     3.7     88.0
dec     0.8     80.0
```

By default, this method utilizes a linear interpolation method, but a wide variety of interpolation techniques is available.

8.3   Specific Types of Data

Pandas can deal with a wide range of data types beyond numerical data. In the following, we discuss some features related to specific data types and how they can be handled within *DataFrames*.

8.3.1   Categorical Data

Categorical data can be of numerical, textual, or other nature, but they rely on a discrete basis. Each data point falls into a specific category and the number of available categories is finite. There may be an underlying hierarchy for the available categories (ranked data), but this is not necessary. To stick with our weather-based examples of this chapter, the "UV-index" (ranked *integer* values) or "cloudiness" (ranked textual data) would be good examples for categorical data:

```
df2 = pd.DataFrame(
    {'clouds': ['cloudy', 'cloudy', 'partly cloudy',
                'mostly clear', 'clear', 'clear', 'partly cloudy'],
     'uv': [0, 0, 1, 3, 5, 5, 1]},
    index=['mon', 'tue', 'wed', 'thu', 'fri', 'sat', 'sun'])

df2
```

```
        clouds  uv
mon            cloudy   0
tue            cloudy   0
wed    partly cloudy    1
thu    mostly clear     3
fri            clear     5
sat            clear     5
sun    partly cloudy    1
```

In order to get a *list* of **unique elements** for a specific column (or *Series* in general), you can use the **df.unique()** method:

```
df2.clouds.unique()
```

```
array(['cloudy', 'partly cloudy', 'mostly clear', 'clear'],
      dtype=object)
```

The method **df.value_counts()** returns a *Series* object that counts how often each unique element appears in a *Series*:

```
df2.clouds.value_counts()
```

```
partly cloudy   2
clear           2
cloudy          2
mostly clear    1
Name: clouds, dtype: int64
```

Finally, if you would like to extract only those rows in your *DataFrame* for which one **column containing categorical data has a specific value**, you can use the .loc property introduced in Section 8.2.2:

```
df2.loc[df2.clouds == 'partly cloudy', 'uv'].mean()
```

```
1.0
```

In this example, we first extract a *Series* object containing the UV-index for those rows for which the clouds column holds the value partly cloudy and then we apply the mean() method of the *Series* class.

8.3.2   Textual Data

As we have already seen, *Series* objects, and therefore *DataFrame* columns, may contain *strings*.[2] Since many functions and methods in Pandas require numerical data, we

---

[2] In this case, the data type of the underlying *Series* is typically shown as object, which may also refer to other data.

need a slightly different toolset. As mentioned, we can utilize the loc property to filter textual data. Unfortunately, this approach requires knowledge of the exact value for which to filter. If, instead, you would like to filter all rows for which different nuances of cloudiness are present, we could try to find all rows that contain the word "cloudy" (i.e., either "cloudy" or "partly cloudy"). For this purpose, Pandas provides as part of the **pd.Series.str** submodule vectorized *string* functions that can be applied to *Series* and *index* objects containing textual data. In order to filter all those rows of the *DataFrame* for which the column clouds contains the *string* cloudy, we can utilize the **str.contains()** function:

```
df2.clouds.str.contains('cloud', regex=False)
```

```
mon      True
tue      True
wed      True
thu      False
fri      False
sat      False
sun      True
Name: clouds, dtype: bool
```

contains() requires as its sole positional argument a pattern *string* that is matched against each element of the *Series*. By default, this pattern is treated as a regular expression; since we are checking for a simple sequence of characters, we deactivate this feature by setting regex=False. Furthermore, contains() assumes that this pattern is case sensitive unless case=False is used. Finally, calling contains() results in a *Series* of *booleans* that can be combined with the loc property to return a *DataFrame* containing only those days that are subject to significant cloud coverage:

```
df2.loc[df2.clouds.str.contains('cloud', regex=False)]
```

```
          clouds  uv
mon       cloudy  0
tue       cloudy  0
wed  partly cloudy  1
sun  partly cloudy  1
```

Beyond contains(), pd.Series.str contains a wide range of vectorized *string* functions that are close relatives of those which we have already met in Section 3.5.7. For instance, we can find and replace specific *strings* in our *Series* object. Consider the following example, which will perform replace() on the *Series* to replace occurrences of the word "cloudy" with the word "sunny" in the clouds column:

```
df4 = df2.copy()
df4.loc[:, 'clouds'] = df4.clouds.str.replace('cloudy', 'sunny')
df4
```

```
clouds  uv
mon           sunny  0
tue           sunny  0
wed   partly sunny   1
thu   mostly clear   3
fri           clear  5
sat           clear  5
sun   partly sunny   1
```

We leave it to the reader to explore the other *string* operations that are available as part of pd.Series.str.

8.3.3   Dates and Times

Pandas can help you to convert *strings* containing dates and times to ***datetime64*** objects that allow you to deal with time-series data properly. Consider the following *Series* that contains *strings* referring to points in time provided in the format YYYY-MM-DD HH:MM:

```
dates = pd.Series(['2020-01-01 12:34', '2020-03-01 08:47',
                   '2020-06-01 14:23', '2020-09-01 22:56',
                   '2020-12-01 13:45'])
dates
```

```
0    2020-01-01 12:34
1    2020-03-01 08:47
2    2020-06-01 14:23
3    2020-09-01 22:56
4    2020-12-01 13:45
dtype: object
```

pd.to_datetime() is able to convert this *Series* of *strings* to a *Series* of *datetime64* objects:

```
dates = pd.to_datetime(dates)
dates
```

```
0    2020-01-01 12:34:00
1    2020-03-01 08:47:00
2    2020-06-01 14:23:00
3    2020-09-01 22:56:00
4    2020-12-01 13:45:00
dtype: datetime64[ns]
```

Note how the date representations barely change, but the data type of the *Series* changed from *object* (which, in this case, refers to *string* data) to *datetime64*. Now, what can we do with the data? Pandas provides a number of functions as part of the **pd.Series.dt** submodule. For instance, we can isolate times with **pd.Series.dt.time**:

```
dates.dt.time
```

```
0    12:34:00
1    08:47:00
2    14:23:00
3    22:56:00
4    13:45:00
dtype: object
```

In a similar way, we could also extract information like the year, month, day, hour, minute, and second. Furthermore, we can compute **time differences** based on *date-time64* objects:

```
datedelta = dates − dates.iloc[0]
datedelta
```

```
0      0 days 00:00:00
1     59 days 20:13:00
2    152 days 01:49:00
3    244 days 10:22:00
4    335 days 01:11:00
dtype: timedelta64[ns]
```

Here we derive the time difference relative to the first row in our *Series*. Note how Pandas outputs the time differences in a way that makes it easily readable for humans. If you prefer a more quantitative measure, you can convert the time difference into any appropriate unit, e.g., seconds:

```
datedelta.astype('timedelta64[s]')
```

```
0           0.0
1     5170380.0
2    13139340.0
3    21118920.0
4    28948260.0
dtype: float64
```

8.4   Functions

In Section 8.1, we saw that the *Series* class contains methods (e.g., pd.Series.mean() to compute the mean value of a *Series*) to perform computations based on the underlying

Table 8.1 A collection of common Pandas methods for descriptive statistics and other related operations. The methods listed here are applicable to *Series* and *DataFrame* objects; in the latter case, operations are by default applied along rows, but can also be applied along columns (keyword argument axis=1). Aggregating methods result in scalar results, while results of nonaggregating methods have the same length as the input data. Methods listed here should be self-explanatory; if in doubt about their use case, please refer to the Pandas reference (see Section 8.8).

Aggregating methods::		
count()	sum()	prod()
median()	mean()	max()
min()	mode()	abs()
std()	var()	quantile(x)
Nonaggregating methods::		
cumsum()	cumprod()	cummax()
cummin()		

data. Naturally, similar method implementations exist for the *DataFrame* class. Before we investigate this functionality, we create a new *DataFrame* to experiment with:

```
df = pd.DataFrame({
    'temp_C': [12.3, 13.5, 9.2, 8.2, 10.2, 11.3, 13.5]},
    index=['mon', 'tue', 'wed', 'thu', 'fri', 'sat', 'sun'])
df = pd.concat([df, df2], axis=1)

df.loc[:, ['temp_C', 'uv']].mean()
```

```
temp_C    11.171429
uv         2.142857
dtype: float64
```

The resulting *Series* object contains the mean values of all numerical columns in df; nonnumerical columns are ignored where methods are not defined for such data.

A wide range of standard functions and methods are available. Table 8.1 provides an overview of the most common ones. Note that some functions and methods are of aggregating nature and result in scalar results, while others result in output of the same shape as the input data. Furthermore, some methods like mean(), std(), and sum() ignore missing data (see Section 8.2.4) in their computations.

In order to aggregate the results of multiple methods as those listed in Table 8.1, you can use the **aggregate method, df.agg()**, to conveniently collate their results in a *Series* or *DataFrame* object. For instance, if you are interested in deriving the *min*, *max*, and *mean* of all numeric columns in your *DataFrame* you can call:

```
df.loc[:, ['temp_C', 'uv']].agg(['min', 'max', 'mean'])
```

```
         temp_C        uv
min     8.200000   0.000000
max    13.500000   5.000000
mean   11.171429   2.142857
```

You can simply provide a *list* of method names (see, e.g., Table 8.1 or the Pandas reference min Section 8.8) as individual *strings* to the `df.agg()` function. If you prefer to aggregate the results of different functions for the individual columns, you can also provide a *dictionary* that contains *lists* of the measures to be computed for the different columns:

```
df.loc[:, ['temp_C', 'uv']].agg(
    {'temp_C': ['min', 'max', 'mean'], 'uv': 'median'})
```

```
          temp_C    uv
min      8.200000   nan
max     13.500000   nan
mean    11.171429   nan
median        nan   1.0
```

The resulting *DataFrame* contains four rows – one for each measure that we want to compute. However, those rows only contain values for the columns to which they have been previously assigned. Therefore, `df.agg()` allows you to compute tailored aggregated statistics for your *DataFrame*.

Despite the wealth of functions and methods already implemented in Pandas, you might want to be able to provide your own functions. This is possible with the **`df.apply()`** method. Imagine we would like to apply some polynomial function to the numerical data and then sum up the results of each column. We can define a function that includes the polynomial and the summation and then provide this function to the `df.apply()` method:

```
def func(x):
    """some function"""
    return np.sum(3*x**2+3*x)

df.loc[:, ['temp_C', 'uv']].apply(func)
```

```
temp_C    2932.8
uv         228.0
dtype: float64
```

There are a few important details that we need to discuss. First of all, we can apply our function `func` only to numerical data, so we have to use the `loc` property to isolate

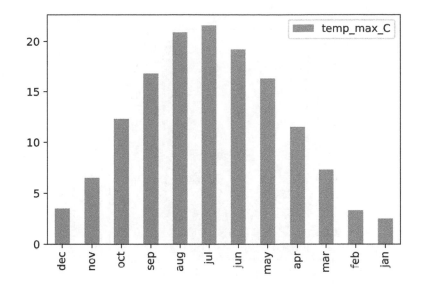

Figure 8.1 A simple bar plot, generated with df.plot().

the two numerical columns in our *DataFrame*. Furthermore, we provide func as an object to df.apply(), which means without specifically calling the function (e.g., as func(x)). Here df.apply() will evaluate func on each column of df; if you would like to evaluate it on each row, you need to specify that with the keyword argument axis=1. Naturally, if func would not include a summation, the result df.apply() would be another *DataFrame*, preserving the original row structure. This flexibility makes df.apply() a powerful tool for transforming data in a *DataFrame*.

8.5   Data Visualization

Plotting Pandas data is straightforward and allows the use of all functions and methods discussed in Chapter 6. Nevertheless, Pandas also provides a few plotting functions of its own that serve as shortcuts to Matplotlib routines. Consider the following example using the **df.plot()** method:

```
df3.plot(y='temp_max_C', kind='bar')
```

The result is shown in Figure 8.1. By simply providing the label of the column to be plotted on the ordinate, Pandas will default to plotting the *DataFrame* row *index* on the abscissa with corresponding axis labels. Alternatively, a different column label can be provided for the abscissa. In this case, we chose a bar plot; the kind keyword argument defaults to line and features a wide range of options, including box, pie, scatter, and other plot styles. The df.plot() method is highly customizable in ways that closely resemble those introduced for Matplotlib functions in Chapter 6. This is on purpose, since

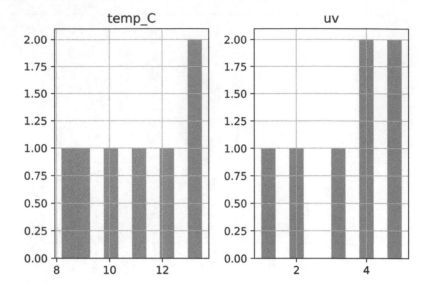

Figure 8.2 A simple histogram plot, generated with `df.hist()`.

the method utilizes Matplotlib functionality and returns an `axes` instance (see Section 6.2). For details on how to customize plots, we refer to the method documentation.

Another convenient method allows you to quickly generate and plot histograms for all columns containing numerical data, **df.hist()** (see Figure 8.2):

```
df2.hist()
```

If you prefer to generate a histogram only for a single column, you can use the `column` keyword argument to provide the column label or a *list* thereof; alternatively, you can apply `hist()` also to an extracted *Series* object. Similarly to `np.histogram()` (see Section 4.5), the `bins` keyword argument allows you to provide an `integer` number of bins or a *list* of bin edges.

Unfortunately, the `df.hist()` method cannot deal with **nonnumerical data**. In order to plot a histogram for nonnumerical data, we must use a workaround that counts the frequency of the different labels and then plots them in the form of a bar plot (see Figure 8.3):

```
df.clouds.value_counts().plot(kind='bar')
```

Note that in this case, we use the `plot()` method of the *Series* class, which of course works very similarly to *DataFrame*'s equivalent. This example showcases Pandas' flexibility in chaining method and function calls for the task of plotting data.

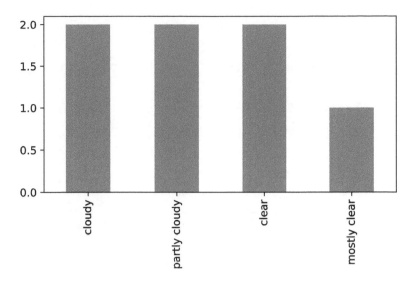

Figure 8.3 A histogram plot, generated from textual data with `df.plot()`. Note how the labels on the abscissa are automatically extracted from the underlying *index* and added to the plot.

8.6   File Input/Output

Pandas supports a wide range of file formats for storing data for different use cases and data sets of different sizes. Most file input/output routines provide a somewhat similar API and, of course, seamless integration into the Pandas environment. We will therefore focus in the following introduction on reading and writing *comma-separated values* (*csv*) files, which constitute a very common means to store modest amounts of tabular data. *csv* files (see Section 4.8) contain data in a comma-separated way, which makes such files readable and editable by humans and does not require any special tools for using this file format. A *csv* file may look like this:

```
mon,12.3,5,clear
tue,13.5,4,clear
wed,9.2,1,mostly cloudy
thu,8.2,2,partly cloudy
fri,10.2,3,partly cloudy
sat,11.3,4,mostly clear
sun,13.5,5,clear
```

The file contains rows of data in four columns that are separated by commas in each row: weekday, temperature, UV-index, and cloudiness; the different columns use different data types (*strings, floats, integers*). Saved as a plain (i.e., unformatted) text file, e.g., `weather.csv`, this file is definitely readable by humans, but finding the proper value of one column for a specific row can be tricky due to the lack of horizontal alignment.

To **read this file into a Pandas** *DataFrame*, the **pd.read_csv()** function can be used:

```
df = pd.read_csv('weather.csv')
df
```

```
    mon   12.3  5           clear
0   tue   13.5  4           clear
1   wed    9.2  1  mostly cloudy
2   thu    8.2  2  partly cloudy
3   fri   10.2  3  partly cloudy
4   sat   11.3  4   mostly clear
5   sun   13.5  5           clear
```

At first, this looks like the *DataFrame* that we expect, but please have a closer look. Something seems off. Have you found it? The problem becomes obvious looking at the row *index*: there are only six rows in this *DataFrame* because the read_csv() function interpreted the first row of the file as the column names. This problem can be fixed easily in two ways. Either, you insert a header row into the file (that might look like this: day,temp_C,uv,clouds), or you explicitly provide column names to read_csv():

```
df = pd.read_csv('weather.csv',
                 names=['day', 'temp_C', 'uv', 'clouds'])
df
```

```
    day   temp_C  uv          clouds
0   mon     12.3  5            clear
1   tue     13.5  4            clear
2   wed      9.2  1   mostly cloudy
3   thu      8.2  2   partly cloudy
4   fri     10.2  3   partly cloudy
5   sat     11.3  4    mostly clear
6   sun     13.5  5            clear
```

This looks much better. As you can see, the first row of the file is now treated correctly. But there is still room for improvement: we could use the column **day** as our row *index*:

```
df = pd.read_csv('weather.csv',
                 names=['day', 'temp_C', 'uv', 'clouds'],
                 index_col='day')
df
```

```
      temp_C  uv          clouds
day
```

```
mon    12.3   5         clear
tue    13.5   4         clear
wed     9.2   1   mostly cloudy
thu     8.2   2   partly cloudy
fri    10.2   3   partly cloudy
sat    11.3   4    mostly clear
sun    13.5   5         clear
```

As you can probably imagine by now, read_csv() is highly customizable and flexible. For instance, the file to be read does not necessarily have to use commas to separate values. The sep keyword arguments allows you to specify the delimiter symbol or a sequence of symbols as a *string* (sep=',' by default); for instance, for a file that uses pipe symbols (|) as delimiters (e.g., mon|12.3|5|clear) you would use the keyword argument sep='|'. If whitespaces are used as delimiters, delim_whitespace=True should be used; the advantage of this keyword argument is that if True, any number of successive whitespaces counts as a single delimiter. Other optional features include the specific selection of relevant columns with the usecols keyword or the skipping of header rows (skiprows) or footer rows (skipfooter), which might be useful to deal with leading and trailing comments and metadata that might be present in such data files. Another useful feature is to define how missing values appear in the file; if, for instance, missing values are indicated as -999, the keyword argument na_values='-999' will turn those instances into *nan* values so that you can use the methods discussed in Section 8.2.4. A long list of additional features is available for this function and we urge users who frequently deal with *csv* files to have a look at those.

Now that we are able to read *csv* files, it would also be useful to write data into such files. The equivalent of pd.read_csv() for **writing data to files** is **df.to_csv()**. As a bare minimum, the function expects the name of the file to be written. In the following example, we will also provide a label for the row *index*, which would otherwise be blank:

```
df.to_csv('weather2.csv', index_label='day')
```

The resulting file, weather2.csv, contains the same data as weather.csv, but also a header line containing the column labels, so that it could be read by read_csv() without having to provide column names:

```
day,temp_C,uv,clouds
mon,12.3,5,clear
tue,13.5,4,clear
wed,9.2,1,mostly cloudy
thu,8.2,2,partly cloudy
fri,10.2,3,partly cloudy
sat,11.3,4,mostly clear
sun,13.5,5,clear
```

Pandas also provides functionality to read other common file formats. For instance, it is possible to parse tabular data stored in sheets of *xlsx* spreadsheet files into a *DataFrame* with **read_excel()** and to write them with **to_excel()**. For users of relational databases, it might be interesting to read and write entire SQL databases into *DataFrame* structures with **read_sql()** and **to_sql()**. Other common file formats for which read and write functions exist include *json*, *xml*, *hdf5*, and others. For a full reference of the file formats that are supported, please refer to the Pandas IO Tools reference listed in Section 8.8.

8.7   Pandas Hints

In this final section, we would like to feature some hints that are hard to squeeze in anywhere else. We hope that some of these hints will help you in being more efficient in using Pandas.

The great strength of Pandas is that it provides vectorization for many functions and aspects. However, sometimes all you need is to **loop over the rows of a *DataFrame*** to process data. This task is simplified with the `iterrows()` method, which allows you to iterate over the rows of the underlying *DataFrame* and returns its values as a *Series* object. A typical use case for **df.iterrows()** might look as follows:

```
for id, data in df.iterrows():
    print('On {} we had {}C and the sky was {}.'.format(
        id.capitalize(), data.temp_C, data.clouds))
```

```
On Mon we had 12.3C and the sky was clear.
On Tue we had 13.5C and the sky was clear.
On Wed we had 9.2C and the sky was mostly cloudy.
On Thu we had 8.2C and the sky was partly cloudy.
On Fri we had 10.2C and the sky was partly cloudy.
On Sat we had 11.3C and the sky was mostly clear.
On Sun we had 13.5C and the sky was clear.
```

Note that `df.iterrows()` returns a *tuple* that contains the row's *index* and data separately.

Pandas **functions typically return modified copies** of *DataFrames* and *Series* objects and almost never changes them in place. However, many Pandas functions provide the keyword argument **inplace**, which defaults to `False`. For those functions, if you use `inplace=True`, Pandas will change the object you are dealing with in place, saving you some typing. But please be careful: applying `inplace=True` on the wrong function call might modify your data irreversibly.

Pandas provides functionality to **group data** in a *DataFrame*. The process of "grouping" involves the splitting of the data based on some criteria, the application of some function to each group separately, and the combination of these results into a new *DataFrame* or *Series* object. Since this sounds rather abstract, let us have a look at a practical example. Consider the case that, based on our weather data stored in df, we would like to compute the average temperature and UV-index for different levels of cloudiness. The default workflow to achieve this goal would be to identify the different unique levels of cloudiness (stored in column clouds), isolate the rows associated with each level of cloudiness, calculate the mean temperature and UV-index for each data set and then combine all the results back into a *DataFrame* object. Pandas' **df.groupby()** function in combination with mean() does all that for you in one line:

```
df.groupby('clouds').mean()
```

```
               temp_C        uv
clouds
clear           13.1   4.666667
mostly clear    11.3   4.000000
mostly cloudy    9.2   1.000000
partly cloudy    9.2   2.500000
```

Here we group the data based on the labels stored in the clouds column. For more complex *DataFrame* objects, it is possible to group the data on multiple column labels. df.groupby() can also group data based on arbitrary conditions, like, for instance, the value of the UV-index:

```
df.groupby(df.uv < 3).mean()
```

```
        temp_C   uv
uv
False   12.16   4.2
True     8.70   1.5
```

Note that calling df.groupby('clouds') by itself only provides a generator object that has to be combined with any of the functions and methods introduced in Section 8.4 to provide a meaningful output.

8.8   References

Online resources

☐ General Pandas resources

Project website
https://pandas.pydata.org

Documentation
`https://pandas.pydata.org/docs`

API reference
`https://pandas.pydata.org/docs/reference`

User guide
`https://pandas.pydata.org/docs/user_guide`

Getting started
`https://pandas.pydata.org/docs/getting_started`

☐ *Series/DataFrames*

Introduction
`https://pandas.pydata.org/docs/user_guide/dsintro.html`

Series reference
`https://pandas.pydata.org/docs/reference/series.html`

DataFrame reference
`https://pandas.pydata.org/docs/reference/frame.html`

10 min to Pandas
`https://pandas.pydata.org/docs/user_guide/10min.html`

Indexing and selection data
`https://pandas.pydata.org/docs/user_guide/indexing.html`

Merging data
`https://pandas.pydata.org/docs/user_guide/merging.html`

Missing data
`https://pandas.pydata.org/docs/user_guide/missing_data.html`

☐ Specific types of data

Categorical data
`https://pandas.pydata.org/docs/user_guide/categorical.html`

Working with text data
`https://pandas.pydata.org/docs/user_guide/text.html`

Time-series/date functionality
`https://pandas.pydata.org/docs/user_guide/timeseries.html`

☐ Functions

General functions
`https://pandas.pydata.org/docs/reference/general_functions.html`

☐ Data visualization

    Chart visualization
       https://pandas.pydata.org/docs/user_guide/visualization.html

☐ File Input/Output

    IO tools
       https://pandas.pydata.org/docs/user_guide/io.html

☐ Pandas hints

    Grouping data
       https://pandas.pydata.org/docs/user_guide/groupby.html

9   Performance Python

Python is typically considered a slow programming language: its computational performance is lower than that of other programming languages like C/C++ or Fortran, which are typically used for numerical simulations and other computationally intensive tasks. As we already saw in Section 2.1, this is because Python is an *interpreted* language, which means that it does not fully compile its code to machine code prior to its execution. Instead, Python code gets compiled into *bytecode*, which is then interpreted and executed by CPython. As a result, Python code performs typically slower than, for instance, C or Fortran code.

However, there are ways to improve the performance of Python code significantly – to a degree that makes it comparable to C/C++. This is possible as Python is using C in the background (through CPython). In this chapter, and the corresponding Jupyter Notebook (cambridge.org/9781009029728/ch9), we will discuss how to take advantage of this close relationship to C, as well as other methods to improve the performance of your Python code.

For further reading on this topic, we can recommend Gorelick (2020).

9.1   How to Write Efficient Python Code

The more efficient your code, the fewer resources it takes during runtime, the faster it runs, and the sooner it completes. In the case of short scripts, efficiency is typically not an issue. However, if you are working on a computationally intensive problem like a numerical simulation or a complex data preparation pipeline, tiny details in coding can have a huge impact on the runtime of your code. This is especially true if you run many iterations of your code: a difference of 1 second in runtime adds up to an additional 16.7 minutes for only 1,000 iterations.

There are different ways to make your code more efficient. The following sections introduce some measures you can take, in order of increasing complexity. But first, we need to learn how we can objectively quantify the performance of your code.

9.1.1   Measuring performance

The easiest way to measure the runtime of code is to utilize the **time** module. The **time.time()** function returns the time in seconds since some epoch as a floating point number. On most Windows and Unix systems, this epoch is January 1, 1970, 00:00:00 (UTC) and the time that has passed since then in units of seconds, often referred to as *Unix Time*. For instance, the timestamp of writing this very sentence can be represented in *Unix Time* as:

```
import time

time.time()
```

```
1641285970.1614494
```

In order to measure the time required to run some piece of code, we can simply subtract timestamps taken before and after the corresponding code lines. Consider the following example:

```
start = time.time()
x = 0

for i in range(1000):
    x += i

print(time.time()-start)
```

```
0.00023126602172851562
```

start here refers to the timestamp before the loop. After evaluating the loop, we generate a new timestamp and subtract start, resulting in the number of seconds that passed in the meantime. Naturally, such a simple expression and short loop evaluate very quickly; it took only 0.2 ms. However, there is an issue. Reevaluate the code cell and you will see that you will get a different time span. This is perfectly fine since the runtime of one or more lines of code depends on many factors, including memory, disk and core processing unit (CPU) usage of background tasks, and can vary widely even on the same computer. This effect is pronounced for short code elements that evaluate in subsecond time spans; evaluating longer scripts that take seconds or minutes to run, this effect is much weaker and runtime estimates become more stable. Therefore, using the time module to estimate runtimes makes sense for long evaluation times, whereas in the case of short code snippets, other tools should be preferred.

But why would you want to know the time it takes for a single line of code to evaluate? Scientific programs oftentimes rely on solving the same equation over and over again. Consider numerical simulations or data processing: for each sample in a data set or each position on a grid in space, you apply the same task, which is often repeated millions of times. Therefore, to make your code as efficient as possible, it makes perfect sense to optimize this "*bottleneck*" in your code and make it run as fast as possible.

Python provides a very convenient interface for benchmarking the performance of small pieces of code. The `timeit` module is able to measure the runtime of code repeatedly and provides you with some meaningful statistics on the results. There are different ways to make use of the `timeit` module; since we utilize Jupyter Notebooks in this book, we focus on how to use this module in the Notebook environment. Conveniently, Jupyter Notebooks allow you to access `timeit` functionality as magic commands. We consider a simple example using `timeit` line magic (see Section 2.4.2):

```
%timeit 5**20
```

```
6.46 ns +- 0.0513 ns per loop (mean +- std. dev. of 7 runs, 100000000
    loops each)
```

The output provided by the `timeit` magic command is very detailed and may vary in appearance. Here, it contains the mean and standard deviation evaluated over a given number of runs, each of which contains a specific number of loop iterations. Therefore, evaluating this entire cell takes much longer than the 6.46 ns specified by the output. The number of runs and loops utilized in the analysis are determined by the magic command itself, based on the computational complexity of the code. In this case, the statement (`5**20`) is evaluated in each run in a loop with 100,000,000 iterations. Why so many iterations? Whenever you run code, there is overhead involved, for instance, to allocate memory and move data into the right places. While technically necessary, this one-time preparation process should not really count against the runtime of the code as it is highly dependent on your computer and its current state. Estimating this overhead is hard, but a way around this issue is to run the same code many times, minimizing the one-time overhead's impact on the overall runtime of the looped code. Therefore, if the evaluation is repeated n times, the runtime of this loop can be measured and the resulting duration divided by n to obtain a better estimate of the actual runtime of the code. This is exactly what `%timeit` does: it measures the runtime over 100,000,000 iterations and scales it down to a single iteration; the mean and standard deviation of the runtime are then derived from seven independent runs.

If you prefer to set the number of loop iterations and the number of runs yourself, you can do so as follows:

```
%timeit -n 10000 -r 10 5**20
```

```
7.73 ns +- 0.928 ns per loop (mean +- std. dev. of 10 runs, 10000
    loops each)
```

The meaning of the options should be obvious: -r sets the number of repetitions or runs and -n sets the number of iterations per loop. As you can see, the resulting runtime is different but overlaps with the previous result when accounting for uncertainties.

So far, we used %timeit as a line magic command (see Section 2.4.2), but there is also a cell magic version, **%%timeit**, that allows you to benchmark several lines of code, i.e., an entire cell, at a time. Consider the following example:

```
%%timeit

x = 0

for i in range(10):
    x += i
```

```
448 ns +- 19.9 ns per loop (mean +- std. dev. of 7 runs, 1000000
    loops each)
```

timeit and time provide us with the means to efficiently benchmark our code and individual elements of it. Now that we have these tools, we will look into how we can improve the efficiency of our code.

9.1.2   Optimization Starts before Coding

Optimizing your code should start at the design level and not just when your code is written and done. You have already learned many of the tools to write efficient code and in the next sections you will get some more hints on how and why to use them, and you will learn some new tools. Once you feel familiar with these tools, you should try to use them regularly. Most importantly, when you start writing code, one of the first questions to ask yourself should be: which of these tools can or should I use?

If you plan to process large amounts of tabular data stored in files, you probably should not use *string* functions to parse this data from a *File* object (see Section 3.9.3). Instead, try to use functionality from the NumPy (see Section 4.8) or Pandas (see Section 8.6) packages. While it is true that importing large modules such as Pandas adds some overhead to your runtime, you will usually make up for such overhead due to the superior efficiency of the implemented functionality, which is often highly optimized.

As a different example, consider numerical simulations, which are typically computationally expensive. In this case, you would not want to deal with *lists* for storing intermediate results (for reasons you will learn in Section 9.1.3). Instead, you should absolutely build on NumPy *arrays* and their vectorized functionality. In some cases, it might be worth taking it one step further by implementing methods to expedite computations even more by exploiting your computer's hardware as shown in Section 9.2. The next sections will introduce some of these techniques and provide some hints on how to improve your Python code.

9.1.3   Optimizing Basic Python

Most users who are new to Python will mainly utilize basic, or so-called built-in, Python components, which we encountered in Chapter 3. Although built-in functionality is somewhat limited compared to the wealth of functionality offered by NumPy (Chapter 4), SciPy (Chapter 5), or Pandas (Chapter 8), it already offers rich opportunities to optimize your code.

For instance, *lists* **can be expensive** (see Sections 3.5.1 and 3.5.5 for more on *lists*). Building *lists* by repeatedly calling append() is especially resource demanding: whenever you use append(), memory is dynamically allocated to store the current *list* plus some extra margin based on its current length. Once the *list* outgrows a certain threshold length, this memory allocation process is repeated to enable the storage of an even longer *list*, assuming that it will grow even longer in the future. This is not an issue if you are dealing with short *lists*; but if your *list* has thousands or millions of elements, you should avoid using append() due to its dynamic memory allocation. Consider the following practical example: we generate a sequence of 1 million *integer* numbers and square each of them. How long will this take if we create an empty *list* and sequentially append squared *integer* numbers in a loop?

```
%%timeit

l = []

for i in range(1000000):
    l.append(i**2)
```

```
264 ms +- 5.78 ms per loop (mean +- std. dev. of 7 runs, 1 loop each)
```

Well, how can we make this process faster? Since we know how long our *list* will be, we could define a *list* of the corresponding length with dummy values and overwrite those through indexing:

```
%%timeit

l = list(range(1000000))

for i in l:
    l[i] = i**2
```

```
247 ms +- 4.85 ms per loop (mean +- std. dev. of 7 runs, 1 loop each)
```

Indeed, this is slightly faster. However, be aware that the square operation can be quite expensive, too, especially for large numbers. In this case, the runtime might be mainly driven by the computation of the squares. To get a better impression of the performance improvements, let us do the same comparison for a computationally lighter operation:

```
%%timeit

l = []

for i in range(1000000):
    l.append(i+1)
```

```
98.7 ms +- 517 microsec per loop (mean +- std. dev. of 7 runs, 10
    loops each)
```

```
%%timeit

l = list(range(1000000))

for i in l:
    l[i] = i+1
```

```
83.9 ms +- 182 microsec per loop (mean +- std. dev. of 7 runs, 10
    loops each)
```

Indeed, now the difference between the two methods amounts to ~15%, which is quite significant. In conclusion, the **use of the `append()` method is rather expensive and should be restricted to shorter** *lists*.

Another way to solve this task would be to use a ***list comprehension*** (see Section 3.7.5). How does it compare to the other approaches performance-wise?

```
%timeit [i**2 for i in range(1000000)]
```

```
238 ms +- 3.99 ms per loop (mean +- std. dev. of 7 runs, 1 loop each)
```

The runtime of a corresponding *list comprehension* compares very well to the case in which we created a *list* of the correct length and then changed its elements through indexing. Indeed, this is exactly what the *list comprehension* does, so it makes sense to take about as much time as that scenario. Therefore, *list comprehensions* are rather efficient as they create *lists* of a static length.

If the length of our *list* is static and fixed, we might also consider replacing the *list* with a *tuple*, which is immutable. Let us do this with the following ***tuple comprehension***, the equivalent of the *list comprehension* we used earlier:

```
%timeit (i**2 for i in range(1000000))
```

```
465 ns +- 5.58 ns per loop (mean +- std. dev. of 7 runs, 1000000
    loops each)
```

The result is astounding! Simply by replacing the *list* with a *tuple*, we achieve a performance boost of a factor of 5×10^6. Why is that? *Tuples* are immutable and therefore require less memory than *lists*; this means, they are significantly more efficient and data can be stored as a *tuple* much faster than as a *list*. Admittedly, this is an extreme example. But even for smaller sequences there is a measurable effect. As a result, if you are about to create a *container* for a static sequence (one that will not change over time), you should absolutely **consider the use of *tuples***.

Finally, before we change topic slightly, we would like to point out that, almost generally, the most efficient way to deal with sequences of any type is to store them as NumPy *arrays* (see Section 4.1) with their superior vectorization capabilities. We discuss the advantages of NumPy in detail in Section 9.1.4.

One more, less obvious, example for how to improve the performance of your Python code is to **decrease the amount of output generated during runtime**. Especially in the case of complex computations or numerical simulations, it makes sense to output some parameters or results to see whether your program is still on the right track during runtime. However, you should be aware that i/o operations, plotting, file access, or even something as simple as `print()` function calls, or in general any kind of output, is surprisingly time consuming. In case you are looping over such an operation many times it is easy to slow down your code considerably. Therefore, if you encounter a slow-down due to outputting results or parameters, you could, for instance, reduce its frequency to every *n*th iteration.

We conclude this section with two final remarks. Firstly, there are myriad ways to improve the performance of code. You can probably spend hours improving your code to save a few minutes on its runtime. But is it worth it? Here you have to trade off the overall runtime of the code and how often you will actually use it against the time that you are willing to invest into making the code faster. There is probably no point in optimizing a script that takes a few seconds or even minutes to run if you use it only once a week. However, if you wrote some code to perform numerical simulations with parameters that need to be carefully tuned, then it is probably worth spending a few hours trying to improve the runtime. Secondly, you can probably replace every loop structure in your code with a *list comprehension* to make it run faster. But in turn, you will make it harder for others (and your future self) to read and understand what your code does. This is just one example, but there are others. Therefore, in agreement with the Zen of Python (see Section 2.1.2), we support the notion that optimization should not happen at the cost of readability.

9.1.4   NumPy

The most important advice to improve the performance of your code, especially in a scientific setting where computationally expensive code is common, is to **use NumPy wherever possible**. We discussed the reason for this recommendation in Chapter 4: *arrays* and NumPy functionality are implemented in such a way that they support vectorization. Vectorization means that functions and other operations on *arrays* are not sequentially applied to the elements one at a time; instead, they are applied to all elements at the same time. Naturally, vectorization boosts computational performance significantly – but how is it done? NumPy cheats a little bit in that it utilizes compiled mathematical libraries under the hood that are implemented in the C language. NumPy serves as a Python layer on top of these libraries so that users can take advantage of their computational advantages and not have to bother with the quirks of using C.

Let us quantify how fast the use of *arrays* is by looking at the same task as in Section 9.1.3: we square 1 million *integer* numbers and store the result as an *array*:

```
%timeit np.arange(1000000)**2
```

```
2.47 ms +- 469 microsec per loop (mean +- std. dev. of 7 runs, 100
    loops each)
```

This approach is a factor of 100 faster than our original approach that uses *lists* and their `append()` method (see Section 9.1.3). We note that it is also significantly slower than using *tuples*, which is easily explained by the more complex memory structure of *arrays* compared to that of *tuples*. While *tuples* might appear faster in this case, we nevertheless recommend the use of *arrays* wherever possible, simply due to the wealth of functionality that is implemented in NumPy, and, of course, optimized for computational performance.

Let us compare the performance of a more complex mathematical operation to get a better sense for the power of vectorization. We compute the variance over a sequence of 10,000 *integer* numbers. With basic Python, this requires computing the mean and then deriving the expectation over the squared residuals from the mean:

```
%%timeit

a = list(range(10000))
mean = sum(a)/len(a)
sum((x-mean)**2 for x in a)/len(a)
```

```
1.61 ms +- 76.9 microsec per loop (mean +- std. dev. of 7 runs, 1000
    loops each)
```

Now, we use the `np.var()` function (see Section 4.5) that allows us to compute the variance in a single line:

```
%%timeit

a = np.arange(10000)
np.var(a)
```

```
55.1 microsec +- 602 ns per loop (mean +- std. dev. of 7 runs, 10000
    loops each)
```

Not only does the use of NumPy improve the readability of the code, it also improves computational performance significantly. It is therefore safe to assume that if there is functionality implemented within NumPy (or most other official Python packages for that matter), it is optimized for computational performance by using vectorization, underlying C code, and potentially some other tricks.

Since vectorization is important for performance, it would be great if we could use this trait in functions that we define ourselves. In fact, this might already be the case. Consider a function that converts temperatures from units of Celsius to Fahrenheit:

```python
def C_to_F(T):
    """Convert Celsius temperatures to Fahrenheit."""
    return T*1.8+32
```

Naturally, this function works with scalar input data:

```python
C_to_F(16)
```

```
60.8
```

However, the way Python works, the input argument is not required to be a scalar, which means that we can pass an *array* to the function. Also, since the inner workings of the function support vectorization (T*1.8+32 is well-defined for *arrays*), the output will be an *array*, too:

```python
C_to_F(np.arange(10, 30, 2))
```

```
array([50. , 53.6, 57.2, 60.8, 64.4, 68. , 71.6, 75.2, 78.8, 82.4])
```

Therefore, if a function supports vectorization, it will by default benefit from the same performance boosts we have already seen. But when exactly does a function support vectorization? The short answer is: when it behaves like a universal function (*ufunc*, see Section 4.2.1), which means that it operates on *arrays* and supports broadcasting and type casting. Generally, if you build your function on *ufuncs*, it will also behave like a *ufunc*. But not all self-defined functions meet these requirements; the following function, for instance, does not behave like a *ufunc* as it fails to process *arrays* as input arguments:

```python
def greater(a, b):
    """Return the greater of a or b."""
    if a > b:
        return True
    else:
        return False
```

The function fails as the use of the *greater than* operator is ambiguous when applied to *arrays* (see Section 4.2.3 for a discussion). Assume that we would like to evaluate this function on a large number of values that are stored as an *array*. Of course, it would be possible to modify the function so that this ambiguity is resolved and the function works natively with *arrays*. However, in this case, we choose a different path that generalizes better. We will take advantage of NumPy's `vectorize()` function that allows you to vectorize any function:

```
vgreater = np.vectorize(greater)
vgreater(np.arange(5), 3)
```

```
array([False, False, False, False,  True])
```

Note that the two input arguments to `vgreater()` have different dimensionalities: NumPy defaults in this case to the broadcasting rule (see Section 4.1.4). It goes without saying that `vgreater()` returns an *array*.

The advantage of the `vectorize()` function is its general applicability: it can utilize almost any function and turn it into a vectorized function. However, be aware that `vectorize()` is not able to magically improve the performance of the underlying function!

Let us summarize what we have learned in this section: you should use NumPy functionality and *arrays* as much as possible in your code. In order to take full advantage of NumPy's performance, try to design computationally intensive functions in such a way that they vectorize. For functions that cannot be vectorized, the `vectorize()` function might be a way to improve their performance if applied to long *arrays*.

9.2   Parallelization

A different approach to efficient and performant computing is parallelization. Virtually all computers nowadays contain CPUs with more than one "core." Even laptop computers now contain multicore architectures, containing four or even more cores, that allow them to run many different processes in parallel: several instances of web browsers, multimedia players, and other pieces of software. This parallelization is rather complex and not suitable for every problem. In the scope of this book, we will only consider parallelization for problems that are ***embarrassingly parallel***; a problem falls into this category if it can be separated into independent and parallel tasks at no significant cost. An example of an *embarrassingly parallel* problem would be to solve the same equation for a range of different parameter combinations – the key is that each evaluation of the equation is independent from all other evaluations. A problem that would not be *embarrassingly parallel* would require some way to exchange parameters or results between the different evaluations. Naturally, the handling of *embarrassingly parallel* problems is much easier than general parallelization problems. However, they also tend to be much more common as they apply to most situations in which you apply the same function or algorithm to large amounts of data.

Parallel computing is a rather complex task as it requires a deeper understanding of the inner workings of computers. Each computer contains one or more CPUs that perform the heavy lifting when it comes to computations. In order to enable parallelization, modern CPUs support hyperthreading, which enables each core to work on two things at a time and in some way to act as two separate processors; such a virtual component is called a *thread*. A running program or *process* can run on a single thread or on multiple threads to improve its performance. By design, Python only uses single threads, enforced by the Python *Global Interpreter Lock*, which precludes the use of multiple threads by default.

However, Python provides two packages that support threading in different ways: threading and multiprocessing. Although their syntax is rather similar, both concepts are very different and should be applied in different situations. Multithreading generally speeds up tasks that spend time waiting for external events to happen (network-bound problem), while multiprocessing speeds up code that relies heavily on computations (CPU-bound problem). In the following, we provide some brief examples showcasing what is possible with these techniques.

9.2.1   Multithreading

The **threading** module enables you to run processes in parallel in different threads. This method helps you to perform tasks in parallel that are network-bound but not really computationally intensive. Consider the following example in which we simulate a function that accesses data from a file or a website and adds it to a *list*:

```python
import time
import threading


def retrieve(sources, results):
    """Simulate retrieval of data from file or website."""
    for i, source in enumerate(sources):
        print('retrieving data from:', source)
        time.sleep(0.3) # wait
        results[i] = 'data from {}'.format(source)

websites = ['website1', 'website2', 'website3', 'website4',
            'website5']
files = ['file1', 'file2', 'file3', 'file4', 'file5']
```

The code in this cell might require some explanation, so let us go through it line by line. The cell starts with importing the time and threading modules; the latter provides the multithreading functionality that we introduce here and the time modules provide a function, **time.sleep()**, which simply waits for the number of seconds provided as its argument. We then define a function, retrieve() that has two positional arguments: sources, which is a *list* of data sources (filenames or website urls), and results, which is a *list* of the same length as sources, the content of which is irrelevant for now. Inside retrieve(), we loop over all elements from *list* sources, print the current data source on the screen and simulate waiting for the data retrieval (file access or website download and scraping) with time.sleep(). In each iteration, we replace the corresponding element in *list* results with a dummy *string* as a placeholder for the data that we retrieved. This final line of the function reveals the purpose of results: by passing a placeholder *list* of the same length as sources to function retrieve(), we can modify this *list* inside this function and these changes will persist outside the *scope* of this function. Therefore, results acts as a means to return data from function retrieve(). This seemingly complicated way is necessary due to the way the threading module works. Finally, we create two *lists* that contain dummy website names and file names.

We showcase the outcome of running function retrieve() in the following code cell and measure its runtime without utilizing multithreading:

```
%%timeit -n 1 -r 1

results_websites = [None] * len(websites)
results_files = [None] * len(files)
retrieve(websites, results_websites)
retrieve(files, results_files)
```

```
retrieving data from: website1
retrieving data from: website2
retrieving data from: website3
retrieving data from: website4
retrieving data from: website5
retrieving data from: file1
retrieving data from: file2
retrieving data from: file3
retrieving data from: file4
retrieving data from: file5
3.01 s +- 0 ns per loop (mean +- std. dev. of 1 run, 1 loop each)
```

We see that the function sequentially runs through the *lists* of website names and file names, which takes a bit more than 3 seconds ($\sim 10 \times 0.3$ s). Note that we generate here two *lists* that contain Nones, which we use to store our data in and pass to retrieve() as positional arguments.

We will run the function again, but this time we will take advantage of the multithreading module and we will again measure how long the runtime is. We start this cell by creating our empty results *lists* for websites and files. Now follows the multithreading functionality: we create two threads, which we call t1 and t2. Each thread receives as target the name of our function (retrieve, note the missing parentheses: we only pass the function and do not call it, yet) and as arguments (`args`), we provide a *tuple* of *list* pairs containing the different data source *lists* and their corresponding `results` *lists*. After defining our threads, we start them individually and terminate them subsequently.

```
%%timeit -n 1 -r 1
results_websites = [None] * len(websites)
results_files = [None] * len(files)

# define threads
t1 = threading.Thread(target=retrieve, args=(websites,
    results_websites))
t2 = threading.Thread(target=retrieve, args=(files, results_files))

# starting threads
t1.start()
t2.start()

# terminate threads
t1.join()
t2.join()
```

```
retrieving data from: website1
retrieving data from: file1
retrieving data from: website2
retrieving data from: file2
retrieving data from: website3
retrieving data from: file3
retrieving data from: website4
retrieving data from: file4
retrieving data from: website5
retrieving data from: file5
1.5 s +- 0 ns per loop (mean +- std. dev. of 1 run, 1 loop each)
```

The output shows that data from websites and files are retrieved in an alternating fashion, suggesting that both threads indeed run in parallel. This notion is supported by the runtime of the function call: 1.5 seconds are exactly half the runtime of the sequential processing without multithreading – half the runtime, since we use twice as many threads as before. We leave it to the user to check that both `results` *lists* are properly populated. The implementation of multithreading now reveals why we need to take a detour in returning the results from function `retrieve()`: threads are unable to handle objects that are returned from functions using the `return` keyword.

This example shows how multithreading can be used to speed up network-bound processes. Be aware that if your threaded function is computationally intensive, and therefore CPU-bound, multithreading will not help you to improve its runtime. Instead, you should be looking at multiprocessing for your code.

9.2.2 Multiprocessing

The **multiprocessing** module enables multiprocessing within Python to expedite large CPU-bound computations in which a large data set is mapped to a function. We showcase the effects and use of multiprocessing on a simple example involving the numerical integration of an intricate scalar function for a large number of input values:

```python
from scipy.integrate import quad


myfunc = lambda x: np.exp(x)/np.sin(x)*(1+np.tanh(x))


def myintegral(z):
    return quad(myfunc, 0, z)


x = np.random.rand(100)
```

We define function `myfunc()` implicitly as a `lambda`-function (see Section 3.8.6); the integral over `myfunc()` is encapsulated in function `myintegral()`. *Array* x contains 100 random numbers that are uniformly distributed (see Section 4.4). Please note that `myintegral()` is defined for a scalar input z, i.e., a single element from x. As a baseline evaluation, we loop through x, extract a single element for which we evaluate the integral, and append it to a *list* containing all the results:

```python
%%timeit -n 3 -r 3

output = []


for xi in x:
    output.append(myintegral(xi))
```

```
7.74 s +- 1.23 s per loop (mean +- std. dev. of 3 runs, 3 loops each)
```

Evaluating the integral for all elements from x takes almost 8 seconds.

Now, let us take advantage of multiprocessing and compare the runtime to this baseline. We will use the `multiprocessing` module by defining an instance of the class `multiprocessing.Pool`. A *pool* is an object that takes care of most multiprocessing aspects for you. All we have to do is to define an instance:

```python
from multiprocessing import Pool


pool = Pool()
```

and use this instance to map our function, `myintegral()`, to each element of our data set (`x`):

```
%%timeit -n 3 -r 3

output = pool.map(myintegral, x)
```

```
2.51 s +- 288 ms per loop (mean +- std. dev. of 3 runs, 3 loops each)
```

As you can see, the runtime is significantly reduced as the workload is shared over all the cores available on your computer. This can be best seen by looking at the load on your CPUs (e.g., using the `htop` command under Linux or MacOS or the `Task Manager` under Windows): in the multiprocessing case, the load of all CPUs should be maximized, whereas in the nonparallelized case, the entire work is done by a single CPU.

It should be pointed out that other ways to utilize the `multiprocessing` module exist, but, especially in the case of *embarrassingly parallel* problems, the `Pool` class and its `map()` method provide a convenient way to implement multiprocessing capabilities.

9.3   What Else?

The methods and approaches discussed here will help you to improve the performance of your code in most cases. However, sometimes, turning your computer up to ten might not be enough and you may need a little extra help to go all the way up to eleven. Of course, Python supports you in squeezing out that very last bit of performance. In the following, we briefly outline some of these methods on a very high level. We deliberately refrain from briefly introducing their functionality as it would not pay justice to their complexity and functionality. Instead, we provide links to useful references, which we propose to the interested reader for self-study to learn more about these approaches.

Dask is a Python module dedicated to parallel computing. In addition to enabling parallelization on single multicore machines, Dask also enables distributed computing on clusters of computers. Furthermore, Dask provides *big data collections* (*DataFrames*, *Bags*, and *Arrays*) that support parallelization and the handling of data sets that are too large to fit into your computer's memory. At the same time, the API to use these collections is derived from familiar modules such as Pandas or NumPy, making their use extremely intuitive if you are already familiar with these modules. Dask is an excellent choice if you plan to use multicore architectures on single or across multiple computers and/or if you plan on utilizing extremely large data sets. For more information, we simply point to the Dask documentation, which provides some excellent introductions and tutorials on how to utilize its functionality.

A different approach to improve performance that is relevant to a specific type of problem is to utilize **graphics processing units**. *GPUs* are hardware components that were initially developed to accelerate the creation of images, for instance, to create highly complex and increasingly photo-realistic renderings for computer games in real time. With this purpose in mind, *GPUs* are highly efficient in performing large-scale matrix multiplications. However, people quickly found other use cases for *GPUs* such as Deep Learning applications. Harnessing the power of *GPUs* for your own research is easier than you might think as dedicated Python modules for this purpose are available. These modules are most commonly utilized by the Deep Learning community to build, train, and utilize Neural Network architectures. Therefore, most of these modules mainly cater to the needs of this community, but they are modular and flexible enough to be useful in other contexts as well. The most common Deep Learning frameworks available for Python are PyTorch and Tensorflow; they provide a consistent interface to performing *GPU* computations with PyTorch generally having a more *pythonic* interface than Tensorflow. Another notable package to perform large-scale *GPU* (and CPU) computations is Aesara (formerly Theano), which is less focused on the Deep Learning community. Here, we simply refer to the respective documentation for more information and tutorials.

Finally, we would like to point out an entirely different approach to improve performance. As we saw in Section 9.1.4, NumPy owes a large part of its computational efficiency to the fact that it is actually built upon compiled C code and specialized math libraries implemented in C. As a Python user, you can take advantage of the same mechanisms that NumPy utilizes: the **ctypes** module enables **language binding** for C functionality from within Python code. Similar language binding capabilities are also available for the Fortran language with the **f2py** module. Language binding enables you to run precompiled code in the form of a Python function. The advantages of this approach are obvious: you generally gain from the high computational performance of precompiled code, while at the same time benefiting from the simplicity of working from a Python environment. For researchers utilizing legacy code available in C or Fortran there is one more advantage: you can continue using your C or Fortran code within Python without having to translate it to Python. Setting up language bindings is, unfortunately, nontrivial, especially in the case of extensive code bases. However, it might well be worth mastering it to improve performance, or simply to benefit from existing legacy code. We refer to the Python documentation for details on the implementation.

9.4   References

Online resources

☐ How to write efficient Python code

   `time` reference
      https://docs.python.org/3/library/time.html

   `timeit` reference
      https://docs.python.org/3/library/timeit.html

☐ Parallelization

    `threading` reference

        `https://docs.python.org/3/library/threading.html`

    `multiprocessing` reference

        `https://docs.python.org/3/library/multiprocessing.html`

☐ What else?

    Dask project page

        `https://dask.org`

    Pytorch project page

        `https://pytorch.org`

    Tensorflow project page

        `https://tensorflow.org`

    Aesara documentation

        `https://aesara.readthedocs.io`

    `ctypes` reference

        `https://docs.python.org/3/library/ctypes.html`

    `f2py` user guide

        `https://numpy.org/doc/stable/f2py/`

Print resources

Gorelick, Micha and Ian Ozsvald. *High Performance Python: Practical Performant Programming for Humans.* 2nd ed., O'Reilly Media, 2020.

10 Software Development Tools

What we have learned so far should be sufficient to write code that is useful for scientific (and other) applications. But there is so much more out there. Professional software developers have built their own ecosystems of methods and software, which can also be of use to researchers and programmers.

This chapter briefly outlines some more advanced concepts related to and borrowed from professional software development. We will learn about version control, which enables the user to keep track of changes in their code, and we will discuss how to publish code so that it can be used by others.

10.1 Version Control

Consider the following common problem in coding: you have a piece of code that works perfectly fine and all you want to do is to add this final feature to make it perfect. After you are done with your changes, you run the code again to check if it is still working – and it fails. If you changed your code in many different places, it might not be obvious which of those changes caused the code to fail, so you have to undo your changes – one by one. Wouldn't it be nice if you could just restore your code to the state it was in before you changed anything?

This is what **version control** does. Version control allows the user to keep track of all the changes (including changes implemented by others) applied to their code. The use of version control software is standard procedure in professional software development, but not so much in research, although everybody should really use it: version control enables you to back up your projects – programming code but also paper or thesis manuscripts – in a dynamic way. If you find that you would like to undo some changes that you applied a while ago, you can simply undo them and restore the state of your project before you applied those changes. Similarly, you can change every aspect of your project and try out new things; if you decide to keep those changes, you can do so, but if you decide against it, you can simply restore your project. So why is version control uncommon in research environments? It is uncommon because it is somewhat tedious to learn how to use version control properly and even then it means some additional steps in your workflow that it is just too tempting to skip.

In the following, we will briefly introduce how to use git, which is probably the most common version control system.

10.1.1   git

git is an open-source distributed version control system, meaning that you can track your project locally as well as on a remote server. The system was originally developed for Linux (as a matter of fact, it was developed to keep track of changes in the development of the Linux kernel) and is now available without cost for a range of operating systems. It is perfectly suited for the coordination of large collaborative software development projects or to provide version control for small coding projects run by a single person – and everything in-between.

git can be run from the terminal, or using one of many different GUIs. In fact, many serious IDEs (e.g., *pycharm*, *vscode*, and many others) come with excellent support for git.

In the following examples, we will run git from the terminal; most GUIs will use the same terminology as is used in the terminal for the different steps, so you should be able to easily identify the same functionality in any GUI tool. Please note that git has a much higher complexity than is shown here. It is an extremely flexible and versatile tool, which unfortunately adds to the impression that its use is complex and hard to learn. In the following examples, we will focus on the bare minimum that you need to turn git into a useful tool for your work. For more details on how git works, have a look at the corresponding references.

Setting up git

Before you can use git, you have to configure a few things. We do this in the following in the terminal or console (indicated by the leading dollar sign, $), where we call it **git**.

For instance, you have to tell git your name and email address, as those are tracked within your project. This is required even if you are the only person working on your project and you only need do it once if you do it *globally* – i.e., for all git repositories on your computer – by typing the following into your terminal, console or powershell:

```
$ git config —global user.name "<your name>"
$ git config —global user.email <your email address>
```

Once this is done, we can create our first git repository by initializing it with the **init** command. To do so, create a new directory for your project and run[1]:

```
$ git init
```

---

[1]   `git init` can also be used in a directory that is not empty, but for this example we will use an empty directory.

This will create a hidden directory `.git/`, which contains all the information that git requires for tracking files and the entire evolution of our project. The safest thing to do is to simply ignore the existence of this hidden directory.

Tracking Changes

Suppose we have a Python script named `script.py` in the project directory that we would like to track. This file, although it lives in the project directory, is not yet being tracked, which we can see by using git's **status** command:

```
$ git status
On branch main

No commits yet

Untracked files:
  (use "git add <file>..." to include in what will be committed)
  script.py

nothing added to commit but untracked files present (use   "git add"
    to track)
```

The `status` command tells us that there is one untracked file, which is `script.py`. It also tells us that we are on branch *main* (we will learn about branches in a bit) and that there are no files available to commit (again, we will learn about this in a second).

To enable the tracking of this file, we must go through a two-step process. First, we have to add this file to the **staging area**, which is to tell git that we intend it to track this file in its current state. The second step is to **commit** changes, which will store the individual files' states in the history of the project. Each commit can be seen as a time step in the evolution or timeline of your project.

We can stage `script.py` using the **add** command:

```
$ git add script.py
$ git status
On branch main

No commits yet

Changes to be committed:
  (use "git rm —cached <file>..." to unstage)
  new file:   script.py
```

The `status` command now tells us that `script.py` is staged and ready to be committed. If you have multiple files that you would like to track in their current state, you can add them to the staging area with the `add` command. Once you are done staging, you can **commit** all your changes, which is typically done by including a very brief note to yourself or others working on the same project to remind them of the changes that you applied. Let's commit our single file for now with a note that we added this file:

```
$ git commit —m 'added script.py'
[main (root—commit) 99a773d] added script.py
 1 file changed, 1 insertion(+)
 create mode 100644 script.py
$ git status
On branch main
nothing to commit, working tree clean
```

Only after finishing this commit, the file script.py is being tracked by git – a snapshot of the current version of the file is added to the history of your project. Your commit receives a unique alphanumeric identifier, in this case (99a773d), which allows you to reference this point in the development of your project in the future. status now tells us that there is nothing to commit and that the *working tree (is) clean*; the **working tree** means your repository directory with all tracked and untracked files. Since there are no untracked files in the directory, it is *clean*.

So what does *tracking* mean? Let's assume we change the content of script.py after we started tracking it. Any changes to the content of the file will be noticed by git:

```
$ git status
On branch main
Changes not staged for commit:
  (use "git add <file>..." to update what will be committed)
  (use "git restore <file>..." to discard changes in working
    directory)
  modified:   script.py

no changes added to commit (use "git add" and/or "git commit —a")
```

The status command informs us that our changes to script.py have not been staged. It does not matter how big those changes are, git will notice them, even if we only changed a single character. To save changes to the file, we need to use the same two-step process that we used before to add this file to the repository: add for staging and commit:

```
$ git add script.py
$ git commit —m 'minor changes'
[main 90fc0b8] minor changes
 1 file changed, 1 insertion(+)
```

It is necessary to stage the file again, since you are staging a new version of the file. It is possible for you to work on several files at the same time, but then you might decide to track the changes on only one of them; in this case, you would stage and commit only this one file, while restoring the other files (see below).

To get an overview of the history of all your commits, you can use the **log** command:

```
$ git log
commit 90fc0b8ef4def14c851889cb2e4cfd517c81251b (HEAD -> main)
Author: <your name> <your email address>
Date:   <date>

    minor changes


commit 99a773d1344ada55df82ee02900c769d72f0fdf9
Author: <your name> <your email address>
Date:   <date>

    added script.py
```

Note how the commit identifier is actually much longer than the seven characters that are presented to the user at the time of the commit. Also, now it should be clear why we have to provide our name and email address to git: every commit – and thus every change to the project – is unambiguously assigned to the project team member who performed that commit.

Undoing Changes

git provides a number of strategies and tools to undo changes in your project, depending on where you are in the development process.

☐ Consider the case that you modified some file but you have not yet staged it. If you decide not to stage it but instead to return it to its original state (i.e., its state during the most recent commit), you can simply **restore** it using:

```
$ git restore <filename>
```

Note that there is no way to restore the changes that you undo here.

☐ If you already staged the file and decide to remove it from the staging area, the following commands will first "un-stage" the file and then undo all changes:

```
$ git restore —staged <filename>
$ git restore <filename>
```

☐ If you want to **restore** a single file from a previous commit, you can use:

```
$ git checkout <commit-id> <filename>
```

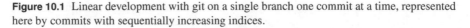

Figure 10.1 Linear development with git on a single branch one commit at a time, represented here by commits with sequentially increasing indices.

This will overwrite your file completely; if instead you only want to restore part of that file, you can use the -p option of the **checkout** command to interactively patch the file.

☐ Finally, if you decide to go back to a past commit and abandon all changes (and commits) that you applied in the meantime, you can use

```
$ git reset —hard <commit-id>
```

Note that this command will **reset** your entire project history to this commit and thus irretrievable delete any changes that happened after this commit. Use this command very carefully.

There are many other ways of undoing and restoring files; for more information and learning materials, please refer to the references section.

Working with Branches

So far, the development process in our project directory is linear, as shown in Figure 10.1: we gradually add and modify files in order to improve our project step by step.

Of course, real-life coding projects typically follow a more complicated path: you try out code snippets, modify elements to make them more efficient or easier to read, and you discard many things along the way. Instead of a linear development process, this much more resembles a tree-like structure, where you start at the root and follow branches, most of which end along the way, typically leaving one branch that represents the most mature state of your project.

git adopts this picture by introducing the concept of *branches*. Branches are development states of your project that allow you to experiment by taking your project into a new direction without compromising the structure of your project.

So far, in the linear development of your project, we have only used a single branch, the *main branch* (this name has been provided by git and is actually displayed when invoking the **status** command). The *main* branch should always be the main development branch of your project, representing the most mature state of your project.

Let's assume that you want to try a new idea for `script.py`, but you also have a list of other important changes you know will take some time so you defer their implementation. Since you do not want to wait to try out your idea, you decide to create a separate *branch* which you call `experiment`:

```
$ git branch experiment
```

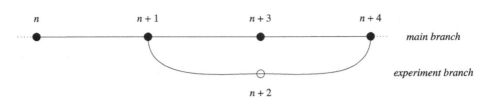

Figure 10.2 An example development graph using branching in git. Based on the *main* branch at commit $n + 1$, we create the *experiment* branch. We apply changes to both branches and commit the corresponding changes (commits $n + 2$ and $n + 3$). Finally, we merge the *experiment* branch into the *main* branch (commit $n + 4$).

You can now switch to this new branch and start modifying your code:

```
$ git checkout experiment
Switched to branch 'experiment'
```

This process is visualized in Figure 10.2. We create the *experiment* branch at commit $n + 1$ and modify the code on this branch as we wish. Note that the project files in both branches are identical before applying any changes.

At some point, we feel the pressure to work on the other open issues. Since those changes are not part of your experiment, we will implement them on the *main* branch. In order to go back to the *main* branch, we have to stage and commit our changes to the *experiment* branch (commit $n + 2$ in Figure 10.2) and go back to the *main* branch:

```
$ git checkout main
Switched to branch 'main'
```

Now it should become clear why branches are a useful tool: all our project files are in the exact same state they were in before we even created our *experiment* branch (commit $n + 1$). We can implement our changes on the *main* branch without having to interfere with our experiment – and vice versa.

Once we are done on the *main* branch, we can stage and commit ($n + 3$) our changes again, and switch back to the *experiment* branch. Similarly, none of the changes that we applied to the *main* branch were applied to the files on the *experiment* branch. Instead, all files are in the same state we left them in when we returned to the *main* branch (commit $n + 2$). The files in the two branches are treated like two separate projects.

We can repeat the process and implement changes in both branches by switching between them and committing changes. But at some point, we need to decide what to do with the *experiment* branch. If we are not interested in keeping the work done on this branch, we can simply delete it:

```
$ git branch –d experiment
Deleted branch experiment (was 90fc0b8).
```

The alternative would be to keep the work done on the *experiment* branch and to implement it into the *main* branch. This process of combining two branches is called *merging*. To merge both branches, we have to switch to the *main* branch first and then tell git to **merge** the *experiment* branch with the *main* branch:

```
$ git checkout main
Switched to branch 'main'
$ git merge experiment
Updating 90fc0b8..aab72f1
Fast-forward
 script.py | 2 ++
 1 file changed, 2 insertions(+)
```

In this example, both branches were merged without any problems and the resulting project files will contain all changes previously applied to the *main* and *experiment* branches. To do so, git will identify new or modified code elements in both versions of each file and apply all changes to the *main* branch file versions. But what happens if the same line of code was modified on both branches in different ways? Which version to keep and which version to scrap? git cannot make this decision – only the developer can. In this case, you have a **merge conflict**:

```
$ git merge experiment
Auto-merging script.py
CONFLICT (content): Merge conflict in script.py
Automatic merge failed; fix conflicts and then commit the result.
```

The merge conflict has to be resolved manually. Open the conflicting file (in this case `script.py`) and modify it. To support you, git will highlight the conflicting lines and present both code versions so that you can simply delete or alter those lines of code that you do not want to keep. Once you saved the conflicting files after resolving the conflicts, you have to run:

```
$ git commit
```

As a result of all of this, any changes that you applied to the *main* branch and the *experiment* branch are now applied to the *main* branch. If you like, you can now delete the *experiment* branch.

This concludes our brief git introduction, which only touches the surface of what git is actually capable of. If you find git useful, we encourage you to have a look at Section 10.3.1 and the additional reading references provided in Section 10.4.

10.2   Create Your Own Python Module

In case you wrote some useful code that you would like to use frequently in the future, you should consider packaging your code into a module. The advantage is simple: you can install your module on your system in a way similar to the way pip (see Section

2.2.2) does, which means that you can import your module from anywhere in your filesystem and you don't have to be in the same directory in which your module code resides. Creating your own module is remarkably simple due to tools like **setuptools** that do all the heavy lifting for you.

The first requirement for your own module – let's call it mymodule – is to provide your code in a **specific directory structure** relative to some project root directory (in this case we use the current working directory, ./, but it could be anywhere on your system):

```
./
./__init__.py
./setup.py
./mymodule/
./mymodule/__init__.py
./mymodule/mymodule.py
./mymodule/mysubmodule/
./mymodule/mysubmodule/__init__.py
./mymodule/mysubmodule/submodule.py
```

Note that our module mymodule contains a submodule, which we call mysubmodule. Why do we need this specific file and directory structure?

☐ The file **setup.py** defines your module and has to be located in your project root directory. In its simplest form, setup.py can look like this:

```
from setuptools import setup, find_packages

setup(name='mymodule',
      version='0.1',
      packages=find_packages())
```

In this example, we define a module named mymodule with version number 0.1. This information is being managed by **setuptools.setup()**. The function **find_packages()** simply walks through your project directory tree and collects all modules it can find and adds them to mymodule. The setup() function has many more parameters that can (and should) be set to provide more information on your module and to simplify its use. For instance, it is possible to define requirements on other third-party modules that will be installed alongside your module, if not yet present. We point to some resources describing these mechanisms in Section 10.4.

☐ Each directory in your project directory tree should contain a file called **__init__.py**. This file marks a module or submodule and is called when the corresponding module or submodule is imported in Python; it can be used to define the module structure, but it can also be left empty without any consequences.

The file `./mymodule/__init__.py` may have the following content:

```
from . import mymodule
```

and `./mymodule/mysubmodule/__init__.py` may look like this:

```
from . import mysubmodule
```

This syntax involving dots is different from a typical `import` statement and can only be used in the context of module definitions. It simply means that `mymodule` uses the content of `mymodule.py` and `mysubmodule` uses the content of the file `mysubmodule.py` (mind that the suffix `.py` is omitted in the `import` statement).

Once the module is defined and the files and directories are arranged in the right order, how do we use our module? All you need to do is to go to your project root directory and run

```
$ python setup.py install
```

This command will install the module in your Python path. Now you can use your module from anywhere on your system like any other Python module:

```
import mymodule                     # import the entire module
from mymodule import somefunc       # import a single function
from mymodule import mysubmodule    # import only mysubmodule
```

One more additional hint: if you are still working on the code of your module, you can use

```
$ python setup.py develop —user
```

to install it in development mode: any changes to the code will trigger a recompilation of the code so that your module always uses its latest version. There is no need to reinstall the module between changes.

10.3   Publish Your Code

If you find your code useful, others might too. Hence, you should consider publishing your code. Publishing code that you used to generate results in your previous publication increases the reproducibility of your work and might even enable some other researcher to continue your work or apply it to a completely different field. The following sections introduce two concepts for how to publish your code and make it accessible to others.

One important consideration that applies to both concepts is that of **licensing**. It is good practice to publish your work (your code – or anything else for that matter) with proper licensing. The reason for this is manifold: maybe you want to restrict the use of your code for certain purposes, or at least you may want to rule out liability, but most certainly you want others using your work for their purposes to acknowledge your contribution. There is a wide range of licenses available from which to pick and your choice should rely on your own motivations and thoughts. Instead of making suggestions here, we would like to point out a service provided by GitHub (see Section 10.4) that helps you pick an appropriate license for your code.

10.3.1   GitHub

The easiest way to publish your code is to simply upload it to a public repository in the form that works best for you. GitHub is a free service that hosts public or proprietary repositories; it strongly relies on the git version control software.

If you already organized your project in the form of a git repository (we call this the *local* repository, see Section 10.1.1), you can simply push its content to GitHub. To do so, you must sign up with GitHub and create an empty repository (we call this the *remote* repository) and link it to your local repository.

In your *local* repository you have to register your *remote* repository:

```
git remote add origin https://github.com/<username>/<project>test.git
git push —u origin main
```

The second line will upload content from your local project git repository to your remote GitHub repository. As you work on your *local* repository you can and should regularly push your code to the *remote* repository on GitHub.

Just like git, GitHub allows you to track and store code files, text files, webpages, data files... pretty much anything.

If you want people to find and use your repository, you should add a README file and a LICENSE file. The former allows you to briefly describe your code, what it does, how it can be used, etc. For simple formatting, you can use the *markdown* language (README.md; see Section 2.4.2 for a brief introduction into the markdown language) or *restructured text* (README.rst). The LICENSE file is important to inform potential users of how they are allowed to use your code. For a discussion of different license types, we refer to resources listed in Section 10.4.

10.3.2   Python Package Index

In case your code is already available as a module as defined in Section 10.2, there is a much more elegant solution: you can add your module to the Python Package Index (PyPI). The reward is that you – and anybody else for that matter – can install mymodule by simply invoking

```
$ pip install mymodule
```

The process of publishing your code with PyPI is not necessarily complicated but it is extensive enough that we will only outline it here. For a detailed description of the process, please refer to the official PyPI guidelines (see Section 10.4). In a nutshell, the following steps need to be taken to post your module to PyPI:

1 your code has to be stored following a specific directory structure;

2 you have to create a file that contains meta information, such as the name of the module and a short description of what it does;

3 you create a README file with a short description;

4 you create a LICENSE file that contains information on the software license under which you provide your module;

5 you generate a distribution archive that bundles everything; and finally

6 you upload your distribution archive to PyPI.

Providing your code on PyPI is a great opportunity to not only showcase your work, but may also be a great contribution to your research community. As a good citizen, you should definitely consider it!

10.4   References

Online resources

☐ Version control

> git project page
> https://git-scm.com/

> git documentation
> https://git-scm.com/docs

> git pro book
> https://git-scm.com/book/en/v2

> Bitbucket git tutorial
> https://atlassian.com/git/tutorials

> GitHub git cheat sheets
> https://training.github.com

☐ Create your own Python module

> setuptools documentation
> https://setuptools.pypa.io

> Building and distributing packages
> https://setuptools.readthedocs.io/en/latest/setuptools.html

☐ Publish your code

Licensing
https://choosealicense.com

GitHub
https://github.com/

Python Package Index
https://pypi.org/

Index